Illinois

Crossroads of a Continent

DISCARD

Illinois

Crossroads of a Continent

LOIS A. CARRIER

UNIVERSITY OF ILLINOIS PRESS
Urbana and Chicago

Illini Books edition, 1998
©1993 by the Board of Trustees of the University of Illinois
Manufactured in the United States of America

P 5 4 3 2 1

This book is printed on acid-free paper.

Library of Congress Cataloging-in-Publication Data

Carrier, Lois, 1934-
    Illinois : crossroads of a continent / Lois A. Carrier.
      p. cm.
    Includes bibliographical references and index.
    ISBN 0-252-06808-4 (pbk. : alk. paper).
      1. Illinois—History. I. Title.
F541.C34   1993
977.3—dc20   92-31041
                                            CIP

Digitally reprinted from the first cloth edition

For Neil
in gratitude for his unstinting help and encouragement
and his prodigious patience

Contents

Preface ix

Part 1: Beginnings

1 The Early Inhabitants of Illinois   3
2 The French in Illinois   11
3 How the Illinois Country Became American
   Territory   22
4 Steps toward Statehood   32
5 The Twenty-first State   39

Part 2: Early Development

6 Patterns of Settlement   49
7 A Sampler of Frontier Towns   60
8 The Challenge of the Prairies   69
9 Red Ink in Illinois   77
10 Illinois at Mid-Century   84

Part 3: The Civil War Era

11 Prelude to War   95
12 Illinois Pitches In   104

13   The Long Road to Peace   114

Part 4: New Directions

14   The Winds of Change   125
15   The Pace of Industrial Growth Picks Up   135
16   Trouble in the Factory   145
17   A New Image for Illinois   154
18   A Different Perspective   167

Part 5: Illinois in the Modern World

19   The Reform Era   177
20   Illinois in World War I   188
21   The Wild and Reckless Twenties   195
22   The Lean Years   207
23   A World Spinning out of Control   217
24   Peace and Progress   227
25   The Decades of Conflict   238
26   Contemporary Illinois   245

Appendixes

1   State Symbols   255
2   Governors of Illinois   257
3   Important Dates in Illinois History   259

    Bibliography   263

    Index   269

Preface

What do the following prominent Americans have in common?

Jane Addams, Louis Armstrong, Saul Bellow, Jack Benny, Gwendolyn Brooks, John Deere, Walt Disney, Benny Goodman, Ulysses S. Grant, Ernest Hemingway, Wild Bill Hickok, Jesse Jackson, Florence Kelley, Julia Lathrop, Abraham Lincoln, Cyrus McCormick, King Oliver, Ronald Reagan, Carl Sandburg, Adlai Stevenson, Raquel Welch, and Frank Lloyd Wright

They are just a few of the many gifted men and women who were born or lived in Illinois. In doing research for this book I not only found that Illinois had many illustrious sons and daughters, but I also learned that much more has happened in Illinois than I had imagined.

The earliest inhabitants of Illinois built the largest prehistoric earthen structure in North America. Spain, France, and England struggled for control of the strategically located Illinois country. A blitz campaign led by George Rogers Clark made it American territory. During the early phases of the westward movement Illinois *was* "the West." Under the golden prairie grasses pioneer farmers found soil so rich that it would not need to be fertilized for a hundred years. Cowboys and cattle kings had their day in Illinois, and Galena with its rich lead deposits became the first boomtown in the West. Chicago was once a moviemaking capital, and the National Baseball League had its beginnings there. Popeye, Dick Tracy, and Moon Mullins were all "born" in Illinois, and the inventors of the Ferris wheel and Crackerjack performed their wonders there, too.

You may not find your city or town mentioned in these pages. This book is meant to be a beginning, not the whole story. There were many interesting aspects of Illinois history that I regretfully had to omit for lack of space.

Related books that I particularly enjoyed are listed at the end of each chapter. A general bibliography at the end of the book includes many of the classics of Illinois history for readers who wish to investigate further. Your own community may have resources unavailable to me, including older people who can give you firsthand information about the past, as well as museums and newspaper archives.

Good and evil, success and failure, make up the history of all states and nations. In doing my research I learned that it often takes more than one try to right a wrong. But at least in a democracy the mechanisms that allow for the correction of mistakes or the making of changes to meet new conditions are in place. All we have to do is learn how to use them—and to have the will to do so.

As we move forward into century twenty-one, Illinois remains the crossroads of a continent, striving to overcome its problems with the same perseverance and innovative spirit that stood the pioneers in good stead. Pioneering is not confined to a particular era: it is a state of mind.

I wish to express my gratitude to Richard L. Wentworth, who took an interest when the manuscript was still in the rough; to editor Karen Hewitt for her patient and efficient follow-through; to Theresa L. Sears, managing editor; to Susan L. Patterson for her thoughtful copy-editing; and to other members of the staff of the University of Illinois Press who contributed to the design, production, and promotion of the book.

My thanks also to those who read and critiqued the manuscript at various stages and made many valuable suggestions, especially Marcia Murphy who understood my audience and whose comments jolted me into yet one more round of revisions.

I also acknowledge those who helped me locate illustrative materials, namely, David Koch and Sheila Ryan, Morris Library, Special Collections, Southern Illinois University, Carbondale; Galen Wilson, Archivist, Chicago Public Library, Special Collections Division; Mary Michals, Curator, Audio-Visual Collection, Illinois State Historical Library, Springfield; Mary Ann Bamberger, Archivist, University of Illinois at Chicago, the University Library, Special Collections Department; Emily Clark, Assistant Librarian, Chicago Historical Society; Pat Chism, Gulf States Paper Corporation, Fine Arts Department; and Daryl Watson, Executive Director, Galena/Jo Daviess County Historical Society and Museum; and to staff members of the Carbondale

Public Library who retrieved information for me through interlibrary loan.

My thanks also to all the young visitors to the University Museum, Southern Illinois University, who, during my decade as a docent there, delighted me with their interest and enthusiasm and convinced me that this book was necessary.

Last but not least, I acknowledge those friends who saw potential when the book was only an idea: Donna Butler, who was present at its inception; Mary Russell Muchmore, whose response to young people has been an inspiration to me; and Carol Christensen, who pried me loose from the project long enough to do some remedial walking.

PART ONE

Beginnings

Illinois . . . a land of gently flowing streams and endless tall-grass prairies . . . of mastodons and great herds of bison . . . of high bluffs and heavily wooded hills. That is what the earliest human inhabitants found when they arrived ten or twelve thousand years ago. And that is very nearly what the first Europeans who came to the Illinois wilderness found. But the landscape slowly changed as American pioneers began arriving in the late 1700s. In those days Illinois was "the West."

1

The Early Inhabitants of Illinois

Prehistoric Cultures

Various histories of Illinois begin at different places in time. We have chosen to begin with the arrival of humans on the continent on which we live. Although there is evidence of human existence millions of years ago in other parts of the world, the arrival of people in North America is a relatively recent phenomenon.

During the world's great ice ages, much of the planet's water became locked up in sheets of ice, causing the sea level to fall. This permitted the Stone Age peoples of Asia to walk across the Bering Strait to Alaska and Canada, arriving as early as 38,000 years ago. As they followed the herds of wild animals on which they depended for food, they were unaware that they had reached another continent, North America. Between periods of glaciation, some of the ice melted and corridors to the south opened, allowing bands of these early people to drift southward and fan out across America. Ten or twelve thousand years ago, some of their descendants arrived in what is now Illinois.

Although the most recent ice age was over, the climate was still chilly. Mastodons, bison, tapirs, ground sloths, and camels roamed the plains. Having no horses, small bands of hunters followed the herds on foot. Constantly on the move, the hunters and their families built no permanent homes but instead used rock overhangs or caves as temporary shelters. If you stand under the Modoc Rock Shelter, which rises above the quiet, two-lane road near the village of Prairie du Roche in southern Illinois, you can get some idea of how precarious the lives of these ancient people were.

About 8000 B.C. the climate of Illinois became warmer and drier. Changes in vegetation may have made it impossible for large game to continue to live in the area, or perhaps some species were hunted to extinction. As the Indians learned to make greater use of the food resources near at hand, seasonal migrations replaced their constant wanderings. Some clever persons among them began making baskets. Basketry may seem like a small advance, but it enabled the people to gather and store large quantities of berries, nuts, herbs, and other woodland plants, thus supplementing their meat diet.

By 1000 B.C. these early people began growing squash, sunflowers, and the corn that eventually became their most important crop. They continued to send out hunting parties, but having better control over their food supply, they were able to settle in villages along the waterways. They built small domed houses by bending saplings into an arched framework, then weaving branches horizontally between the uprights and covering the outside with grasses, mud, or animal skins.

During their nomadic days, the Indians had not been able to carry much with them. After adopting a more sedentary way of life, they began to accumulate more personal goods. They learned to make pottery for cooking, storing, and ceremonial use and constructed a greater variety of stone implements, tools, and weapons; however, they did not develop a technology for heating and forming metal.

Step by step their culture became more complex. We know that they were building small burial mounds before 1000 B.C. Pots, tools, and weapons have been found in some of these early graves, but later more exotic goods begin to appear, many of which were made of materials not ordinarily found in Illinois. Objects fashioned from marine shells from the Gulf of Mexico and Atlantic Ocean, obsidian from the Southwest, and copper from the North and Northeast provided luxuries for the rich and for funeral goods for chiefs and priests. Archeologists surmise that these people had already set up extensive trade networks.

Between 900 A.D. and 1400 A.D. the Indians built a spectacular city on the Mississippi flood plain near present-day Collinsville. The ancient city that once stood on the present Cahokia Mounds site covered six square miles and had a population of more than 20,000. Monks' Mound, the largest ancient earthwork in North America, was the centerpiece of this metropolitan area. It rose from the surrounding plain in four terraces to a height of 100 feet, covered fourteen acres, and had a base larger than that of the famous pyramid of Cheops in Egypt. The remains of more than 120 smaller mounds have been found nearby.

The city was not a random concentration of buildings, but a highly organized community. The temple on Monks' Mound overlooked a

A model of the Cahokia Mounds site. The city once located here is thought to have been the capital of the prehistoric mound-building peoples of the Mississippi Valley. Courtesy of the Illinois State Historical Library.

plaza where sacred games and rituals took place. Engravings on copper and marine shell ornaments depict a bird-man warrior, a feathered serpent, a long-nosed god, and a player of sacred games, giving tantalizing glimpses of the religious and ceremonial life of the Indians of this period.

While excavating at Cahokia, a team of archeologists uncovered the remains of a mysterious circle of wooden posts that immediately reminded them of Stonehenge in England. Appropriately, they named this circle Woodhenge. Priests may have welcomed the sun there with prayer and chanting each morning. Woodhenge probably also served as an astronomical calendar. The sunrise lined up with certain posts at certain times of the year, giving the priests a way of keeping track of the passing days and seasons and determining the correct time for the planting and harvesting ceremonies.

About 1500 A.D. the bustling city suddenly fell silent, and the area was abandoned for reasons still not understood. Perhaps nearby resources had been used up, and the area could no longer support so large a concentration of people. Diseases carried by Europeans to the New World may have spread by way of trade routes, causing epidemics. Intertribal warfare or a revolt of the lower classes could have brought about the decline of this marvelous city.

The Illini and Their Competitors

Some time after the prehistoric cultures disappeared, probably between 1500 and 1550, a group of Indian tribes calling themselves the

"Illini" or "Illiniwek" ("The Men" or "The People") came to live in a large area extending from southern Wisconsin and Iowa to southern Illinois, southeast Missouri, and Arkansas. They were members of one of the largest groups of American Indians, the Algonquian-speaking peoples. When Europeans began settling North America, Algonquian tribes occupied much of the eastern half of the continent, and some lived as far west as the Rocky Mountains. The Illini had chosen the prairies and woodlands of the Midwest as their homeland.

The Illini consisted of about twelve tribes, including the Kaskaskia, Peoria, Michigamea, Tamaroa, and Cahokia. Although they lived apart from each other, they organized themselves into a loose confederacy with a grand chief and a coat of arms by which other tribes could recognize them. The Illini population in the early 1500s is thought to have been about 8,000.

How closely related the prehistoric Indians were to the historic tribes of Illinois still puzzles archeologists. When European explorers questioned the Indians about the ancient mounds, the Indians seemed to know little about the early people who had made them, yet they still revered the mounds as sacred places. Some scholars point to similarities in building, hunting, and agricultural techniques as evidence that the ancient people were the ancestors of the modern Indians. Others think that the modern Indians moved into the area and intermarried with the last of the ancient people.

The Illini lived in villages along the waterways of their territory. Their groups of rectangular houses faced each other, and the large open area between them served as a public gathering place for ceremonies and games. Their everyday clothes were simple breechcloths, skirts, and tops made of deerskin, but old engravings also show Illini dressed in full regalia. Belts, garters, and sashes woven of dyed bear and buffalo hair enhanced their costumes, as did the bright feathers with which they made exotic headdresses and the jewelry they fashioned of bone, animal teeth, beads, and shells. The men tattooed their bodies and painted designs on themselves.

The Illini worshiped Manitou, the Great Spirit, and many other lesser spirits or manitous. They said that they had received their most sacred object, the calumet, from the sun. This was a ceremonial pipe having a bowl carved of stone and a two-foot-long wooden pipestem decorated with the heads and necks of birds or with colorful feathers. Priests offered the smoke of the calumet to the sun when they prayed for good growing conditions. Calumets were offered to guests who had come in peace, smoked by the parties ratifying a treaty, given to travelers to ensure their safe passage through Illini territory, and sent as declarations of war to neighboring tribes. The war calumet had only red feathers.

Each young Illini man had to find a superhuman helper and guardian, and this he did by prayer and fasting. A manitou then appeared to him in a dream, giving him instructions for being able to contact his protector when necessary. Upon awakening, the man gathered the objects mentioned in the dream and put them in a packet made of painted matting. Thereafter, when he needed help, he opened the packet and went through the ritual that had been described to him in his dream.

When a man killed his first game, a special feast was given to thank his guardian spirit for having given him success. The young hunter was then considered eligible for marriage because he had proven that he could provide for a family. When he married, he and his family followed the traditional pattern of village life.

The yearly cycle began with the spring planting of crops. Then in June everyone set off on the summer buffalo hunt. They had no horses, so they traveled in dug-out canoes or on foot. They returned to their villages in time to harvest the first corn crop in July. In the leisurely summer months, the men hunted and fished while the women tended the crops, dried meat and fish, and gathered acorns, nuts, and wild fruit.

In October all of the able-bodied villagers set out in high spirits for the winter buffalo hunt on the prairie. When they sighted a herd, they encircled it, set grass fires at intervals, then killed the animals with spears and bows and arrows as they tried to escape. The women cured the meat and dressed the hides. In January everyone returned to the village.

By February parties of braves were on the trail again, making surprise attacks on neighboring tribes and taking captives, some of whom were made slaves while others were adopted into the tribe to replace people who had died. A raid was considered particularly successful if no Illini were killed. If any warrior did meet his death, the leader of the raid had to recompense his family for the loss.

In early spring the women collected sap from the sugar maple trees while men and boys fished, sometimes spearing the fish and sometimes shooting them with bows and arrows. When the weather was warm enough, the first seeds were planted, thus beginning a new cycle.

Most years at least a few of the villagers died. The Illini believed in an afterlife, so they buried their dead carefully, dressing them in their best clothing and painting their faces, then performing a dance in their honor. Corn and a pot to boil it in were left by the side of the dead

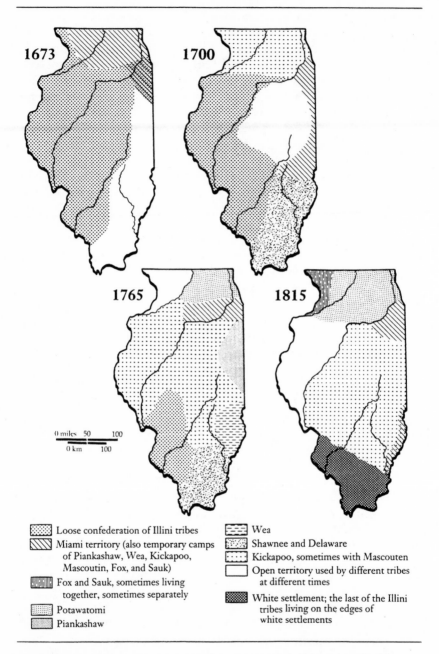

Movement of Indian Tribes in Illinois, 1673–1815. These maps reflect the gradual loss of territory that the Illini suffered as other tribes crowded in upon them and white settlers began arriving.

person, and sometimes pendants, bracelets, and other items were placed in the grave.

This simple way of life was not to continue. In the 1500s five non-Algonquian tribes living in present-day New York and Pennsylvania banded together to form the powerful League of Five Nations, also known as the Iroquois. The Iroquois put great emphasis on military training and acquired a reputation for being fearless and fiendish warriors. They were also the first tribes to have firearms, which they got from the Dutch and English in return for furs. One Frenchman said of them, "The Iroquois approach like foxes, fight like lions, and fly away like birds." They were feared wherever they went.

When the Iroquois had depleted their traditional hunting grounds, they swooped down on neighboring tribes to the west, including the Huron, Sauk, Fox, Potawatomi, Shawnee, Kickapoo, Miami, and others. These tribes fled in terror to the west and south, invading the lands that had traditionally been Illini territory. Soon the pressure for living and hunting space caused strife and dislocation there.

By 1650 the Iroquois had begun making forays directly into the lands of the Illini. The Illini confederacy, never as well organized and disciplined as the Five Nations, was no match for them. A long period of decline began.

❧

We have looked at the early inhabitants of Illinois, beginning with the hunter-gatherers who arrived about 12,000 years ago. After they developed a primitive system of agriculture, they were better able to control their food supply. Eventually they built a complex culture that came to a climax in the mound-building era. Then, suddenly, they were gone.

The Illini moved into the Illinois country some time after 1500. Archeologists have not been able to establish for certain whether they were related to the previous inhabitants. The Illini lived a life that cycled with the seasons until that rhythm was disrupted by the invasions of other tribes.

The French were the first Europeans to reach Illinois. When they arrived, the beleaguered Illini welcomed them. But, as we shall see, the French were unable to help the Indians in the long run.

For Further Exploration

David Brose, James Brown, and David Penney. *Ancient Art of the American Woodland Indians.* New York: Harry N. Abrams, in association with the Detroit Institute of Arts, 1985.

The many fine photographs in this beautiful book bring to life the unique cultures of the prehistoric Indians of the eastern United States. Some of the artifacts pictured are from Illinois.

Richard W. Jefferies. *The Archaeology of Carrier Mills: 10,000 Years in the Saline Valley of Illinois.* Carbondale: Southern Illinois University Press, 1987.

Cooperation between the Peabody Coal Company and a team of archeologists resulted in this survey of a rich prehistoric site that otherwise would have been lost to mining. Extensive salt springs in the area were of great importance to the early inhabitants and, later, to the first European settlers.

Stuart Struever and Felicia A. Holton. *Koster: Americans in Search of Their Prehistoric Past.* New York: Anchor Press/Doubleday, 1979.

For many years, spring plowing on the Koster farm in west-central Illinois turned up a scattering of artifacts. When the site was eventually excavated by archeologists, more than ten levels of occupation dating back more than 5,000 years were uncovered. Thousands came to watch the dig in progress.

2

The French in Illinois

Into the Wilderness

In the 1700s the most important town in the French colonial district of southern Illinois was Kaskaskia. Located on a fertile flood plain near where the Kaskaskia River flows into the Mississippi, it became the main link between French Canada and the Gulf of Mexico and an island of civilization in the overwhelming isolation of the wilderness. People of that day called it the "Paris of the West." Much later it became the first state capital of Illinois.

The Mississippi River brought about both Kaskaskia's prosperity and its downfall. Because of the river, Kaskaskia became a bustling commercial center. But each spring, rains and the runoff from melting snow and ice upstream transformed the river into a roiling menace. After surviving many spring floods, old Kaskaskia was finally wiped off the map by the great inundation of 1881. The river changed its course, rushing right over the town. If the water were clear, you might be able to look down and see traces of the old village lying at the bottom. But as the Mississippi is silt-rich and muddy, you can see only the brown water moving by and, jutting up out of the water on the other side of the river, a small remnant of land that is still attached to Illinois. Now called Kaskaskia Island, it has the distinction of being the only part of Illinois that lies west of the Mississippi.

How did it happen that the French made their way so deep into the interior of the continent while for many years the English stayed between the Atlantic and the Appalachian Mountains? The answer to this question lies in the difference between the immediate goals of these two great colonial powers. The English wanted to use their American

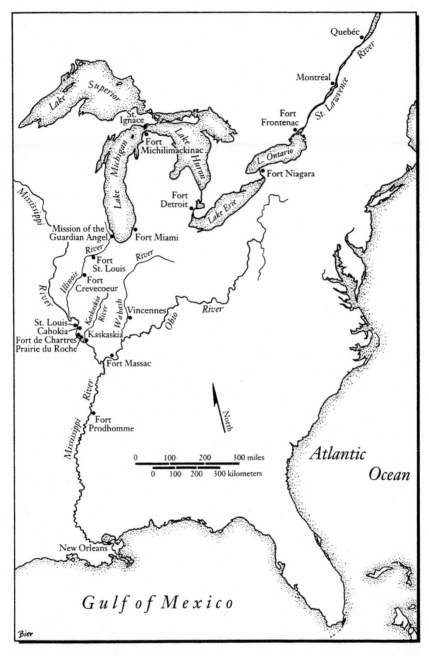

Twenty important French settlements in the New World. The French hoped
to control the interior by controlling the inland waterways. Illinois outposts
linked French Canada with New Orleans.

colonies as sources of raw materials for British industries and as markets for goods manufactured in England, so they began by building substantial towns and cities with large and stable populations along the Atlantic seaboard. The French hoped to build colonies for the same purpose eventually, but first they wanted to gain control of the lucrative fur trade far inland. Using the waterways as highways, they built a line of forts, missions, and trading posts from eastern Canada to the Great Lakes. By the 1600s they had reached the Midwest. In 1750 the English are thought to have outnumbered the French about eight to one, but the French had spread out over a much larger area.

The French Explore the Mississippi Valley

It was the French explorers who gave Illinois its name. They added a French ending to the name of the Illini, referring to the land where these Indians lived as "the Illinois."

The French listened carefully when the Indians spoke of a river that they called Misi Sipi (big river). It lay to the west, they said, but they did not know how far it went or in what direction it eventually flowed. Could this be the long-sought passage to the Pacific Ocean, the French wondered. If so, they wanted to be the first to claim it. They also felt a sense of urgency about exploring the river because they feared that it might have a tributary flowing into it from the East, which the English could use to make their way from Virginia into the interior. Anxious to monopolize the fur trade, the French certainly wanted to prevent that.

The Discoveries of Jolliet and Marquette

The governor of New France (Canada), Louis Frontenac, chose an experienced young explorer and fur trader named Louis Jolliet to lead the first expedition into the Mississippi Valley. France had long been a stronghold of Catholicism, and all of its foreign endeavors included the spreading of the Catholic religion. Hoping to Christianize and educate the Indians, the French always sent at least one priest along on such journeys. To accompany Jolliet, Frontenac chose a young Jesuit priest, Jacques Marquette.

Marquette had been an earnest seminary student in France and had been encouraged to continue his studies there. But he was filled with missionary zeal and begged to be sent to a distant land where he could carry the message of his beloved church to those who had had no chance to hear it. His request was at last granted, and he made the long journey to Canada. He was assigned to the mission located at St. Ignace in what is now upper Michigan. Jolliet met Marquette at St. Ignace, and on

May 17, 1673, they set out to explore the Mississippi River, accompanied by a crew of five men.

In two canoes the party paddled across Lake Michigan to Green Bay. There they met friendly Indians who advised them not to travel down the Mississippi River, as they would be in great danger from river monsters and hostile tribes. Marquette explained that his mission was to carry the word of God to all Indians, regardless of the dangers ahead.

Miami Indian scouts guided the Frenchmen down the Fox River and helped them portage (drag or carry their canoes a short distance) to the Wisconsin River. At that point, the Miami turned back. On June 17 the explorers entered the Mississippi, passing into territory that few, if any, white men had seen before.

The two leaders recorded seeing spotted deer, buffalo herds, and monstrous fish, one of which almost capsized one of the canoes. But for more than 300 miles they encountered no Indians. Then one day they saw human footprints in the mud along the shore. Ordering the men to guard the canoes, Jolliet and Marquette followed the footprints until they came to a settlement of Illini Indians on the west bank of the Mississippi near present-day Keokuk, Iowa. These Indians, probably of the Peoria tribe, may have been driven across the river by the Iroquois.

Men, women, and children came running out of the houses, shouting and gesturing. They had never seen Europeans before. Marquette and Jolliet were led to the house of the chief. Marquette had taken the trouble to learn six Algonquian languages, so he was able to converse with these people. He explained that he had come to teach them about God and to tell them that French soldiers had vanquished their enemies, the Iroquois. They then gave him information about the river and about the people through whose territory they would be passing.

Next a four-course feast was served: corn porridge, followed by fish, dog meat, and buffalo. As a sign of respect and friendship, the visitors were fed with a spoon as a parent would feed a small child. Marquette explained that they did not eat dog, so that dish was quickly whisked away. The next morning 600 Indians escorted them to their canoes.

Near present-day Alton the Frenchmen passed a bluff on which a picture of two winged monsters had been painted. Marquette recorded that they had calflike bodies covered with scales, men's faces, red eyes, tiger beards, deer horns, and long serpentine tails winding around their bodies. Seen by travelers a century later when the painting had grown fainter and only one figure was visible, the creature became known as the Piasa Bird. It may have had magical or religious significance. Similar creatures appear on prehistoric pottery.

After passing the mouth of the Ohio, the Frenchmen came upon tribes of Indians who had guns, cloth, glass beads, metal knives, and hoes, indicating that they had had contact with Europeans, probably the Spanish. The Indians told them that they were about ten days' journey from the mouth of the Mississippi. When they began encountering roaming bands of Indians who were not as friendly and trusting as the previous Indians had been, the explorers decided to turn back rather than to risk being captured by the Spanish or killed by hostile Indians. They now knew that the Mississippi River emptied into the Gulf of Mexico and not the Gulf of California and agreed that it was more important to return to Canada with that information than to see the mouth of the Mississippi.

On their return trip, they entered the Illinois River and met members of another Illini tribe, the Kaskaskia. They were well received and invited to come back. The journey had been hard on Marquette, but he was pleased to have found a large group of willing Indians to work with and promised that he or another "black robe" would come the following year to start a mission among them. A band of Kaskaskia then escorted the Frenchmen to the Lake of the Illinois (now known as Lake Michigan) by way of the Des Plaines and Chicago rivers. Marquette had become quite ill by the time the explorers reached Green Bay in late September.

In the spring of 1684 Jolliet set out for Montréal carrying a copy of Marquette's journal, his own report, maps they had both made, and papers relating to his fur-trading business. Within sight of the first houses of Montréal, his canoe capsized. The two people with him were drowned, and all the papers were lost. Later, Jolliet dictated an account of the Mississippi expedition from memory. It is believed that a second copy of Marquette's journal, which had been deposited for safekeeping at St. Ignace, eventually reached Montréal.

Marquette never entirely regained his health, but sheer determination carried him back to the Kaskaskia settlement where he founded the Mission of the Immaculate Conception. Again he became very ill. After a short rest he tried to make his way back to St. Ignace, but the 300-mile trip was far beyond his endurance. He died in the wilderness on May 18, 1675.

The Tribulations of La Salle and Tonti

Robert Cavelier, a wealthy Frenchman better known by his title, sieur de La Salle, dreamed of establishing a French empire in the New World. The spirit of the expeditions he led contrasted sharply with that of the Marquette-Jolliet expedition. Proud and combative, he possessed a love of country equaled only by his personal ambition.

La Salle was able to interest both Governor Frontenac and King Louis XIV in his ideas. Frontenac commissioned La Salle to organize a company to develop the West, and the king promised La Salle control of the fur trade south of the Great Lakes. However, financial support for the venture was harder to come by. In addition to spending much of his own fortune, La Salle had to make several trips to France to persuade rich relatives and friends to invest in his venture.

On one of these trips he met an Italian soldier of fortune, Henri de Tonti, who had lost a hand in combat and had had it replaced with an iron hook. Tonti became La Salle's faithful lieutenant and confidant. The Indians were also impressed with him. They were amazed by his iron "hand" and thought he had special powers.

La Salle had enough bad luck to make any but the most stalwart turn back. He and Tonti built a small fort at Niagara as well as a boat that they named the *Griffon*. The *Griffon* was the first sailing vessel to travel the inland waters. Recruiting a crew to go on an expedition into a wilderness thought to be peopled by fierce savages was no easy task. La Salle had to accept anyone who would go, and some of his recruits turned out to be misfits and renegades. To make matters worse, La Salle was not known for his diplomacy and tact. Strife with his men became a hallmark of his expeditions.

The first disaster La Salle suffered was the loss of the *Griffon*. He had sent it back to Fort Frontenac with a load of furs that the crew was to sell or barter for more supplies. They were then to return to Fort Miami near present-day South Bend, Indiana. Meanwhile La Salle, Tonti, and the rest of the party canoed down the Kankakee to the Illinois River and built a fort that La Salle named Fort Crevecoeur.

Having had no word of the *Griffon* for several months, La Salle made an arduous cross-country trip back to Fort Frontenac only to discover that his boat had probably gone down in a storm. When he returned to Fort Miami, he found it wrecked. He pushed on to the Indian camp near which Tonti was to have constructed a second fort. The village was deserted, and mutilated corpses were strewn about the cabins. His one comfort was that Tonti's body was not among them. La Salle next went to Fort Crevecoeur and found that the men he had stationed there had deserted, wrecking the building, stealing the supplies, and leaving the half-finished frame of a second boat they had agreed to build lying on its side like a beached whale.

It is hard to imagine how one man could possibly hope to track down another in the vast wilderness of mid-America in the late 1600s. Nev-

ertheless, La Salle canoed down the river, asking all of the people he
met if they had seen a white man with an iron hand. Eventually he was
overjoyed to learn that Tonti was safe and had made his way to Mackinac
in upper Michigan. La Salle went there, too.

By December 1681 La Salle and Tonti had collected a band of
forty-nine people, including some Indians and their families and were
at last able to set out for the mouth of the Mississippi. They reached
the Gulf of Mexico early in April 1682. In a solemn ceremony La Salle
claimed the Mississippi River, all of the rivers that flowed into it, and
all of the land surrounding those rivers for France. Both the Missouri
and Ohio rivers flow into the Mississippi, so he was laying claim to
more than half of the continent. La Salle named this vast area Louisiana
in honor of his king, Louis XIV of France.

La Salle and Tonti returned north and built a new fort, Fort St.
Louis, on a site occupied today by Starved Rock State Park. La Salle
left Tonti in charge there and went back to France to round up support
for a naval expedition to the mouth of the Mississippi.

The king and his advisors were well aware of the Spanish presence
in Mexico and were anxious to counter it with French forts and colonies
along the Gulf of Mexico. La Salle said that if he were given two ships,
he could establish such a colony. He was so persuasive that he was given
four ships with crews and supplies and was made governor of all the
territory between Lake Michigan and the Gulf of Mexico.

On July 24, 1684, La Salle left France with a force of about 250 men,
including four priests, one of whom was his brother. But misfortune
continued to plague him. One ship was captured by the Spanish. The
remaining ships sailed right past the Mississippi Delta without seeing
it, probably because bad weather had shrouded it in rain and fog. When
La Salle realized that they had gone too far west, he could not persuade
the captain, with whom he had previously quarreled, to turn back. In
desperation, La Salle took one of the ships in for a landing, and it ran
aground. Most of the ammunition and supplies that were to have been
used to establish a colony were lost. The captain insisted on returning
to France, leaving La Salle and his party stranded some four hundred
miles west of the Mississippi on the coast of Texas, probably near
Galveston. They built a small fort and planted crops, but the crops
failed because of a drought.

Still determined to reach the Mississippi, La Salle set sail in the last
ship. It, too, ran aground. Some of the crew were drowned, and others
were killed by Indians. Only forty of the 180 who had come ashore
with him were still alive. In January 1687 he decided that their only
hope was to try to reach Fort St. Louis. He set out with the twenty-eight

men he thought were still strong enough to travel, but when the party reached the Trinity River that May, La Salle met his final misfortune. He was murdered by four of his own men.

French Settlements in the Mississippi Valley

La Salle's death did not bring an end to French aspirations in the Midwest. French traders continued to travel from New France to the Gulf of Mexico by water. By 1699 the French had managed to establish two settlements on the Gulf coast: Biloxi (in present-day Mississippi) and another near the mouth of the Mississippi. New Orleans was founded about 1718.

Because of increasing Indian unrest and warfare, building outposts in the northern part of the Illinois country became a risky business. As a result, the French concentrated on southern Illinois, and their settlements there became important way stations and supply depots between Canada and lower Louisiana.

Tonti remained in Illinois for fifteen years after La Salle's death. Priests, government officials, Indians, and settlers relied on him for information, maps, and moral support. In 1698 François Laval, the bishop of Québec, asked Tonti to recommend a location for a new mission in southern Illinois. Tonti suggested that missionaries be sent to the Tamaroa and Cahokia Indians who were living across the Mississippi from present-day St. Louis. Following his advice, Laval sent three priests there in 1698. They built the Church of the Holy Family and named the village that grew up around it Cahokia.

Kaskaskia, the town with which we began this chapter, was located about fifty miles south of Cahokia. Another group of French colonists settled about fifteen miles north of Kaskaskia, calling their village Prairie du Roche because the fertile land on which it was built had a backdrop of imposing limestone bluffs. (Today these bluffs are a honeycomb of caves created by the quarrying of limestone).

In 1720 the French built Fort de Chartres about five miles west of Prairie du Roche, to serve as the military and administrative center for the Illinois country. That same year black slavery began in Illinois. Philippe Renault, the French director of mines, had come to the area hoping to find gold; finding none, he began a lead-mining operation. On his way to the Illinois country he stopped at the Island of Santo Domingo in the Caribbean and purchased a number of black slaves, perhaps as many as 500. A few years later, when he left to prospect for metals in Missouri and northern Illinois, Renault sold the slaves to the French families of Kaskaskia.

French villagers in the Illinois country enjoying their leisure time in traditional French ways. Courtesy of the Illinois State Historical Library.

The French and Indian War

By 1750 La Salle's dream of building a French empire in the New World seemed about to be realized. The French had a secure hold on Canada, the Mississippi River, and several seaports on the Gulf of Mexico. But by this time the English had begun showing greater interest in the lands beyond the Appalachian Mountains.

In 1749 a group of English colonists formed the Ohio Company and asked King George II for a land grant of half a million acres in the Ohio Valley. He honored their request, much to the consternation of the French. The French accused the English of trespassing, insisting that La Salle had claimed the interior of North America for France long before the English had arrived. Not so, said the English, maintaining that explorer John Cabot had claimed the whole continent for England two hundred years before La Salle's explorations.

The Seven Years' War broke out in Europe in 1756. France and England declared war on each other, and the fighting spread to their colonial possessions. The American phase was known as the French and Indian War. Although all of the major battles took place in the East, far from the Illinois country, the war had a profound effect on the future of Illinois.

At first the French had the advantage because they had been able to recruit many Indians as allies and were more skillful at fighting wilderness battles. However, the balance shifted when the new English foreign minister, William Pitt, poured manpower and supplies into the struggle for half a continent. British soldiers and colonial militia fighting side by side managed to capture some of the French-held forts.

The French did not receive such support from their home government, and some of their Indian allies grew disheartened and withdrew. In 1759 the English victories reached their climax with the fall of the French city of Québec. Within a year, all of Canada was in the hands of the English, and the French were ready to acknowledge defeat. However, the Seven Years' War was still in progress in Europe. Until that ended, no peace agreement could be final. At last, in 1763, England, France, and Spain stopped fighting and met in Paris to negotiate an official end to the war. They signed the Treaty of Paris, according to which France agreed to give up all its possessions in North America. The French era in the Illinois country had come to an end.

❧

Marked out on a map, the French outposts in the North American wilderness are impressive. The courage, tenacity, religious ardor, and spirit of enterprise that the French showed in penetrating the interior brought them to the brink of success. But without consistent and reliable support from the mother country, the French in North America could not confine their English competitors to the area between the East Coast and the Appalachian Mountains. When they lost the French and Indian War, they lost half a continent, including the Illinois country.

It did not take the jubilant English long to discover that they had saddled themselves with a rich but unyielding wilderness. In the next chapter we will follow their unfruitful attempts to establish themselves in Illinois.

For Further Exploration

Natalia Belting. *Kaskaskia under the French Regime*. Urbana: Graduate College of the University of Illinois, Illinois Studies in the Social Sciences, Vol. XXIX, No.3, 1948. Polyanthos edition, New Orleans: Polyanthos, 1975.

This slender volume, based on court and parish records, gives an authentic picture of life in the French villages in the Illinois country, particularly Kaskaskia. Isolated as they were, the villagers retained their religious beliefs, language, and traditions—and their gaiety of spirit.

Donald Barr Chidsey. *The French and Indian War*. New York: Crown Publishers, 1969.

Although not specifically about Illinois, this book makes clear how valuable the lands of the interior of North America were to the Europeans who fought over them.

Virginia S. Eifert. *Louis Jolliet: Explorer of Rivers*. New York: Dodd, Mead, and Co., 1962.

This account of the activities of the early French explorers highlights the exploits of Jolliet and explains the supporting roles played by the church, the French government, and the fur traders and their crews.

3

How the Illinois Country Became American Territory

The Proclamation of 1763

Having vanquished the French, the English found themselves in possession of half a continent. The Illinois country formed more than a third of the western border of the new lands; its location on the greatest river of the interior made it strategically and militarily important. Realizing this, the English were determined to occupy Fort de Chartres and other wilderness outposts. However, there was much disagreement over whether the time was ripe for starting settlements so far from the seaboard colonies.

In 1763, at the end of the French and Indian War, King George III of England issued a proclamation saying that no settlements were to be made west of the Appalachian Mountains. He and his advisors hoped that if the western lands were left to the Indians for the time being, they would stop attacking settlements east of the Appalachians.

However, the proclamation proved ineffective. For one thing, some settlers were already living west of the mountains. Others who had waited for the war to end so they could move there were determined to proceed with their plans. Speculators and promoters wanted to start colonies, buy and sell land, and set up businesses. Benjamin Franklin and other colonial leaders went to England to argue the case for settling the western lands. They pointed out that the French had lost their possessions in North America because they had failed to establish strong colonies.

While these debates raged on, the king's proclamation was ignored. Traders, trappers, and adventurers continued to head westward, and soon backwoodsmen, farmers, and their families followed. There was, after all, not much the colonial governors, the king, or Parliament could do to stop them.

Pontiac's Uprising

Although the war had been lost by the French, Pontiac, a powerful Ottawa chief, still believed that he could drive out the English and return the French to power. Like many other Indian leaders, he felt that if a European presence in the wilderness was inevitable, it would be far preferable to have the French rather than the English.

The French did not disrupt the Indian way of life as much as the English did. French villages remained small, and the settlers made no attempt to uproot the Indians. The French assumed that someday the Indians would change their way of life and settle on farms and in villages next to their white brothers. Many French fur traders sincerely liked the Indians and participated in their social rituals and ceremonies of friendship. During their months in the wilderness, they lived as the Indians lived. Some married Indian women.

The English, on the other hand, cut down the forest, plowed and planted, and drove out the wildlife, making it difficult for the Indians to live in their customary manner. Impatient when they encountered Indians on land they wanted, the English tried to buy them out, drive them out, or exterminate them.

Pontiac realized that he and his braves could not do the job alone. He visited other tribes living in the Great Lakes area and in the Ohio Valley and persuaded them to take part in a joint action against the English. In May 1763 raiding parties attacked fourteen widely separated forts that the English had recently taken over from the French. Because of the secrecy and surprise with which the Indians conducted their campaign, they were able to overrun all but four of the forts. Pontiac is thought to have coordinated the skirmishes and sent in reinforcements.

Detroit was one of the forts that did not fall. Pontiac therefore laid siege to it, but after five months his warriors became restless. Lying around outside the fort waiting for something to happen or carrying out small harassments was not their idea of warfare. Many of them returned to their villages. By then his old allies, the French, were much weaker than the English and could no longer help him. In fact, the French government had already signed a peace treaty with England.

When news came that the English would soon reinforce Fort Detroit, Pontiac saw that the situation was hopeless and lifted the siege. A formal peace treaty between Pontiac and the English was confirmed at Oswego, Illinois, in 1766. The English reestablished garrisons in the wilderness forts that the Indians had ambushed and moved to occupy the forts the French had built in the Illinois country.

The English at Fort de Chartres

On October 9, 1765, Captain Thomas Stirling and a hundred English soldiers marched into Fort de Chartres. The next day, the last French flag to fly in the Illinois country was quietly lowered, the English flag was raised, and Captain Stirling read a proclamation stating that French settlers who wanted to stay and were willing to take an oath of allegiance to the British crown would be treated like all other English subjects. They would not be required to give up their language, religion, or traditions. Those not wanting to live under British rule were free to leave without hindrance.

Shortly after these ceremonies were completed, Louis St. Ange de Bellerive, the French commandant, and his twenty-one soldiers crossed the Mississippi and took up residence in Spanish territory. The French settlers loved their quiet little villages and did not want to leave, but they did not trust the English promises. Being Catholic, they did not want to be ruled by Protestant Englishmen. An estimated one thousand French settlers living in or near Kaskaskia moved west of the Mississippi or went back to France. About two thousand of their countrymen stayed behind, hoping for the best.

The English soon found that they had taken on an almost impossible task. Supplies were slow to reach the isolated fort. Officers and soldiers sickened and died in the hot and humid summers to which they were not accustomed. There were no trained officials to establish a civil government. When settlers had complaints, they had no reliable court or law enforcement system on which to depend.

Fort de Chartres was to have been the military and administrative headquarters for the English in Illinois, but within a few years it was in a state of disrepair. The Mississippi River undermined the buildings during spring floods, even though British engineers did all they could to prevent it. In 1772 the English destroyed Fort de Chartres so that no enemies could make use of it and moved to Kaskaskia. A short time later, they put Kaskaskia under the care of a Frenchman who had become an English subject, Phillippe de Rocheblave, and left the Illinois country.

George Rogers Clark and the Campaign for Illinois

Most of the battles of the American Revolutionary War (1776–83) took place in the East, but one important campaign took place in the Illinois country. Some of the American colonists living in the wilderness west of the Appalachians felt so far removed from the conflict that they took little interest in it. But others were more far-sighted, realizing that if the British lost their colonies on the East Coast, they might attempt to take over the Ohio and Mississippi valleys. They could then keep the Americans boxed in on the East Coast, just as the French had tried to do to the English. The East Coast was already heavily settled, and the freedom to expand westward had to be protected.

A Virginian named George Rogers Clark became the hero of the Revolution in the Illinois country. Clark had made several expeditions down the Ohio River and owned land near present-day Louisville, Kentucky. He hoped the British would be driven out of North America entirely so that they would no longer be able to interfere with American progress. His ultimate goal was to take Detroit, the most important British fort in the West. But first he wanted to secure the Illinois country. If the forts there could be won, links could be forged among the East Coast, the Kentucky settlements, and the Mississippi Valley. These garrisons would provide bases for future operations against the British.

Clark Consults Patrick Henry

As far away from Virginia as Illinois was, the Virginians still considered it part of their territory. In 1606 King James I had signed a charter authorizing the London Company to begin settlements between the 34th and 45th parallels north latitude, stipulating that the Colony of Virginia could extend from sea to sea. To the Virginians, the old charter meant that they were entitled to occupy all the lands due west of Virginia. A glance at a map of the United States shows that part of Illinois lies within this area.

Clark therefore traveled to Virginia to consult the governor, Patrick Henry. He told him that spies sent to the Illinois country had reported that the British had only a few men stationed there and that the French settlers felt little loyalty toward the English. He then explained his plan to Governor Henry. He wanted to smuggle troops—two or three hundred men if he could get them—into the Illinois country. He planned to take Kaskaskia by surprise, then quickly move on to Cahokia before the British stationed at Detroit had time to react. Next he would march on Vincennes, a village on the east bank of the Wabash River.

Clark emphasized that with such a small army, his only hope of success lay in secrecy and speed.

The resources of the thirteen colonies were being drained by the war effort in the East, and there was little to spare for the campaign Clark outlined. Nevertheless, Henry gave his approval and promised Clark limited financial help. On January 18, 1778, Clark left Williamsburg, Virginia, and set off on an adventure that would make the Illinois country American territory.

Kaskaskia and Cahokia

Clark and the 175 men he recruited traveled down the Ohio River as far as Fort Massac. There they hid their boats and made an overland trek of more than 120 miles to Kaskaskia. Had they continued by boat, they would have been too visible.

They arrived at Kaskaskia in the dark of the night of July 3, 1778. Rocheblave, the official in charge there, was quietly captured as he slept in his bed. Then, on Clark's orders, the soldiers created enough of a

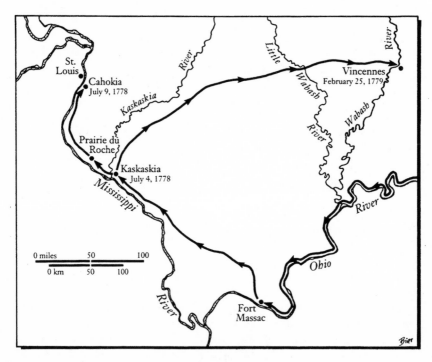

George Rogers Clark's route, 1778–79.

disturbance in the streets to make the people believe their town had been invaded by a large army. Experiencing no resistance, the soldiers told the apprehensive people that they had nothing to fear and should stay in their homes until morning.

Early on July 4, Clark met with the leading citizens of Kaskaskia and explained why he had come. Telling them that the Americans no longer wished to live under the English flag and were fighting for their freedom, Clark promised that if they became Americans, they would have the same privileges and protections all other Americans would have as soon as the British were defeated. He ended his speech with an important piece of news that had not yet reached the Illinois wilderness: France had agreed to help the Americans fight the English. Upon hearing that, the Kaskaskians quickly agreed to cooperate and joined in the celebration that followed. During the festivities, the bell that hung in the village church was rung. It later became known as the Liberty Bell of the West. (After the great flood of 1881 it was found in the river and is now located on Kaskaskia Island.)

Having taken Kaskaskia, Clark sent one of his most trusted officers, Captain Joseph Bowman, to the French villages north of Kaskaskia. Some of the villagers volunteered to accompany Bowman to help him explain the situation. Within three days, Clark had control of all the Illinois settlements, and no blood had been shed.

Vincennes Won and Lost

Clark next turned his attention to the British fort at Vincennes. He wanted to capture it to protect the supply lines between Kentucky and the Illinois country. Clark consulted Father Pierre Gibault, the priest serving the French settlements in the Illinois country at that time. Father Gibault told him that the French people of Vincennes would receive the Americans in much the same way as the people in the other French villages had.

Clark then wrote them a letter summarizing what he had already said to the people at Kaskaskia. A Frenchman, Dr. Jean Laffont, agreed to deliver the message, and Father Gibault went along to answer questions. Just as Father Gibault had said, when the letter was read and the people had discussed it, they decided to put themselves under the protection of the Americans. After swearing allegiance, they marched to the fort and demanded that the British flag be taken down and the American flag raised. The few English soldiers who were manning the fort quickly surrendered, and a small contingent of Clark's men took over. Vincennes, too, had been taken without bloodshed.

Meanwhile, word of what had happened in the Illinois country reached the British officer in charge at Detroit, Lieutenant Henry Hamilton. Hamilton had a bad reputation among the Americans. Some claimed that he had urged the Indians to raid isolated villages and kill American settlers. He was known as "The Hair Buyer" because he was said to offer the Indians bounties for American scalps. His duty, as he saw it, was to keep Americans out of the West. Clark's successes embarrassed and angered him.

Hamilton hurriedly set out from Detroit with the few men who could be spared: thirty-five English soldiers, seventy-eight Frenchmen, and about sixty Indians. On the way he enlisted the help of several hundred more Indians. Clark got word that Hamilton was on the move but did not know his destination. Then, in mid-December, Clark, who was in Kaskaskia, received a desperate note from Vincennes saying that Hamilton and his army were within three miles of the fort. By December 17 Hamilton had recaptured Vincennes and made prisoners of the few Americans there.

Final Victory at Vincennes

News of Hamilton's success made the Kaskaskians exceedingly apprehensive, for they feared the English would march on Kaskaskia next and punish them for having cooperated with the Americans. To stem the panic, Clark showed little concern over the matter and let it be known that he was expecting reinforcements from Kentucky. In private, he felt considerable unease because he had little hope that any reinforcements would actually reach him.

Clark had a friend named François Vigo, a Sardinian merchant who lived in St. Louis, a settlement that was at that time in Spanish territory. Vigo had gone to Vincennes to arrange for the shipment of more supplies to the Americans stationed there. Only after he arrived did he learn that the British had recaptured the town. He was arrested, but when the British learned that he was a Spanish citizen, they released him after making him promise to return directly to St. Louis. He did as he had promised but then hurried back to Kaskaskia to tell Clark what he had been able to find out.

Vigo informed Clark that Hamilton had sent word to all of the Indian tribes in and around Michigan to fight with him in the spring. He had promised that together they would wipe out all the American frontier settlements west of the Appalachians. They were to spend the winter making small raids on American settlements, then return to Vincennes in the spring for the great battle. Vigo also told Clark that at present only a small British force was manning the fort at Vincennes.

George Rogers Clark and his men crossing the Wabash River as they approach Vincennes. Courtesy of the Illinois State Historical Library.

Realizing that Hamilton would never expect him to attack in the dead of winter, Clark decided upon an immediate assault. On February 5, 1779, he and his men set out on the long march eastward across Illinois from Kaskaskia to Vincennes. At first, rain was more of a problem than cold. However, as they advanced toward their goal, the weather worsened. The bottomlands were so flooded that for hours they had to wade through icy waters, the heavy mud clinging to their boots. Some nights they were unable to keep a fire going long enough to cook and to dry their clothes. As they neared their destination, Clark ordered them not to hunt or build fires, as the light of a fire or the sound of a gunshot might alert the enemy.

With provisions running low, the men dragged themselves along, hungry, tired, and cold. Some came down with fevers and grew almost too weak to walk. Just when it seemed almost impossible to go any farther, they reached the Wabash River. The sight of the fort they had come so far to take put new life into Clark's bedraggled little army.

On February 23 Clark and his men moved toward the fort, shooting their rifles. When Hamilton heard the first shots, he thought it was just a few partying Indians having a good time. However, as the gunfire continued far into the night, it became obvious that the fort was under attack.

Toward morning Clark had his men dig a trench just beyond the reach of the fort's guns and installed several of his expert sharpshooters in it. Whenever the British opened a gunport to fire out at their attackers, Clark's riflemen shot at them. They seldom missed. Hamilton's losses mounted, but the Americans suffered no casualties.

The next day Clark sent a message to the fort asking Hamilton to surrender. At first Hamilton refused, but by the middle of the day he saw that further resistance was futile. At ten o'clock on February 25 Hamilton and his men marched out of the fort to become prisoners of war. The American flag was raised, and the cannons were fired in honor of the occasion. Clark's final victory at Vincennes had made the Illinois country American territory.

After the French and Indian War it took the British two years to reach Fort de Chartres, partly because Pontiac's uprising had to be quelled before they could proceed westward. By the time the Revolutionary War broke out (1776), the English had become so discouraged with the overwhelming task of protecting and governing isolated villages deep in the Illinois wilderness that they wrecked the fort, turned the civil government in Kaskaskia over to a Frenchman who had become an English subject, and left.

During the Revolution, most Americans were preoccupied with the fighting in the East, but George Rogers Clark recognized the golden opportunity that lay open in the West. He planned and carried out the conquest of the Illinois country.

The thirteen seaboard colonies gained more than their independence as a result of the Revolutionary War. Great Britain ceded all of its North American possessions except Canada and East and West Florida to the new nation, more than doubling the size of the United States. Clark's far-sighted campaign had extinguished all British claims to the Mississippi Valley. Now it was up to the Americans to succeed where older and more powerful nations had failed. In the next chapter we will see how the Illinois wilderness became the Illinois Territory.

For Further Exploration

George Rogers Clark. *The First American Frontier: Col. George Rogers Clark's Sketch of His Campaign in the Illinois in 1778–9.* Cincinnati: Robert Clarke & Co., 1869. Reprint, Dale Van Every, advisory editor. New York: Arno Press and the New York Times, 1971.

Without George Rogers Clark's campaign, the western boundary of the United States might well have been the crest of the Appalachian Mountains. Included in this book are a short biographical sketch of Clark, Patrick Henry's instructions to him, Clark's own account of the campaign, and Major Bowman's journal of the final victory at Vincennes.

David Goodnough. *Pontiac's War, 1763–1766.* New York: Franklin Watts, 1970.

Historians disagree on Pontiac's place in history. Was he a brave patriot, making a last-ditch effort to save his people, or a ruthless renegade? This author places him midway between these extremes but sees the uprising as disastrous for the Indians. The fear the ambushes created solidified the determination of white setters to drive the Indians out.

4

Steps toward Statehood

Illinois as a County of Virginia

When the news of George Rogers Clark's success in the Illinois country reached Virginia, the Virginians declared Illinois a county of Virginia. However, defending and governing a distant and sparsely settled wilderness was no easier for the Virginians than it had been for the English or the French. In 1784 Virginia ceded the county of Illinois to the federal government. Within a few years, other states that had claimed lands in the west followed suit. Congress was then faced with the task of integrating the new area into the United States.

In 1785 Congress passed the Land Ordinance Act, which set up a system for surveying the territory. The Northwest Ordinance, a plan for governing it, followed two years later. The ordinance named the land west of the Appalachian Mountains as far as the Mississippi River and north of the Ohio River the "Northwest Territory." (Later, when the Pacific Northwest was added to the United States, the Northwest Territory was often referred to as the "Old" Northwest.) Lawmakers stipulated that not less than three nor more than five states should be created from the 265,878 square miles that comprised the Northwest Territory. Illinois along with Ohio, Indiana, Michigan, and Wisconsin became the new states, a process that took more than a hundred years.

Arthur St. Clair, who had been appointed the first governor of the Northwest Territory, arrived in what is now the state of Ohio in 1788, a year after the ratification of the new Constitution. Using Marietta as his headquarters, he set to work on the difficult task of establishing civil government in the wilderness.

Four chaotic years had passed since Virginia had ceded the Illinois country to the federal government. The following letter, dated September 1789 and sent to the commandant at Vincennes by the people of Kaskaskia, pictures their distress: "The Indians are greatly more numerous than the white people, and are rather hostilely inclined. . . . Our horses, horned cattle, and corn are stolen and destroyed without the power of making any effectual resistance. Our houses are in ruin and decay; our lands are uncultivated; debtors absconded and absconding, our little commerce destroyed. . . . Ever since the cession of this Territory to Congress, we have been neglected as an abandoned people, to encounter all the difficulties that are always attendant upon anarchy and confusion."

St. Clair promised to visit the settlers and reached Kaskaskia in March 1790. Within a few weeks he created the first county in what would eventually become the state of Illinois, naming it after himself. He appointed his cousin, William St. Clair, court clerk for the new county. Although the troubles of the settlers were by no means over, at least a beginning had been made.

While at work on the Northwest Ordinance, the members of Congress had feared that the spread of slavery might hinder development because many New Englanders would not settle where slavery was allowed. Southerners who would have objected to the abolishment of slavery within their own borders did not insist on its expansion, feeling that allowing slavery in the West might make it possible for westerners to compete with them in the cotton and tobacco trades. Congress therefore included the following statement in Article VI of the Northwest Ordinance: "There shall be neither slavery nor involuntary servitude in the said territory, otherwise than for the punishment of crimes, whereof the party shall have been duly convicted."

Some of the settlers living in what is now Illinois had slaves and were concerned that they might be required to give them up. Governor St. Clair tried to appease them by misinterpreting Article VI. He told them it meant that no *new* slaves could be brought into the territory but that slaves already there were in no way affected.

The Indians living in the Northwest Territory could not help noticing the influx of white settlers. They terrorized isolated settlements in a last-ditch effort to save their lands. After General Anthony Wayne, a Revolutionary War hero, had defeated the Miami Indians in the Battle of Fallen Timbers (1794), the Northwest Territory became safer for settlers, but Indian troubles farther west and north continued until 1832. Fort Wayne, Indiana, is named for General "Mad" Anthony Wayne, the "Mad" referring both to his bravery and quick temper.

Illinois as Part of the Indiana Territory

According to the Northwest Ordinance, a territory could organize its own General Assembly as soon as it had a population of five thousand free, white males twenty-one years or older. At that point it could also elect one delegate to the U.S. Congress. When the Northwest Territory reached that point, voters chose Indian fighter William Henry Harrison to represent them in Washington. Through Harrison's efforts, a bill creating the Territory of Indiana was passed by Congress in 1800.

The Territory of Indiana included all of the old Northwest Territory except for the portion that became the state of Ohio in 1803. Harrison became governor of the new Indiana Territory, and Vincennes became the capital. At this point, Illinois was part of the Indiana Territory, but not happily so. Illinois settlers complained that they were not receiving adequate protection and insisted that the seat of government at Vincennes was too far away from their main settlements.

The Territory of Illinois

After nine years of trying, those who wanted separation from Indiana found a way to accomplish their goal. They agreed to help elect Jesse B. Thomas as the delegate to Congress from the Indiana Territory. In turn, Thomas pledged to work for the enactment of a law that would allow Illinois to become a separate territory. He won the election and made good his promise. The law creating the Illinois Territory went into effect on March 1, 1809. Kaskaskia was named the territorial capital.

President James Madison appointed Ninian Edwards of Kentucky governor of the Illinois Territory. Edwards met with the territorial judges and worked out a legal code for the new territory, adapting most of the thirty-eight laws in it from the laws of the Indiana Territory.

In the next few years Congress remedied two important complaints of Illinois settlers. The Northwest Ordinance stated that a settler had to be a landowner before he could vote, but only about 220 of the 12,000 inhabitants of Illinois owned the land on which they were living. Congress agreed to drop the land ownership requirement.

The other complaint was that families who had been living on the frontier for several years could not be sure that the land they had cleared would someday be theirs. The federal government had not finished surveying the land or setting up land offices to which people could go to buy acreage, so many of these early settlers were technically squatters. When the federal government was ready to sell, newcomers and speculators might suddenly appear to compete for the land. Congress therefore passed a preemption law that gave squatters the first chance to buy the land they were living on.

An Event Long Remembered

About 2 A.M. on the morning of December 17, 1811, people throughout the Midwest were awakened by a violent trembling of the earth. Residents of the little town of New Madrid, Missouri, who were at the epicenter of the quake, ran outdoors thinking the end of the world had come. Fields rippled like waves on an ocean. Trees swayed, became tangled together, and snapped off with sounds like gunshots. People were afraid of being swallowed up by the earth as it cracked open. In some places, sand, coal, and smoke blew up into the air as high as thirty yards. People as far away as Québec, Canada, and Washington, D.C., felt the tremors.

Boatmen on the Mississippi and Ohio rivers heard harsh scraping sounds as if they had run aground. Some boats were swamped while others had the water suddenly sucked out from under them. Bluffs fell into the river, creating tidal waves. New islands suddenly appeared, and old ones disappeared. Even the course of the Mississippi River changed in several places. Although the Richter scale did not exist in those days, experts have estimated that the New Madrid earthquake would have registered over 8.0. Fortunately, few people lost their lives on land because the quake was centered in a sparsely populated area. No one knows how many people died on the rivers.

Indian Troubles and the War of 1812

Indian troubles broke out again shortly before the War of 1812. A Shawnee chief named Tecumseh and his brother who was known as "The Prophet" had tried to form yet another coalition of tribes to oppose the invasion of American settlers into their traditional lands. Tecumseh advised tribal leaders not to sell or cede any more land to the Americans and gathered an army of braves at an encampment on the Tippecanoe River in Indiana. The governor of the Indiana Territory, William Henry Harrison, met with Tecumseh and listened to what he had to say, but he considered Tecumseh a thorn in his side. In November 1811, while Tecumseh was away, an American sentry was killed. Harrison attacked the village at Tippecanoe and wiped it out, effectively ending Tecumseh's challenge. Later Harrison made a successful bid for the presidency of the United States, running under the slogan of "Tippecanoe and Tyler, too." (He was the hero of Tippecanoe, and John Tyler was his running mate).

Although the Illini tribes were no longer a threat, other tribes that had come to Illinois later, such as the Kickapoo, Potawatomi, and Winnebago, far outnumbered the settlers. Had Tecumseh succeeded, these Indians might have joined together to make meaningful deals with white officials or fought as members of a cohesive group against the encroachment of white settlers. Instead, small bands of Indians continued to harass isolated settlers. In desperate circumstances themselves, they struck with little warning, killing men, women, and children and stealing horses and other goods.

The violence increased to such a point that in 1811 Congress assigned four companies of mounted rangers to Illinois. Governor Edwards constructed Fort Russell near Edwardsville and had small block-houses built along the line of settlement so that people could reach a place of safety when necessary. Farther north, Peoria's Fort Clark was rebuilt. The sixty soldiers stationed at Fort Dearborn on the site of present-day Chicago were put on alert.

By February 1812 Governor Edwards was alarmed enough to tell the secretary of war that Illinois was likely to lose half of its population within the next few months if something was not done about the Indian problem. He wrote: "No troops of any kind have yet arrived in this Territory, and I think you may count on hearing of a bloody stroke upon us very soon. I have been extremely reluctant to send my family away, but, unless I hear shortly of more assistance than a few rangers, I shall bury my papers in the ground, send my family off, and stand my ground as long as possible." A bloody stroke came, but not in southern Illinois.

The Massacre at Chicago.

The original causes of the War of 1812 had more to do with freedom of the seas than with life in the Illinois wilderness. However, the British in Canada had made allies of some of the Indian tribes and encouraged them to raid American settlements. Shortly after the war began, the British and their Indian allies overwhelmed Fort Michilimackinac at the northern tip of Michigan's lower peninsula.

In a moment of panic the American commander at Detroit sent word to his subordinate at Fort Dearborn, Captain Nathan Heald, telling him to give the blankets, tools, and other goods stored there to friendly Indians, to destroy all but a small amount of the ammunition, and to evacuate the fort.

Fort Dearborn massacre, 1812. Courtesy of Illinois State Historical Library.

John Kinzie, a fur trader and silversmith who was liked and respected by the Indians, had a trading post near Fort Dearborn. Kinzie knew the Indians were restive and thought they might be planning an attack, as there had already been several skirmishes nearby. He told Heald it would be much better to stay in the fort and try to hold out until help arrived. Officers under Heald agreed, but Heald was reluctant to disregard the orders he had received. Kinzie warned him that if he were going to evacuate Fort Dearborn, he should do so immediately.

Unfortunately, five days went by before Heald made up his mind. By then the Indians had had time to plan an attack. No sooner had the soldiers and civilians filed out of the fort and started eastward across the prairie than their Indian guides turned on them and were quickly joined by other Indians hiding nearby.

Kinzie managed to get his family safely aboard a boat, and he himself was spared by the Indians, as was Captain Heald's wife. Many of the others were not so fortunate. About sixty men, two women, and twelve children were killed. Five women were taken captive, and several children were never accounted for. Heald surrendered to the Indians but was eventually released.

For a few years after the Fort Dearborn massacre, fear of the Indians made some Illinois settlers retreat to more densely populated areas. Immigration into Illinois virtually stopped, and land sales fell off. But by the time the war officially ended early in 1815, the Indians had suffered enough defeats to see that even their alliance with the British would not stop the tide of white settlement. The raids on isolated settlements all but ceased, and within a few years the Illinois frontier was again bustling with new life.

☙

The complicated sequence of events that led to the establishment of the Illinois Territory began when the state of Virginia claimed the Illlinois country as a county of Virginia. Defending and governing a distant province became such a burden that Virginia soon ceded Illinois to the federal government. In 1787 Congress drew up the Northwest Ordinance, and Illinois became part of the newly organized Northwest Territory. By 1800 Ohio was ready to become a separate territory, and a large portion of what had been the Northwest Territory became the Indiana Territory, of which Illinois was a part. But Illinois settlers wanted more control over their own affairs. After a little wheeling and dealing on the part of leading citizens, Illinois became a separate territory in 1809.

Illinoisans were so pleased with their new status that they were not particularly anxious to achieve statehood. But that changed in 1817, due mainly to the efforts of a young lawyer from Kentucky, Daniel Pope Cook. An account of the eventful years in which Illinois became the twenty-first state follows in chapter 5.

For Further Exploration

William Atkinson. *The Next New Madrid Earthquake: A Survival Guide for the Midwest*. Carbondale: Southern Illinois University Press, 1989.

Basically a preparedness manual, this book also includes a brief account of past seismic activity along the New Madrid fault as well as an up-to-date survey of what scientists now know about predicting earthquakes.

Otto A. Rothert. *The Outlaws of Cave-in-Rock*. Cleveland: Arthur H. Clark Company, 1924. Reprint. Evansville, Ind.: Whipporwill Publications, 1984.

Operating in the wilderness where they felt safe from government interference, the river pirates and bands of outlaws along the Ohio and Mississippi rivers added to the hazards and uncertainties of pioneer life and made settlers eager to have law enforcement agencies nearby.

5

The Twenty-first State

Preliminaries: Cook and Pope

Daniel Pope Cook arrived in Illinois in 1815. Although in poor health, he was an ambitious young man looking for a job. Governor Ninian Edwards, who later became his father-in-law, appointed him auditor of public accounts. Cook also bought a share in the territory's first newspaper, the *Illinois Herald*.

In 1817 Cook began publishing articles that pointed out the undemocratic aspects of territorial government: the governor's absolute veto power; a General Assembly that could not appoint public officials; territorial representatives elected to the U.S. Congress who could voice their opinions during congressional sessions but who could not vote. Cook acknowledged that statehood would be costly because the federal government would no longer pay the salaries of public officials, but he maintained that it would bring new waves of settlers that would, in turn, increase the value of land in Illinois.

Cook was elected clerk of the House of Representatives of the Illinois Territory, a good position from which to continue his campaign. At his urging a committee drew up a petition requesting statehood. Governor Edwards ordered a population census, but Cook and others were too impatient to wait for it to be completed. Instead, they estimated the population at forty thousand and named that figure in the petition. On December 10, 1817, the Illinois General Assembly approved the petition and sent it to Washington.

Congress appointed Nathaniel Pope, the territorial representative from Illinois and Cook's uncle, chairman of the committee to consider the petition for statehood. The committee discussed the petition, then drafted an enabling act to present to Congress. At that point, Pope proposed several amendments, the most important of which concerned the northern border of Illinois. That proposed border was south of Lake Michigan and would have given Illinois no shoreline. Pope argued that if Illinois had a shoreline, it would be securely linked to the East Coast via the Great Lakes. He requested that the boundary be set forty miles to the north, and Congress approved this amendment. If Pope had not brought this matter up, eight thousand square miles of Illinois— parts of fourteen counties—would be in Wisconsin today. So would Chicago.

Congress approved and the president signed the enabling act in April 1818. The people of Illinois could then turn to the task of developing a state constitution.

The Constitutional Convention

In July 1818 Illinois voters chose thirty-three delegates to attend Illinois's first constitutional convention. Early settlers did not pay much attention to political parties. They voted for people they knew and liked or whose opinions mirrored their own. Among the delegates they chose were three physicians, two sheriffs, three lawyers, a minister, a store-keeper, a flatboater, and a land office official. These men gathered in Kaskaskia the first Monday in August and chose Judge Jesse B. Thomas as their chairman.

Their first problem occurred when the delegates could not officially come up with the required population figure of forty thousand. The closing date of Governor Edwards's census was changed from June to December so that settlers who arrived after June could be included. Still there were not enough people, so more had to be "found." Some people were counted twice and families just passing through were included as though they had come to stay. The final report stated that the population was 40,258. No one argued the point. Later, a federal report showed that Illinois had actually had a population of only 34,620 when it became a state, but by 1820 the national census showed the population of Illinois to be 55,211. Counting people living in clearings in the woods must have been an inexact science at best!

Next a committee of fifteen, including one person from each county, was chosen to work up a rough draft of the constitution. Elias Kent Kane, a young delegate from Randolph County, played much the same role as James Madison had played in framing the U.S. Constitution. Kane studied the constitutions of other states, then offered suggestions

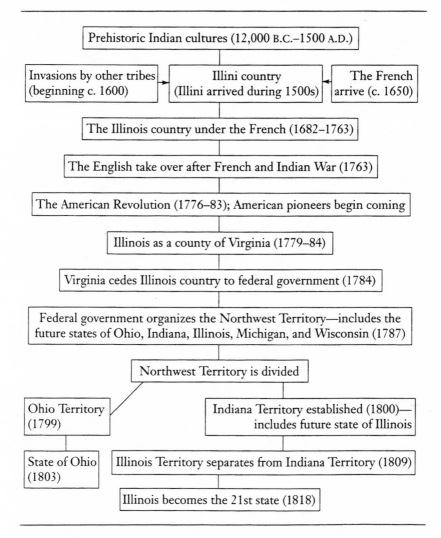

Prehistoric Indian cultures (12,000 B.C.–1500 A.D.)

Invasions by other tribes (beginning c. 1600)

Illini country (Illini arrived during 1500s)

The French arrive (c. 1650)

The Illinois country under the French (1682–1763)

The English take over after French and Indian War (1763)

The American Revolution (1776–83); American pioneers begin coming

Illinois as a county of Virginia (1779–84)

Virginia cedes Illinois country to federal government (1784)

Federal government organizes the Northwest Territory—includes the future states of Ohio, Indiana, Illinois, Michigan, and Wisconsin (1787)

Northwest Territory is divided

Ohio Territory (1799)

Indiana Territory established (1800)—includes future state of Illinois

State of Ohio (1803)

Illinois Territory separates from Indiana Territory (1809)

Illinois becomes the 21st state (1818)

Illinois from wilderness to statehood.

based on his research. Between meetings he rewrote and edited the evolving document.

On August 15, just a week after the committee had begun its work, a draft of the constitution was ready for consideration by the whole convention. The delegates went through the document article by article and voted on proposed changes. A short and simple constitution consisting of a preamble and eight articles was then ready to present to Congress. (Before 1820, the constitution of a new state was not submitted to the voters of that state. It automatically went into effect after receiving congressional approval.)

Illinois voters chose Shadrach Bond, who had been the first delegate to Congress from the Illinois Territory, as their first governor. The General Assembly met in October to celebrate Governor Bond's inauguration but did not convene a regular session because it could not pass any laws until the U.S. Congress had approved the Illinois constitution. Congress did so early in December.

On December 3, 1818, President James Monroe signed the act that made Illinois the twenty-first state of the Union. One wonders what he thought as he put pen to paper. Long before he had become president he had made two official visits to the area and had reported that it was "miserably poor" and that the extensive grasslands "will not have a bush on them for ages" and therefore "will never contain a sufficient number of inhabitants to entitle them to membership in the confederacy."

The Slavery Controversy

The only article of the new constitution over which there had been heated debate was the article prohibiting slavery. In spite of the fact that the Northwest Ordinance prohibited slavery, slavery did exist in Illinois. The French had introduced it in the 1700s, and neither the British nor the Virginians had forbidden it. In fact, Virginia ceded Illinois to the federal government on the condition that the inhabitants be allowed to retain their lands and "property," including slaves. Indiana had gotten around the slavery prohibition in the Northwest Ordinance by passing an indenture law. When Illinois became a territory in 1809, it did the same.

Indenture was originally a form of apprenticeship in which white persons bound themselves to masters for a specified number of years. In return for their labor, their masters provided them with food, clothing, and shelter and taught them a trade. However, the system as applied to black people was much harsher. A white man could bring blacks under the age of fifteen to Illinois and register them to serve until they were thirty-five if they were males and thirty-two if they were females. Children born to indentured servants became the property of their mother's master, and indentured servants could be bought and sold. Although indenture contracts were said to be voluntary, many blacks signed them only because they had no alternative. If they refused, they had no way to obtain employment. The indenture laws were still in effect when the delegates to the constitutional convention met.

Some delegates did not want slavery outlawed because they thought slaves would relieve the labor shortage on the frontier and make it possible for western states to compete with the older states. Also, many Americans thought of slaves as personal property with which the government had no right to interfere.

Those opposed to slavery thought that the western lands were not well suited to slave labor and that in the long run slaves would be an economic burden. Poor white farmers who could not compete with slave owners wanted slavery prohibited, as did some who did not want black people to come and live in Illinois. In addition, a slowly growing minority believed that slavery was morally wrong.

Some people viewed the Illinois constitution as a victory for those who opposed slavery, but, as it turned out, that victory was far from complete. When the General Assembly met the following year, it immediately set about writing the infamous Black Laws, which were not repealed until the end of the Civil War. These laws stated that slaves could not be brought to Illinois for the purpose of freeing them. Free blacks had to prove they were free by presenting a court certificate whenever asked to. Indentured servants could not bring suit or testify in court. When their master or mistress died, they could be disposed of by the executor of the dead person's estate. In other words, they were simply another kind of property.

When the General Assembly met in 1823, the proslavery legislators went even further. They framed an amendment to the Illinois constitution that would have legalized slavery. However, the constitution stated that before any amendment could go into effect, three-fourths of the members of the General Assembly had to approve the calling of a constitutional convention. If they did so, then the voters of the state had to vote on whether such a convention should be called.

The proslavery advocates were greatly disappointed when they were unable to get three-fourths of the General Assembly to vote in favor of a convention, so they illegally unseated one legislator and put their own man in his place. When a second vote was taken, they had the necessary majority, and the matter was referred to the voters of the state.

By this time, Edward Coles was serving as governor. A southerner who had inherited slaves, Coles had brought them to Illinois and freed them before the Black Laws had been passed, helping them toward independence by giving them small farms. At the time of the constitutional convention he had argued forcefully against slavery. Now he led the antislavery forces in another bitter fight.

For more than a year, politicians, preachers, lawyers, and others traveled about denouncing both slavery and the behavior of the pro-slavery faction. People who might otherwise have voted for the convention were influenced by these earnest speakers. When the vote was finally taken, the call for a constitutional convention was rejected and no amendment materialized. Illinois remained a free state—at least in name.

Kaskaskia, the First State Capital

Congress had granted federal land for a state capital to other states, but by an oversight no such grant was made to Illinois. The convention delegates declared Kaskaskia the capital for the present, then directed the General Assembly to petition the federal government for land on which to build a new, more centrally located capital. They specified that the land was to be on the Kaskaskia River considerably to the east of Kaskaskia. Congress eventually granted the land to the state, and two years later the seat of government was moved to a new town surrounded by wilderness, Vandalia.

꿏

Daniel Pope Cook's enthusiasm touched off the movement that resulted in statehood for Illinois. At his urging, the Illinois General Assembly drew up a petition requesting statehood and presented it to Congress. A congressional committee discussed the petition and, on the basis of it, wrote an ennabling act. Congress and the president approved the ennabling act in April 1818. Once these preliminaries had been taken care of, Illinoisans proceeded with the creation of a state constitution.

The first constitutional convention in Illinois history took place in Kaskaskia in August 1818. The short and simple document that the delegates completed in just a few weeks served the state for thirty years. Most of the articles were not controversial, but the volatile slavery issue brought heated discussion. Proslavery advocates agreed to an article forbidding slavery but only because they realized that Congress might not approve the constitution otherwise. Some of them felt sure they could find ways to circumvent the antislavery provision—and they soon did.

While waiting for Congress to approve the constitution, Illinois voters chose Shadrach Bond as their first governor. Then on December

3, 1818, President Monroe signed the act that made Illinois the twenty-first state. Immigration to the state picked up, and development of the state's resources began in earnest. We are now ready to turn to an account of the turbulent first decades of statehood.

For Further Exploration

Janet Cornelius. *A History of Constitution Making in Illinois.* Urbana: Institute of Government and Public Affairs, 1969.

This study of the first three constitutions of Illinois (1818, 1848, and 1870) shows how each solved some problems and created others. The author includes details such as what the delegates to the constitutional conventions did for a living, some of the strange provisions special-interest groups tried to have included in the documents, and reasons why delegates voted the way they did on civil rights issues.

PART TWO

Early Development

When Illinois became a state it was still mostly wilderness. But new people kept coming, creating villages and towns and converting the wild prairies into farms. By the 1850s trains were rolling across the land, carrying crops to market. Illinois had become one of the most important agricultural states in the Union.

6

Patterns of Settlement

The First Waves

Many people think of the westward movement as something that happened west of the Mississippi River. We connect it with movies about wagon trains, Indian ambushes, shoot-outs in taverns and corrals, and stagecoach robberies. Actually, the westward movement began as soon as pioneers began crossing the Appalachian Mountains and heading into the interior of the continent. In those days Illinois was about as far west as one could go.

Backwoods families from Virginia, Georgia, and the Carolinas made up the first wave of settlers in Illinois, and they chose to settle in the southern part of the territory. They were mostly of English, Scottish, or Scots-Irish descent, although there were also small groups of German settlers.

The forebears of these early Illinois pioneers had come to New England and Pennsylvania in the early 1700s. Because they preferred the isolation and freedom of backwoods living, they had gone into the wilderness rather than settling near the established coastal towns. It was said of these strong-willed and independent people that if they could hear the sound of a neighbor's axe or his dog barking, they thought it was time to move.

As the northeastern back country began filling up, they drifted south, again moving inland to avoid entanglement with civilization. But eventually the plantation owners who wanted to bring more land under cultivation forced the backwoods families to retreat ever deeper into the wilderness until they were backed up against the Appalachian Mountains. It was easy for the plantation owners to buy the land out from under the backwoodsmen, many of whom were squatters (that is, they did not own the land on which they lived and could not afford to buy it). Furthermore, these wilderness people did not want to be farmers. They wanted to hunt and fish and live off the land much as the Indians were doing. The cultivation of large tracts of land around them made this impossible.

When they heard that there was an almost endless supply of land west of the Appalachians, the backwoods families headed in that direction, often with no exact destination in mind. Some moved to Kentucky and Tennessee and later pushed on to Indiana and Illinois. Some came directly to Illinois.

Southern Illinois appealed to these early settlers because the wooded hills reminded them of the mountains they had left behind. They were not used to living in an open and exposed environment, so they shunned the prairies. They found an abundant supply of wood in southern Illinois while on the prairies wood was scarce. In those days most people thought that the prairie soil was too poor for crops because so few trees were growing on it.

On the heels of these first pioneers came a wave of backwoods families who were just as interested in bettering themselves economically as in trying to escape civilization. They wanted to create permanent new homes and farms. When they arrived, some of the families who had come in the first wave felt it was time to move farther west. They left behind the land they had cleared, the crude cabins they had built, and the garden plots or small fields they had worked, making life a little easier for the newcomers. Sometimes the newcomers paid them for the improvements they had made.

After the land along the waterways of southern Illinois was spoken for, pioneers began settling between the rivers, then slowly moving northward. Some settled in the Sangamon River Valley and along the Illinois River. By then farmers living on the edge of the prairie had tried drilling holes in the prairie sod and planting corn, hoping to supplement, at least in a small way, the crops they grew in their fields. They were very much surprised to find that they got a better crop from the uncultivated prairie soil than from lands they had cleared of trees. Although this convinced some of the more adventurous that they should move out onto the open prairie, the last challenge from the Indians stopped them for the time being.

Black Hawk's War

The Fox and Sauk Indians lived near each other and had fought side by side in battles with other tribes. At first they were united in their

Black Hawk by Charles Bird King. The Warner Collection of Gulf States Paper Corporation, Tuscaloosa, Alabama.

opposition to the coming of white settlers. After considerable pressure was put upon them by the federal government to move west of the Mississippi, one of their chiefs, Keokuk, agreed to give up tribal lands in Illinois and move his people to Iowa. But Black Hawk, the leader of a small band of warriors, refused to follow. His village in the Rock River Valley stood in the midst of rich cornfields that had taken years to cultivate. In the early 1800s a treaty had been signed ceding the land on which the village stood to the U.S. government, but allowing the Indians to live there until white settlers arrived. When settlers began coming, Black Hawk refused to acknowledge the treaty and said that it did not reflect the will of his people.

The mere presence of Black Hawk's band was enough to terrify the settlers, who asked the government for help. Eventually Black Hawk was persuaded to sign a new treaty in which he agreed to move west. However, when he finally led his followers across the Mississippi River, hostile Sioux attacked them. Facing starvation, Black Hawk and about fifteen hundred Sauk and Fox came back to Illinois in April 1832, hoping to find open land on which to plant corn.

Believing that Black Hawk and his followers had come back to raid, the governor called out the militia. (In his autobiography, Black Hawk says that he and his followers had come in peace, otherwise they would never have brought their wives and children.) Hoping to avoid armed conflict, Black Hawk sent a flag of truce to the commander of the troops that had gathered nearby, but the envoys were killed by inexperienced and undisciplined soldiers. Indians looked upon such killings as the breaking of a sacred trust.

Much to the surprise of the soldiers, Black Hawk retaliated and routed them from the field. It was to be his last success. He and his warriors made a few scattered raids, but they did not receive the aid from other tribes that they had expected, and their movements were hampered by the presence of the women and children. Food supplies dwindled, and many of his braves suffered from malnutrition and disease.

Black Hawk then attempted to lead his band back to Iowa as quickly as possible. They turned north into what is now Wisconsin, but as they were struggling to cross the Mississippi River, pursuing soldiers attacked. On August 2, 1832, they defeated Black Hawk and his braves at the Battle of Bad Axe and ruthlessly slaughtered the wounded braves and many of the women and children as well. Black Hawk was later captured and imprisoned at Fort Monroe in Virginia. After his release, he became a celebrity. People turned out in large numbers to see him as he traveled from town to town. However, he soon grew tired of that life and was allowed to join Keokuk's band in Iowa, where he lived out his days.

When Black Hawk's War ended, all Indian tribes were ordered out of Illinois, whether they had participated in the conflict or not. Even the Kaskaskia, who had fought with the Americans against the Fox and Sauk, had to leave. For the Indians, the Black Hawk War was another in a long series of disasters associated with the coming of white settlers. For the pioneers, it was a signal that they could now safely move into northern Illinois. But by then the earlier settlers from the South had to face new competitors: the Yankees.

The Yankee Invasion

People who lived in the cities and on the farms of the northeastern and mid-Atlantic states had many reasons for wanting to try their luck in the West. The thin, rocky New England soil had been depleted by long years of use, and the small amount of virgin land still available was expensive. It was possible to make a good living growing sheep for wool, but that took more land than most farmers had or could afford to buy.

Some families moved to New Hampshire and Maine, hoping to find cheaper land and start new farms. Others moved to the cities but soon became discouraged by what they found there. Their skills were not needed, as machines were doing the jobs mechanics and artisans had previously done. Also, new immigrants from Europe were willing to work for low wages, so the New Englanders had to accept wages they considered inadequate to keep their jobs. Skilled workers either had to stay where they were and become low-paid tenders of machines or move west to the frontier where their skills would still be valued.

Letters from friends who had already moved to Illinois and lively advertisements in newspapers helped many Yankees make the decision to move to Illinois. They pored over the readily available guidebooks for immigrants that described the good soil, crops, minerals, and other resources of the state and included maps, routes, and estimates of the costs related to starting new lives in the West. One handbook listed the necessary expenses in this order:

Federal land	$1.25 per acre
Fencing	$1 per acre
Yoke of oxen	$40–$60
Milk cow	$10–$14
Team of horses	$80–$100
Plow	$9
Wagon	$80
Harrow	$8
Twelve hens	$0.80–$1.00 each
Swine	$3–$4 each

Although a few Yankees came to Illinois early in the century, the 1830s and 1840s were the big years of migration for them. In terms of

Using rivers as highways, many pioneer families found flatboating easier than a cross-country trek. Courtesy of the Illinois State Historical Library.

comfort and culture, they left a great deal behind, but the long-range possibilities of the frontier were irresistible.

Routes to Illinois

Many of the first pioneers had made the long trek west on foot, walking almost a thousand miles to get to Illinois. They followed Daniel Boone's Wilderness Road from North Carolina through the Cumberland Gap, then down into Kentucky. After that, they used Indian trails and animal traces or cut paths through the woods themselves.

At this early stage of the westward movement, the trails were too primitive to accommodate large wagons. Pack animals carried household goods, provisions, tools, and personal belongings. Two-wheeled carts pulled by oxen, mules, or horses (and sometimes people) were also common. Travelers who had no beasts of burden carried their belongings in bundles on their backs or cut strong forked branches from trees, tied their bundles to them, and pulled them along.

By the time the second wave of settlers came, the Ohio River had become a marine highway. Families made their way across the mountains, then floated down the river on flatboats. The journey by water was certainly less grueling than the overland routes, but the river had its perils, too. People who had no experience at maneuvering the clumsy arks, as the flatboats were called, sometimes ran them aground or capsized them. Snags, shallows, rapids, and sandbars seemed to pop up from nowhere. Indians occasionally attacked boats that drifted too close to shore. River pirates lurked in the woods and enticed boaters ashore, then robbed and murdered them. But in spite of all these difficulties, many flatboats made it "all the way to Shawneetown," as a song of the day put it. For more than twenty years Shawneetown was the most important town in Illinois. Pioneers stopped there to rest and get supplies, then continued down the Ohio or left the river and traveled overland.

Keelboats, the cargo carriers of the early pioneer period, were manned by skilled crews known for their pugnacious behavior ashore. Mike Fink was the most famous of the keelboatmen. This was the kind of boasting "holler" he and his companions shouted as they swaggered down the streets of the little river towns where they landed:

> I'm a ring-tailed roarer
> and a ring-tailed screamer too!
> I was raised on grizzly bear milk
> and cradled with a wildcat.
> I'm half horse and half alligator
> and people call me the Mississippi Snag.
> I can eat a dozen rattlesnakes for breakfast
> and drink a barrel a' whiskey besides.
> I can outrun, out-hop, out-jump and out-fight
> any man in this whole country!
> Ya-hoooooooo! Yip-eeeeeee!
> Stand back and gimme room!

Unlike the flatboats, which were usually broken up for lumber after their one-way trip, keelboats made round trips. The keelboaters had to literally shove the boat along upstream with long poles. About the fastest a keelboat could move against the current was one mile per hour. Eventually steamboats put the keelboats out of business, but by that time the keelboaters had carried millions of tons of goods to people living in the wilderness.

While the Ohio River became the main route for the early settlers, it was not as convenient for the later immigrants from the northeastern and mid-Atlantic states. Fortunately, Congress saw the need for a road that would make the West more easily accessible and would tie the East and the West together. It approved the building of the National Road (also called the Cumberland Pike) in the early 1800s, and construction began at Cumberland, Maryland, in 1815.

It was slow going. Not until 1833 was the section between Cumberland and Columbus, Ohio, completed. Seven years later the builders had reached Indianapolis, Indiana. The section from Indianapolis to Vandalia, Illinois, was graded and ready for surfacing when enthusiasm for completing the road declined. A marvelous new form of transportation, the railroad, had emerged in the East, and it seemed certain that in a few years iron horses would be chugging across the western lands. Many citizens thought roads would soon be obsolete and wanted no more money spent on them. The last stretch of the National Road was left unfinished.

Nevertheless, in the 1830s and 1840s thousands of immigrants from New England, Pennsylvania, and New York, as well as from foreign countries, came as far as they could by way of the National Road, then fanned out across the prairie or headed north to Chicago.

In 1811 Nicolas J. Roosevelt became the first person to pilot a steamboat all the way from Pittsburgh to New Orleans. (He happened to be on the river during the New Madrid earthquake.) Shortly afterward, Captain Henry Shreve showed that steamboats could make the upstream voyage from New Orleans to Louisville in twenty-five days, a trip that ordinarily took three or four months by keelboat. By the 1820s steamboats were navigating many of the waterways of Illinois.

The *Seneca Chief* officially opened the Erie Canal in 1825 by steaming into New York City from Buffalo and dumping a barrel of water from Lake Erie into the harbor. This great engineering project linked the eastern seaboard to the Great Lakes and made the journey to Illinois much faster and more comfortable than overland travel.

Conflicts between Southerners and Yankees

Once they began living in the same areas, it did not take southerners and Yankees long to discover that they did not like each other very much. The southerners tended to be suspicious of outsiders, especially since some of them had been taken in by Yankee peddlers. They did not greet their new neighbors with open arms.

The most serious complaint of the backwoods settlers was that there were just too many Yankees. As one woman put it, "I am getting skeery about them 'ere yankees. There is such a power of them coming that they and the Injuns will squatch out all the white folk." (The backwoods people thought of themselves as the white folk.)

Basic to many of the misunderstandings between the two groups was the difference in attitudes toward the wilderness itself. The earliest wave of settlers loved the wilderness and thought of it as a sanctuary. They more or less disappeared into it and became part of it. Even the farmers who followed them were isolationists to some extent, although they took on the task of taming the wilderness with more vigor than their predecessors had. But the Yankees were in a big hurry to conquer the wilderness and build profitable farms and cities.

The Yankees were, generally speaking, better off financially than the earlier settlers. They had saved money or had funds from houses, farms, and businesses they had sold before moving west. Many were able to bring wagonloads of household and personal goods or ship them by boat. They could afford to hire builders, carpenters, and other crafts-men, as well as farmhands and domestic help. Although they had to start out in log cabins as the southerners had done, Yankee families considered log cabins only temporary shelter. By the 1830s, milled lumber, machine-made nails, windows, and hardware were much easier to obtain, and the Yankees had the money to buy them.

Backwoodsmen regarded Yankees as stiff and proud and liked to tell stories about how one of their own had given a Yankee his comeuppance. For example, there were several versions of a story about a Yankee city-slicker who rode out on his finest horse to court a backwoods girl at a country dance. Not only did he lose the girl, but his fine horse lost its mane and tail, causing him great embarrassment as he rode back to the city.

The Yankees valued hard work, order, thrift, and shrewdness and were single-minded in their desire to succeed. They saw their new neighbors as crude and shiftless, one step up from savages in many cases. Some who had come five or ten years before were still living in cramped and dirty cabins on ragged frontier farms. It took several years before the Yankees came to appreciate the physical strength, courage, and staying power of the settlers who had come before them. Even then, any young Yankee woman bold enough to marry a southerner ran the risk of being ostracized by her family and friends.

The Yankee settlers were usually better educated than the southern-ers and were anxious to establish churches, schools, newspapers, and other cultural institutions. The southerners of the early period had little use for book learning. One man said it might be all right for men to learn how to read, but when would women ever have the time for such frivolity? And book learning just made people proud "like them uppity Yankees," said others. One father refused to allow his daughters to learn to read and write because he had heard of a case in which a girl had made arrangements to elope by writing her lover a letter.

The southerners did not like the way Yankees did business, either. They said that Yankees sewed raccoon tails on to cat pelts and tried to pass them off as raccoon pelts. If anyone was cheated in a business deal he or she was said to have been "yankeed"; any object that had been varnished or decorated to hide its flaws so it could be sold was also said to be "yankeed."

The attitudes of the southerners and Yankees toward each other were slow to change. We will see that even more fundamental differences between them surfaced when the nation faced the crisis of a civil war. At that time some of the southern counties of Illinois thought of seceding from Illinois and joining the Confederacy.

ᴿᴿ

Southern Illinois was the first part of the state to be settled. The backwoods families who came from the southern states chose it because its densely wooded hills reminded them of the homes they had left behind. There was plenty of wood, game, and privacy, so they could continue their old way of life far from the populous regions they were trying to escape.

Northern Illinois was next. The Chicago area began attracting large numbers of settlers after the Erie Canal was completed in 1825 and immigrants could come via the Great Lakes rather than having to make the difficult cross-country trek.

Last to be settled were the mid-state prairies. In the early 1800s many people assumed that the soil was poor because so few trees were growing on the prairie. A little experimentation proved otherwise. Still, East Coast farmers who wanted to try prairie farming held off because of the threat of Indian attack. After Black Hawk's War (1832) the Indian tribes still living in Illinois were forced to move west of the Mississippi, and the prairies began to fill up.

The pioneers who settled in northern and central Illinois were different than the earlier settlers in southern Illinois. Most came from the northeastern and mid-Atlantic states and had never lived in the wilderness before. Ambitious and more prosperous than their southern counterparts, the Yankees set to work converting the prairies into farms. They represented the civilization from which the southerners were trying to escape. Misunderstanding, mistrust, and dislike characterized the relationships between the southerners and the Yankees when they first met in Illinois. The rise of towns, which we will turn to next, brought about more contact—and eventually more tolerance—between the people of these two cultures.

For Further Exploration

Leland D. Baldwin. *The Keelboat Age on Western Waters*. Pittsburgh: University of Pittsburgh Press, 1941.

Keelboaters such as Mike Fink are generally remembered for their boisterous behavior on land, but their feats of strength and courage as they carried tons of cargo down the Ohio and Mississippi rivers made possible the early, presteamboat phase of the westward movement.

Black Hawk. *Black Hawk: An Autobiography*. Edited by Donald Jackson. Urbana: University of Illinois Press, 1955.

Having become somewhat of a celebrity after his surrender, Black Hawk dictated his life story to an interpreter in 1833. Reprinted here with an historian's account of Black Hawk's War, it gives readers a chance to view the conflict from the Indian point of view.

Betty I. Madden. *Art, Crafts, and Architecture in Early Illinois*. Urbana: University of Illinois Press (in cooperation with the Illinois State Museum), 1974.

The privations of the pioneers are often emphasized over all other aspects of frontier living. The many drawings and photographs in this book—and the lively text—present the log cabin era from a fresh point of view.

Christiana H. Tillson. *A Woman's Story of Pioneer Illinois*. Chicago: Lakeside Press, R. R. Donnelley, 1919.

When Christiana Tillson settled with her husband near present-day Hillsboro, she soon found that her New England upbringing set her apart from her backwoods neighbors. She viewed them with some distaste, but also with compassion and humor, and they viewed her with a mixture of mistrust and admiration—and as a source of help in time of trouble. Her autobiography is one of the best firsthand accounts of the clash between two cultures in early Illinois.

Edwin Tunis. *Frontier Living*. Cleveland: World Publishing Co., 1961.

Artist and writer Edwin Tunis is well aware that great events are not the sole content of history. His enthusiasm for the paraphernalia of everyday life in preindustrial America has led to the production of many fine books of drawings with short, explanatory texts, of which this is one.

7

A Sampler of Frontier Towns

New Salem: A Typical Frontier Community

Successful towns changed so much as they grew that only a few if any traces of pioneer life remain in most of them today. New Salem, on the other hand, looks very much as it looked during the frontier years. In 1906 the wealthy newspaper publisher William Randolph Hearst took an interest in New Salem because Abraham Lincoln had lived there. He bought the site and donated it to the state. The buildings were reconstructed on their old foundations, and authentic artifacts from the everyday life of the times were gathered and placed in the homes and workshops, where they can be seen by visitors today.

James Rutledge and John Camron, the founders of New Salem, purchased land near Springfield in the early 1820s and built a combination gristmill and sawmill on the Sangamon River. Before long, people from the surrounding farms were waiting in line to have their grain ground and their lumber milled. Having made a success of their first business ventures, the partners named their town New Salem and began selling lots to newcomers.

By 1830 New Salem had two general stores, a grocery, and a saloon. Several artisans had brought their families there, among them a blacksmith, a shoemaker, a tanner, a barrel maker, a cabinet and furniture maker, and a hatter. Rutledge turned his house into an inn, and another family started a ferryboat operation. The Board of County Commissioners regulated the prices a ferryboat operator could charge:

For each man and horse	12½ cents
One man on foot	6¼ cents
One horse without rider	6¼ cents

One head of cattle	3 cents
One sheep	2 cents
Working wagon and team	50 cents
Pleasure carriage and horse	25 cents

One April day in 1831 a flatboat ran aground on a dam below New Salem and began taking on water. The villagers gathered to watch. One of the crew, a lanky young man in jeans and calico shirt, looked the situation over, then had the men help him unload some of the cargo. He borrowed an awl and bored a hole in the boat, letting out the water in its hull. After plugging the hole, he and the crew were able to float the craft over the dam. The crew rested in the town for a while. Denton Offutt, the owner of the cargo, liked what he saw and decided to come back later and start a store there. Eventually he hired the resourceful young man who had freed the boat, Abraham Lincoln, to run it.

New Salem slipped into decline in the 1830s. It had become obvious that the Sangamon River was not as suitable for steamboat traffic as had been hoped. The depth of the water varied too much from place to place and from season to season. Then when nearby Petersburg was chosen over New Salem as the county seat for the new Menard County and the post office was moved there, New Salem became a backwater village. Unable to make a living there, one family after another left until at last it became a ghost town. The story of many frontier villages ended this way. Others, however, prospered.

Galena, the First Boomtown of the West

Lead brought miners streaming to Galena in the early 1800s. Many years before, the Indians living in northwestern Illinois had showed the French lumps of lead ore. The Indians had no particular use for it, but the colonial powers valued it highly because bullets were made from it. Lack of manpower and transportation stymied efforts to make use of large quantities of the ore until steamboats began traveling the waters of the upper Mississippi about 1820. After that, the "lead rush" was on.

Hopeful miners arrived and staked out claims. Steamboats carried both the ore—and the news of the bonanza—down the Mississippi. Soon miners from every state in the Union and from many foreign countries flocked to the northwest corner of Illinois. Galena, the principal ore from which lead is extracted, became the name of the town that sprang up there.

Fortunes were made not only in mining but also in shipping. Galena became the busiest port on the Mississippi River above St. Louis. Substantial homes and public buildings replaced the log cabins.

Lead miners at Galena, the first boomtown of the West. Galena mines reached their peak of production between 1830 and 1850 but continued on a smaller scale for some years after that. The Galena/Jo Daviess County Historical Society and Museum.

Doctors, lawyers, craftsmen, and merchants came as the rapid growth in population created a demand for their services. By 1845 Galena had become the richest town in Illinois. Pioneers farmed the surrounding prairie land, taking advantage of the market Galena provided for them.

Miners from the southern part of the state found northern Illinois winters unpleasant. They therefore worked their claims in the spring and summer, then returned south before the cold weather set in again. Their pattern of migration was similar to that of a fish called the sucker. Some people claim that is why Illinois was once known as the Sucker State.

Galesburg: A Planned Community

More than twenty Illinois towns began as colonies of settlers from the eastern states, among which were Bloomington, Kewanee, Metamora, Mt. Hope, Ottawa, Princeton, and Galesburg. Buying land jointly had economic advantages and gave shareholders some control over the development of their community. Coming to the frontier as part of a group of families also eliminated some of the drudgery, insecurity, and isolation that made life so hard for the early pioneers.

In 1835 George Washington Gale, a Presbyterian minister, drew up a plan for a settlement. When he explained it to the members of his church in New York, fifty families responded by contributing $20,000 to a fund for purchasing land. A committee of three traveled to Illinois and chose twenty square miles in the northwestern sector. When families began arriving in 1836, each received an eighty-acre parcel of land. One square mile was set aside for a town center. Committed to bringing religion and culture to the frontier, Gale founded Knox College the following year. A thriving community stood where only wild prairie had been before.

For more than a decade, Galesburg was a homogeneous community in which there was general agreement on matters of religion, politics, and social life. Later, when a railroad line was built to the city, people from other backgrounds began arriving. The original families were soon outnumbered, and the population became more diverse.

Chicago's Star Rises

The choice geographical location of Chicago was recognized long before the great city came to life. The French had built the Mission of the Guardian Angel there in the late 1600s but, because of Indian unrest

Jean Baptiste Point du Sable, founder of the first permanent settlement at Chicago. Chicago Historical Society.

in the area, had abandoned it after a few years. For almost a century no other Europeans lived there.

About 1779 a black man, Jean Baptiste Point du Sable, began the first permanent settlement at Chicago. Du Sable is thought to have been born in Santo Domingo. He was involved in the fur trade when he was captured by the British and imprisoned at Fort Michilimackinac during the American Revolution. When he regained his freedom, du Sable went to the Chicago area and started a trading post. He married a Potawatomi Indian woman and had two children. Before long, Indians and fur traders formed a village adjacent to his homestead.

Du Sable prospered during the twenty years he lived there. In addition to running his fur-trading business, he farmed, operated a mill, and was a competent carpenter. His well-furnished house had such luxuries as mirrors and pictures, articles not generally found in a frontier village. He is thought to have moved to Peoria for a while, then to St. Charles, Missouri.

In 1803 the U.S. government built Fort Dearborn near the trading post du Sable had left behind and stationed a small contingent of American soldiers there. A year or so later, a fur trader and silversmith named John Kinzie bought du Sable's place. After the massacre of 1812, he returned to Chicago to reestablish his home and business. He envisioned Chicago as an important trade center and strove to make it a prosperous and attractive frontier settlement.

One early urban pioneer, Jennie Hall, came to Chicago with her family in the early 1830s. When she was an old woman, she described their experiences. They arrived from New York by way of the Great Lakes on one of the first steamboats to make the run. They found only a dozen or so log buildings, including a few stores and three inns. Jennie's father immediately bought a lot for $50. He then cut some trees, floated them down the river to the site, and built a cabin. In the months that followed, he found it easy to earn a living with his carpentry skills, which were much in demand.

Engineers completed a new harbor for the city in 1834. Many more boats were able to dock there, and the tempo of settlement picked up. Newcomers were so anxious to buy land that people made fortunes selling it to them. For instance, Jennie's father bought a lot on Lake and State streets for $500 and a day later sold it for $1,000. He bought three other lots, which he also sold for more than he had paid for them. Men with real estate to sell waited for boats to dock, then rushed up to the people as they disembarked and tried to get them to buy.

By the end of the decade, Chicago was beginning to compete with

St. Louis as the most important trade and transportation center in the Midwest. Chicago's star was rising.

Bishop Hill: A Utopia on the Prairie

Erik Jansson felt that the Lutheran Church in Sweden had become too worldly and complicated. He wanted to return to a Christianity as simple as that described in the Bible. When he began speaking out for reform, he quickly found himself in trouble with both the church and the government. Realizing that he and his followers would not be allowed to live as they wished in Sweden, Jansson made plans to establish a settlement in America. His community was to be based on the New Testament idea that all property should be held in common and all members of the group should be provided for.

In 1846 Jansson and four hundred of his followers sailed for America, then made their way to Illinois. They named their settlement Bishop Hill after Jansson's birthplace. No sooner had they arrived than winter began closing in, leaving them with no option but to dig crude cavelike shelters in the side of a ravine. The cold, crowded conditions, together with a food shortage, resulted in the deaths of ninety-six colonists during that first miserable winter.

In the spring 350 acres of sod were broken, and food crops were planted. Subsequent winters were better. Soon cash crops were being sown, including flax for making linen cloth and broom corn that was sold to broom companies. Within a few years, outsiders began coming to Bishop Hill to purchase the community's high-quality linen, wool fabrics, rugs, furniture, implements, meat, and dairy products. Bishop Hill became a thriving and spacious town with good streets, nicely furnished houses, many shops and stores, and a first-rate hotel.

However, the ideals on which the community were based did not survive. Joint ownership did not work out in the long run. But even after the original company of settlers disbanded, the town retained its Swedish culture. Annual harvest and Christmas festivities based on old traditions still draw many visitors each year.

Nauvoo: The Mormons in Illinois

Joseph Smith, founder of the Mormon Church, claimed to have had a number of heavenly visions, on the basis of which he wrote the Book of Mormon and established a new religion. He soon had a large following in New York state, where he was then living. Under his leadership and that of his assistant, Brigham Young, the Mormons moved first to Ohio, then to Missouri. When they were driven out of Missouri, they came to Illinois.

In 1839 Joseph Smith bought land at nearby Commerce, a run-down, abandoned village on the Mississippi River. The industrious Mormons set to work at this seemingly unpromising site and before long had laid out a new city that they named Nauvoo, the Hebrew word for "beautiful place." As the number of Mormon converts arriving from the East increased, Illinois politicians began to realize that Mormon support was worth having. To get it, they promoted a number of laws that were advantageous to the Mormons.

In 1840 the General Assembly granted the Mormons charters that allowed them to operate almost as if they were a separate state within Illinois. They could make their own laws and organize themselves as they pleased as long as they did not violate state or federal law. They were empowered to establish a militia for their own protection, build a university, and engage in manufacturing. By 1842 the Mormons in Hancock County numbered a surprising sixteen thousand, and three years later Nauvoo had become the largest city in Illinois.

The non-Mormon population of Hancock County found the religious beliefs of the Mormons disagreeable and resented the special

The Mormons moved to Utah before they were able to make much use of this temple built at Nauvoo. Courtesy of Illinois State Historical Library.

privileges that the Mormons had been granted. They also felt intimidated by the well-trained Nauvoo Legion, the largest armed force in the nation except for the U.S. Army.

After scattered incidents of violence, Hancock County became an armed camp. Sure that a war was about to break out, the nervous settlers appealed for help. Finally Governor Thomas Ford called out the state militia and went to Hancock County to evaluate the situation himself.

Smith had been accused of using the Nauvoo Legion to wreck the press of a newspaper that had printed articles criticizing him. When he and his brother, Hiram, went to nearby Carthage to answer the charges, Governor Ford, fearing for their safety, had them jailed. Then, thinking that everything was under control, he dismissed most of the state militia and assigned the job of guarding the jail to only one company, the Carthage Grays. A short time later, when a mob stormed the jail, the Carthage Grays more or less looked the other way while the Smith brothers were lynched.

Hostilities continued for two years. Some of the settlers had become so fanatically anti-Mormon that they were willing to settle for nothing less than driving the Mormons out. With Smith gone and their privileged status breaking down, the Mormons decided to leave. In 1847 Young, who had taken over the leadership of Nauvoo after Smith's death, led his followers on the long trek to Utah, where they founded Salt Lake City. Many buildings in Nauvoo have been restored by the Mormon Church and can be visited by modern tourists.

❧

We have looked at six Illinois communities of the early 1800s. New Salem, the most typical, provided goods and services for the surrounding farmers, who, in turn, supplied the town with agricultural products. New Salem gradually became the center of social and cultural life for the whole area. Boomtowns like Galena seemed to grow up almost overnight as miners rushed in from all over the country and the world to exploit the rich lead reserves there. Chicago attracted settlers because of its superb geographical location. To farsighted people it was apparent almost from the beginning that the village on the lake would one day be the crossroads of the nation.

Other towns were settled by groups rather than individuals or separate families. For example, a group of New Englanders led by George Washington Gale incorporated to buy land and established the town of Galesburg on the Illinois prairie. Bishop Hill, another planned community, was settled by dissenters from the Swedish Lutheran Church.

Nauvoo was the only town in Illinois history to become almost a state within the state. Under the leadership of Joseph Smith, the founder of the Church of Jesus Christ of the Latter-Day Saints, the residents of Nauvoo soon achieved a higher standard of living than was usual on the frontier. However, their religious beliefs and their autonomy (they were permitted to establish their own government and even their own army) kindled the hostility of their neighbors. After several years of conflict between themselves and nearby settlers, the Mormons set out for Utah.

During the years when towns began springing up all across the state, the prairies were also coming under cultivation. Life for the prairie pioneers was in some ways easier than it had been for the backwoods families of southern Illinois, but there were still plenty of hardships to be faced, as we shall see.

For Further Exploration

Charles Boewe. *Prairie Albion: An English Settlement in Pioneer Illinois.* Carbondale: Southern Illinois University Press, 1962.

Another interesting pioneer community, known as the English Prairie, was established by two well-to-do Englishmen who had become dissatisfied with the economic and political systems of their country and immigrated to Illinois. The author of this book weaves together a narrative of the enterprise, using excerpts from the letters and diaries of the founders, Morris Birkbeck and George Flower. He also includes both positive and negative comments of visitors to the settlement.

Olov Isaksson and Soren Hallgren. *Bishop Hill, Ill.: A Utopia on the Prairie.* Stockholm, Sweden: LT Publishing House, 1969.

If you are curious about why utopian communities tend to be short-lived, this book will be particularly interesting. It begins with a general discussion of such communities, then centers on Bishop Hill. Photographs bring the old Bishop Hill to life, as do the paintings of Olof Krans, an artist who came to live in the community in 1850 when he was twelve years old.

Benjamin P. Thomas. *Lincoln's New Salem.* Springfield: The Abraham Lincoln Association, 1934. New and rev. ed. Carbondale: Southern Illinois University Press, 1987.

This valuable little book provides a portrait of a pioneer town in which we can see the transition from strict self-reliance and independence to interdependence and a richer social and political life.

8

The Challenge of the Prairies

Sea of Grass

To pioneers traveling overland to central and northern Illinois, the shady woodlands through which they passed must have seemed endless. In many places the canopy of trees was so thick that it was like traveling all day in twilight. Then, suddenly, they were confronted with a sight unlike any they had ever seen: the country opened out into vast, sun-filled grasslands. They had reached the eastern edge of the great prairies that were later found to extend all the way to the Rocky Mountains. The Grand Prairie, a huge tract of grasslands, began just below present-day Chicago and extended down the eastern half of the state almost to the middle. Smaller prairies covered much of the rest of Illinois.

Thousands of years before, glaciers had covered more than three-fourths of the state. They ground down everything in their paths and, as they retreated, left behind fine particles of rock that enriched the soil with minerals. During the centuries that followed, prairie grasses protected the soil from erosion and added organic material, making it even more fertile. Under the prairie sod lay soil so rich and deep that it would need no fertilizer for a hundred years.

Many settlers seeing the Illinois prairies for the first time thought them breathtakingly beautiful. They loved the grasses moving in the wind, like waves in a green sea, grasses tall enough to hide a person on horseback. One woman said that in a short walk over one corner of a prairie she found forty different kinds of flowers, and another reported gathering a bouquet of 120 different kinds. Birds filled the meadows with song and motion, flocks of waterfowl nested around the ponds, and small game was plentiful.

Other travelers, however, described the prairies as empty and monotonous. They felt small and lonely as they made their way across them without seeing any sign of human habitation. But the prairie pioneers persevered because they understood at least to some extent that the land they were buying had great potential. Illinois was on the verge of becoming a great agricultural state, the breadbasket of the nation.

John Deere's Plow

The graceful grasses and flowers that grew to be six or more feet high often had more of the plant underground than above. Roots as big around as a man's finger extended twelve or fifteen feet down into the soil and tangled with those of other plants. The conventional plows the settlers brought with them could barely do the job. Two men, one leading several pairs of oxen and the other guiding the plow, could work only about an acre a day. Even then, the animals had to work so hard that they sometimes died in the fields. The men felt the strain too as their plows lurched along, jumping out of the furrow every few yards. Farmers who managed to break a total of thirty or forty acres of prairie sod the first year considered themselves lucky.

After the first plowing, the fields lay open to sun and rain, and the stems and roots of the prairie plants decayed. The soil then contained so much organic material that it retained moisture and became sticky. When the farmer did the second plowing in preparation for planting, the mucky soil clung to the cutting edge of the plow. Every few yards he had to stop and clean the plowshare (the iron cutting blade).

In 1837 a blacksmith named John Deere moved from Vermont to Grand Detour, Illinois. He watched the prairie farmers at their frustrating work, then designed a plow especially for them. His most important innovation was the use of steel rather than iron for the plowshare. The smoother and less porous steel allowed the sticky soil to slide off much more easily than it did off iron. Farmers immediately saw that this self-cleaning plow could save them an immense amount of time and labor.

Deere's plow made it possible for farmers to cultivate more land and therefore grow much larger crops. These included grains, fruits and vegetables, and feed crops for hogs and cattle. The farmers were not the only ones to benefit from Deere's invention. The processing and distributing of prairie crops formed the economic basis for the development of Chicago and other Illinois cities.

Deere set up a small factory in Grand Detour, then in the 1840s moved to Moline to have easier access to the steel he needed. By the end of the century his company had become one of the big producers of agricultural implements and machinery. Other manufacturers, including Cyrus McCormick, the designer of some of the earliest harvesting machinery, came to Illinois. The state was well on its way toward becoming the farm equipment capital of the nation.

Illinois Cowboys and Cattle Kings

Illinois shared in the nation's colorful history of cowboys and cattle kings. Drovers traveled around the state, buying pigs and cattle from small farmers, then drove them to Chicago or even to the East Coast. The continued popularity of the lean, long-legged, half-wild varieties of stock was due in part to the fact that they could stand the long marches to market.

Isaac Funk was one of the early cattle barons of Illinois. Funk, a German immigrant, came to Illinois in 1824 with other members of his large family and bought land near Bloomington. Starting out in a log cabin and in debt, Funk eventually became a rich gentleman farmer with a spacious estate. At first he raised cattle on his own land, then began traveling about buying animals from ranchers as far away as Texas. These he drove back to Funk's Grove for fattening, after which he took them to market.

A cattle or hog drive started out from Funk's Grove on a note of high excitement. When the gates were opened, 200 to 300 cattle or 800 to 1,200 hogs rushed out. After an hour or so on the road, they settled down and moved along at a slow, steady pace. It took about twelve days to reach Chicago, where the animals were sold at a good profit.

In the early days, few farmers were interested in scientific farming. What had worked for their fathers was good enough for them. Some still believed old superstitions, such as that driving rusty nails into fruit trees would improve production or that certain crops had to be planted during certain phases of the moon. Men like Funk, on the other hand, saw scientific methods as the key to the future of farming. Funk worked hard to improve the breeds he raised and experimented with new ways of fattening cattle. After he had made his fortune, he devoted much of his time to public service, including trying to get Illinois farmers to update their methods and materials.

For a short time, Illinois farmers who wanted to raise crops came into conflict with those who wanted to allow their cattle to range freely.

Loose stock trampled the fields, damaged young plants, and ate part of the harvest. The farmers insisted that the cattlemen must fence in their herds; the cattlemen countered that the farmers should fence in their crops. Wooden posts and rails were scarce and expensive on the prairie, and no one wanted to pay for them. At last the government worked out a compromise by which the cost was shared.

A man who was to achieve much greater fame than Isaac Funk in a career indirectly related to cattle droving was James Butler Hickok. Born in Troy Grove, Illinois, in 1837, Hickok moved to Kansas Territory where his exploits made him a folk hero and gave him the nickname "Wild Bill" Hickok. An expert marksman, he kept order in the wild, brawling cattle towns he served as marshal.

John Wright and the *Prairie Farmer*

John S. Wright was a businessman rather than a farmer, but he became the farmers' friend and advocate. Born in Massachusetts in 1815, Wright came to Chicago with his father in the early 1830s. He made his first fortune in real estate by the time he was twenty-three. Although he lost most of it when a financial crisis swept the country in 1837, he made a second and larger fortune in the same business. During his lifetime he promoted Illinois in every way he could and involved himself in various innovative business schemes, not all of which were successful. But Wright's restless energy, busy mind, and persuasive personality changed the lives of many prairie settlers. He is best known for the founding of a newspaper called the *Prairie Farmer*.

While trying to drum up support for some of his ventures, Wright traveled widely throughout the state and talked to the farmers. One of their complaints was that the methods and equipment they had used on their old farms were not suitable for use on the prairie. Sparked by these talks, Wright decided to start a newspaper specifically aimed at prairie farmers and their problems. In the first regular issue of the *Prairie Farmer* (January 1841), Wright encouraged his audience to use the paper as a forum for sharing their experiences and exchanging information and ideas. "Farmers, write for your paper," read the masthead on the first page.

Many farmers did contribute letters and articles, and Wright also introduced them to new scientific methods by getting experts to write articles on fertilizers, crop rotation, conservation, improved methods of breeding animals, and new ways of fighting insect pests and plant diseases. There were also practical articles on replacing log structures with frame buildings, preserving foods safely, keeping the costs of fencing down, and using native plants for feeding stock.

Subscriptions rose as farmers identified more and more with their paper. Later, when the battle for public schools was being waged, Wright was able to influence the largest block of Illinois voters, the farmers. He had used the *Prairie Farmer* to make them see how knowledge could bring increased productivity, income, and comfort to their lives; when he wrote editorials on the need for a public school system, many farmers were ready to listen. Wright's newspaper is still published today.

The Hardships of Prairie Life

The lives of the backwoods families who settled southern Illinois were plagued with lack of funds, lack of laborers, Indian raids, ignorance, sickness, and isolation. But they had one great advantage over prairie families from the Northeast: they had lived in the wilderness for generations and knew what to expect. Most of the New Englanders had never lived in wild country before. They had toiled to cultivate their rocky New England farms and knew the capriciousness of nature. But on the prairie everything seemed to happen on a much larger scale. They felt overwhelmed by being so far from help.

Eliza Farnham, a New Englander who lived with her husband on the Illinois prairie for several years, left a written record of those difficult times. She recorded a stormy spring when violent electrical storms accompanied by heavy rain occurred every day from April 24 through the end of June. Eliza, her husband, and their neighbors gathered in one house to wait out the storms together, never dreaming how long that would take. On many days there were no hours of normal daylight at all. On some days, new hope would come with the dawning of a bright, clear day, but then a gray spot would appear on the horizon. Within an hour, the harmless-looking cloud would swell into a life-threatening storm beating down on the cabins and crops and toppling trees in nearby groves. When flashes of lightning lit the horizon or zigzagged down the sky followed by jarring vibrations of thunder, the settlers began to wonder if God was sending another flood like that recorded in the Bible. The small cabin they huddled in certainly did not feel seaworthy enough to be an ark.

When the storms finally abated, the settlers ventured out only to find their early crops rotted in the field and the ground too saturated to plow and plant again. Every little hollow had become a pond, and ponds had become lakes. The standing water made a perfect place for disease-carrying mosquitoes to hatch. People came down with the ague, a disease we know today as malaria. They thought the mist rising from swampy lands caused it, but actually it was transmitted by mosquitoes.

In the fall fires roared across the prairies. Some were caused by lightning strikes, and others were started by people. Indians had known for a long time that the controlled burning of the prairie in the fall killed the seeds of invading plants and insect larvae but did not injure the roots of the true prairie plants. It was their way of keeping the prairie intact, a method used today in the small prairie reserves that still exist in Illinois.

At first the newcomers did not realize the danger of grass fires, and most prairie farmers did not know how to set and supervise controlled burns. It was a powerful experience to see the horizon on fire with livid plumes of purple and yellow smoke rising from the fast-moving flames that devoured the dry grasses. Because they had never seen such a spectacle, many settlers misjudged how fast a prairie fire could travel. They lost their homes, sheds, crops, animals, belongings—and sometimes their lives—by watching just a little too long or not knowing what to do.

In winter the weather was subject to unpredictable and drastic changes in temperature. Illinois and other midwestern states lie in a belt where fronts of icy polar air sweep southward to meet fronts of warm, moist air moving north from the Gulf of Mexico. Tornadoes, blizzards, thunderstorms, and high winds are the spawn of such weather clashes.

In the winter of 1836–37 the weather had been mild and rainy when a shift in the direction of the wind brought such a sudden and sharp drop in temperature that rain turned to sleet and a blizzard soon followed. Geese and chickens froze to the ground before they could be brought in. A hog farmer and his crew who were driving nine hundred hogs to market had to abandon them and find shelter for themselves. (The pigs piled up on each other in a huge heap. Those on top insulated those underneath, and all but twenty of the hogs survived.) During this same storm, a half-frozen man rode up to an inn and called out for help. Several men came out, but finding him frozen to the saddle, they had to carry him into the inn in his saddle, where they thawed him in front of the fire.

Just as river pirates in earlier days had terrorized settlers in the Cave-in-Rock area, prairie pirates formed an armed band about three hundred strong and raided isolated farms in northwestern Illinois. They ransacked cabins and took anything of value. The loss of winter food supplies, clothing that had taken long hours to make, tools, and seeds created hardships for people far away from sources of replenishment. The prairie pirates were also master horse thieves. Having a horse stolen was a real catastrophe for settlers who relied on their horses for transportation and farm work.

At last, settlers in the Rock River Valley had had enough. They tracked down and hanged a few of the thieves. The remaining pirates realized that the time when they could commit crimes without fear of reprisal was over. They disbanded, some moving farther west.

In time the eastern cities began to feel the loss of population. They had fewer consumers and fewer taxpayers, so they tried to stop the flow of immigrants and to persuade families already living on the prairie to return by publicizing the negative aspects of life in the West in newspaper and magazine articles. Some families living on the Illinois prairie did return to their old homes, and few could blame them. They had lost members of their families and much of their fortunes. However, others felt they had reached a point of no return and forged ahead. By doing so, they eventually turned the prairies into one of the richest agricultural areas in the world.

❧

It must have been maddening for the prairie pioneers to know how rich the prairie soil was and to have so much trouble getting at it. John Deere's self-cleaning plow proved to be a significant breakthrough. Then when John Wright founded the *Prairie Farmer*, Illinois farmers took it to their hearts. It became a trusted source of information and a medium for exchanging ideas and experiences related directly to the needs of the prairie farmer. In the 1830s farm productivity began to rise dramatically.

But what good did it do to grow commercial crops if you could not get them to market? Illinoisans rushed to update their transportation system so that they could compete with other agricultural states. They were in such a hurry that their solution to the problem became a problem itself, as we shall see in chapter 9.

For Further Exploration

Eliza W. Farnham, *Life in Prairie Land*. New York: Harper, 1846. Prairie State Edition. Urbana: University of Illinois Press, 1988.

Eliza Farnham's account of a New England bride's adjustment to frontier living is told with a fine sense of drama, humor, and pathos. Vivid descriptions of weeks of unremitting electrical storms, unbelievably swift prairie fires, blizzards, and summers of mosquitoes and fevers are balanced by accounts of social events, political activity, and everyday neighborliness. Farnham returned to the East Coast after four years but retained her love for the Illinois prairies.

Gurdon Saltonstall Hubbard. *The Autobiography of Gurdon Saltonstall Hubbard*. Chicago: The Lakeside Press, R. R. Donnelley, 1911.

While still in his teens, Hubbard persuaded his parents to allow him to go west and work for the American Fur Company. Within a few years he was put in charge of gathering furs in central and eastern Illinois. The Indians called him "Swift Walker" because even in rough terrain he could hike seventy-five miles a day. By 1830 the fur trade was no longer profitable in Illinois, so Hubbard turned to other pursuits in Danville and Chicago.

Juliette Kinzie. *Wau-Bun: The "Early Day" in the North-West*. New York: Derby and Jackson, 1856. Reprint. Urbana: University of Illinois Press, 1992.

Young Juliette Magill married into the John Kinzie family. An open and vivacious young woman with a sense of humor and eyes and ears for all that happened around her, she proved equal to the difficult life in which she found herself. In *Wau-Bun* she relates her own experiences as well as stories she heard from other settlers.

John W. Voigt and Robert H. Mohlenbrock. *Prairie Plants of Illinois*. Springfield: Department of Conservation, State of Illinois, n.d.

Interest in our prairie heritage has led to vigorous efforts to preserve the few remaining virgin prairies in Illinois. This manual with its clear pen and ink drawings includes brief descriptions of native prairie plants, the uses to which they have been or are put, and their habitats.

9

Red Ink in Illinois

Rushing into the Future

A surge of self-confidence and high spirits ushered in the 1830s. Opportunity! Progress! Expansion!—those were the catchwords of the time. By then Illinois, like many other states, had reached a plateau of development beyond which it could not rise without better transportation. Agricultural products needed to be shipped to distant markets without delay. Raw materials had to keep rolling into industrial cities so that manufactured items could roll out. To fill the labor shortages in the West a more efficient way of getting immigrants from East Coast ports to Chicago had to be found. The development of mineral deposits was limited to supplying local needs because it was too expensive to ship the products elsewhere. Faced with such problems, entrepreneurs anxious to move Illinois into the modern age came up with a number of internal improvement projects designed to update transportation in the state.

The Illinois and Michigan Canal

The first major internal improvement project to be put before the General Assembly in Illinois was a canal that would connect Lake Michigan with the Illinois River. The Illinois flows into the Mississippi River, so a canal would provide the missing link in a tremendous waterway extending from the East Coast to the Gulf of Mexico.

Not everyone favored the building of the canal. People living in southern Illinois said it would be of little use to them, yet they would have to help pay for it. They also thought it would bring in too many Yankees. Some people feared the canal would slowly enlarge itself and

Canal boats on the Illinois and Michigan Canal. The canal made it possible to travel from New York to New Orleans entirely by water. Courtesy of the Illinois State Historical Library.

eventually wash away a good part of the state! Strangely enough, few citizens or their representatives in the General Assembly seemed very concerned about the more practical issues. How much would the canal cost? How was it to be paid for? Were there enough engineers and technicians to do it properly? Where would the necessary pool of laborers come from?

Already in 1822, Illinois lawmakers had petitioned the federal government for a land grant. They had hoped to receive enough land for the canal right-of-way as well as additional acreage that could be sold to finance the building of the canal. However, the federal government granted only enough land for the right-of-way plus a ninety-foot strip on each side for towpaths.

Congress was more generous when a second request was made in 1827. It granted a total of 290,915 acres for the building of the Illinois and Michigan Canal. By then it seemed to the members of Congress that such a canal was desirable because it would help tie the rapidly developing western part of the country to the older states in the East and South. However, the actual building of the canal did not begin until 1836. There were several reasons for this delay.

First, it took time to reach agreement on what kind of a canal should be built. Engineers wanted to build a deep-cut canal so that steamboats could use it as well as specially built canal boats. A deep-cut canal would be much more expensive to build than a shallow canal, but enthusiasm for the project was so high that at first voters did not seem to care about the extra cost. Many thought that all the state had to do to pay the bill was to sell some of the land it had been given by the federal government. Unfortunately, when some of this land was put up for sale, it brought disappointingly low prices. Suddenly a shallow-cut canal became the more popular option.

Then a new form of transportation emerged—the railroad. In the 1830s railroads in the East were becoming capable of carrying people and goods faster and cheaper than any other form of public transportation. For Illinoisans who had never seen a locomotive, the idea of railroads becoming a common feature of the landscape seemed far-fetched. But some who had been to the East returned convinced that railroads were the transportation of the future. They claimed that canals were already outdated and that plans for the Illinois and Michigan Canal should be scrapped and a state system of railroads built instead. They thought that railroads would be less expensive to build than the canal. The canal backers did not want the money already put into the canal to be lost and insisted that the canal would pay for itself soon after it was completed.

In 1833 state lawmakers voted to proceed with both projects. In his inaugural address of 1834 Governor Joseph Duncan justified this decision by declaring that if such projects were delayed, Illinois would be unable to compete successfully with neighboring states. He also insisted that the longer the state waited, the more expensive and difficult the task would be. Both the General Assembly and the general public enthusiastically agreed. Times were good, and few stopped to consider the great financial burden the state was about to assume. Governor Duncan borrowed $500,000 to begin construction of the canal, and groundbreaking ceremonies took place on July 4, 1836.

As a first step, contracts for portions of the canal were let to private companies, but before work could proceed, workers had to be found. Because not enough were available in Illinois, recruiters went to Ireland to persuade poor laborers there to come to Illinois. Many did so. Without them, the canal could not have been completed.

Only the most primitve building techniques were available. Workers used black powder to blast a channel, then removed the debris by hand with scrapers, picks, and shovels. Thaws and rains made the soil so soggy that digging was almost impossible in the spring. Progress was slow, and costs greatly exceeded estimates, but at this point there was little thought of turning back.

The Internal Improvements Act of 1837

Just before the General Assembly met for the 1836–37 session, an Internal Improvements Convention was held in Vandalia, and delegates from all parts of the state attended. Speaking on behalf of their districts, delegates described the projects their people wanted. Because politicians stay in office by getting what their constituents want, the members of the General Assembly listened carefully. When the General Assembly convened, it passed the Internal Improvements Act of 1837, which provided funding for some of the projects outlined at the convention.

Funds were allocated for making the Kaskaskia, Illinois, Wabash, Little Wabash, and Rock rivers navigable by steamboat. The Great Western Mail Route between Vincennes and St. Louis was to be improved, as were many smaller roads. But the most visionary project of all was the building of a statewide railroad system.

A First Try at Building a Railroad

The General Assembly debated the question of whether the railroad system should be owned and operated by the state or run as a private business. Deciding in favor of private business, it granted charters to sixteen companies to build stretches of the railroad. However, this plan failed when the companies could not come up with the necessary funds. The state had to take over the enterprise.

Lawmakers allocated $3.5 million for the building of the Illinois Central, as the railroad was to be called. It was to run from Cairo at the southern tip of the state to the Illinois River at the point where the canal would eventually enter the river. From there it was to follow a northwesterly route to Galena. No branch line to Chicago was planned because the legislators thought the completion of the Illinois and Michigan Canal would solve transportation problems in that part of the state, at least until it was more heavily settled.

The railroad was to have two east-west lines crossing the main north-south route: the Northern Cross was to run from Quincy through Springfield and Danville, then to the Indiana state line. The Southern Cross would be built between Alton and Mt. Carmel. Other crosses and connecting lines were to be added later.

In 1837 officials and citizens gathered for a groundbreaking ceremony at Meredosia, a town on the Illinois River, and the building of
the Northern Cross got underway with festivities and great hopes.

The Panic of 1837

An unexpected disaster brought work on both the canal and the
railroad to a halt. A severe financial depression, the Panic of 1837,
spread across the nation. It resulted partly from speculators investing
heavily in land in the belief that its value would quickly skyrocket.
Instead, the price of land fell, and fortunes were lost.

In the past members of Congress had often disagreed about whether
or not the federal government should regulate banks in the various
states. Some lawmakers felt that without government supervision, the
banking system would be unstable, confusing, and subject to corruption.
Others felt that if the federal government was allowed to control
banking, it would have too much power over the nation's economy.

At the time of the Panic of 1837, banks were not federally regulated.
In some states, including Illinois, banking had become chaotic. Some
private banks issued notes meant to be used as money but did not
always keep enough gold in reserve to back them up. When the
financial situation all over the country deteriorated, worried investors
rushed to the banks demanding their money, only to find that their
banks could not pay up. Thousands of people lost all their savings. To
make matters worse, the Illinois General Assembly had sold bonds to
the public to finance state banks. When the state banks failed, the state
government was left with all of those bonds to pay off and no money
for that purpose.

As the situation worsened, people had less money to spend, and
consumer goods accumulated in the stores and warehouses. Prices of
grain and meat dropped, production tapered off, and unemployment
soared. Many businesses had to shut down.

Governor Duncan now saw that the state was headed for bankruptcy
and tried to persuade the General Assembly to repeal the Internal
Improvements Act. The lawmakers refused, even though work on the
two largest projects had to be stopped for lack of funds. Tracks were
laid between Meredosia and Springfield, but the planned schedule of
three runs per week was never realized. By 1844 the one and only
locomotive had worn out, and the line had become a financial disaster.
Three years later the state sold the railroad at auction, receiving for it
about one-fortieth of what it had cost to build.

Booming Economy
High production. Heavy spending.
High employment.

Overexpansion
Wild speculation in land, utilities,
stocks, and bonds. Unwise investments.
Heavy credit buying.

Overproduction
Market flooded with goods. Prices
fall. Manufacturers' and merchants'
inventories rise.

Cutbacks
Investors become skittish. Companies
cut back production. Workers laid off.

Consumer Spending Falls
More production cuts. More unemployment.
People start withdrawing their savings.

A Run on the Banks
Banks cannot meet demands for withdrawals and have
no money to lend. Some close temporarily. Some close for good.

Panic

The boom-to-bust cycle.

The Illinois and Michigan Canal was too far along to be abandoned, even though it was costing millions of dollars more than the planners had originally estimated. In 1842 work on it resumed, and the first boats moved through it in 1848. When completed, the ninety-six-mile-long canal with its seventeen locks was able to carry boats from Lockport near Chicago to the Illinois River at La Salle.

Later, railroads made the Illinois and Michigan Canal obsolete, just as some people had predicted. However, by that time the canal had moved millions of tons of agricultural products and other freight and served as a crucial link in a trade route that extended all the way from the East Coast to the Gulf of Mexico.

❧

In the 1830s the people of Illinois somewhat recklessly plunged themselves deep into debt. The backers of various internal improvement projects sincerely believed that after completion the projects would quickly pay for themselves. But building canals and railroads in the wilderness was much more difficult, took much longer, and cost many times more than anyone had imagined. And few people foresaw the financial panic that swept the nation in 1837. The panic not only put people out of work, but it also brought an end to the wild spending spree. The first try at building a state railroad ended up a dismal and expensive failure. The Illinois and Michigan Canal finally became operable twelve years after the colorful groundbreaking ceremonies.

The future did not look all that bright in the 1840s. Nevertheless, by 1850 Illinois was again in the thick of things, working out its problems, growing vigorously, and participating more fully in national affairs. The next chapter gives us a portrait of Illinois at mid-century.

For Further Exploration

Jim Redd. *The Illinois and Michigan Canal: A Contemporary Perspective in Essays and Photographs.* Carbondale: Southern Illinois University Press, 1992.

Chicago writer and photographer Jim Redd has photographed the remnants of the old canal route as it looks today and has skillfully woven the history of the canal into his travelogue.

Paul Simon. *Lincoln's Preparation for Greatness: The Illinois Legislative Years.* Norman: University of Oklahoma Press, 1965. Illini Books ed. Urbana: University of Illinois Press, 1971.

Chapters 2 through 4 capture the optimism and reckless high spirits that led to the passage of the Internal Improvements Act and set the state on a course toward bankruptcy.

10

Illinois at Mid-Century

Coming of Age

In the early 1800s Illinoisans were absorbed in affairs within their own borders. But by mid-century they were finding themselves more deeply involved in the affairs of the nation as a whole. Certainly the financial panic of 1837 had made it clear that the economy of the separate states was inextricably linked to the national economy. This had been a painful lesson for Illinoisans, dashing the high spirits that had led to the festive groundbreaking ceremonies for several large-scale internal improvement projects. Illinois had such an enormous debt that it could not even pay the interest due on it.

Many people thought the situation hopeless and wanted Governor Thomas Ford to default on the loans and declare the state bankrupt. Governor Ford considered such a solution dishonorable and realized it would make borrowing money from out-of-state investors difficult in the future. Instead of repudiating the debt, he arranged for it be be paid back on a more relaxed schedule. However, he could only get lenders to agree to the new plan by promising that the state would increase taxes. Illinoisans who were still recovering from the panic were not happy with the idea of paying new taxes, but Ford worked out a plan by which they would pay a small amount to begin with, then higher rates as prosperity returned. By the late 1850s Illinois was able to pay the annual interest on its debt, and twenty years later it had paid it off in full.

Meanwhile, soldiers from Illinois officially took part in a war against a foreign power for the first time. When the Mexican War (1846–48) broke out, President James K. Polk asked Illinois to supply three regiments. Enough volunteers responded to fill nine. Illinois troops performed with honor in the crucial battle of Buena Vista, in which the Mexican general, Antonio López de Santa Anna, was defeated.

History is full of strange minor episodes. For example, Santa Anna had a wooden leg. Someone in the American forces decided that the leg would make a good trophy to send back to Springfield. It was taken from him and apparently arrived safely in Illinois. Long after the general had any use for his wooden leg, the question of what to do with it came up for discussion in the General Assembly. The rest of the story will be told when we come to World War I.

A New Capital

By the mid-1800s the upstate counties were growing faster than the southern counties, and people living there wanted a more centrally located capital. When the state house at Vandalia became too small, the General Assembly decided to move to another city. Springfield, Alton, Jacksonville, and Peoria all competed for the honor of becoming the new capital. Springfield won with its offer of a building site and $50,000

The first capitol in Springfield, now known as the "Old Capitol," served as the state building until after the Civil War. Courtesy of the Illinois State Historical Library.

toward the construction of the capitol building. Ground was broken in July 1837, and two years later wagonloads of state property began arriving in Springfield.

For a short time it looked as if Illinois might become smaller than it had been at the time it was granted statehood. People living in nine of the northern counties felt they were not getting their share of attention from the state government; furthermore, they did not want to be held responsible for any part of the state's huge deficit. Wisconsin, needing a larger population to apply for statehood, saw a golden opportunity. It invited the discontented Illinois counties to become part of Wisconsin.

Leaders in the nine Illinois counties petitioned Congress for permission to join Wisconsin, claiming that Nathaniel Pope's 1818 amendment, which had made them part of Illinois, had been in violation of the Northwest Ordinance. Congress rejected the request. Wisconsin became a state in 1848, and the Illinois boundary remained as it was.

A New Constitution

By 1848 the population of Illinois had soared to over 400,000, and the social, economic, and political life of its people had become so complex that the constitution of 1818 was no longer adequate. A new constitution nearly three times the length of the old one was proposed and adopted.

The framers of the new constitution made sure that there would be no more grand schemes for public works backed by enthusiasm rather than hard facts. From then on, any proposal with an estimated cost of more than $50,000 had to be approved by the voters of the state. In another attempt to keep expenses down, delegates to the constitutional convention cut the size of the General Assembly from 162 to 100 members, each of whom was to be paid $2 per day for the first forty-two days of a legislative session and $1 per day for any additional time.

A practice that seems strange to us today, viva voce voting, had been used early in the state's history. People went to the polling place and orally announced their preferences to the clerks who recorded them. As the population grew, this method of voting became highly impractical and undesirable in terms of privacy. The 1848 constitution therefore did away with it.

The new constitution corrected some of the shortcomings of the old one, but it did not look to the future. Some of its provisions soon became obsolete, and only twenty-two years later a third constitution replaced it.

The Land of Promise

Up to this point, we have talked mainly about pioneers who immigrated to Illinois from other parts of this country. We have not said much about the wave of immigrants who came to Illinois directly from foreign lands beginning in the 1830s and continuing until the Civil War. Searching for freedom and economic opportunity, people from England, Scotland, Wales, Ireland, Germany, Norway, Sweden, Denmark, Switzerland, Portugal, Italy, Greece, Belgium, and Poland came to Illinois. Immigrants from other parts of this hemisphere also arrived, including people from Mexico, South America, and the West Indies. Some even came from as far away as Hawaii and China.

Of the 851,500 people living in Illinois in 1850, more than 100,000 had come from other countries. The two largest groups of immigrants were the Germans (38,000) and the Irish (28,000).

German Immigrants

The thousands of Germans who came to Illinois at this time included farmers and laborers, intellectuals, merchants, and craftsmen. During the early 1800s, wars and revolutions destabilized Europe and made life miserable for many people. The kingdoms and principalities from which Otto von Bismarck would later create modern Germany were ruled by oppressive despots who came under attack from some of their own citizens. German officials moved quickly to quell all dissent, and the people who had participated in abortive revolutions had to flee. Many of them came to America in search of political, religious, and intellectual freedom.

Economic conditions also caused Germans to emigrate. Farm land in Germany had been subdivided so often that the plots were too small to support a family. When they heard that in the American West even poor people could own land, they packed their belongings and set out for the New World. Some came to Illinois and bought farms along the Mississippi, Illinois, Rock, and Fox rivers. Industrious and determined to succeed, they were said to have built good barns before they built good roofs over their heads. Germans who were too poor to buy land hired themselves out as farm workers or found city jobs until they had enough money for a down payment. Some found they liked city living and gave up agriculture. Chicago, Peoria, Galena, and Quincy had large German neighborhoods.

The Irish Immigrants

The Irish were even more oppressed in their homeland than the Germans had been in theirs. Irish Catholics, who were in the majority, were governed by Protestant Englishmen living in Ireland and who were by far in the minority. Most Irish Catholics were prevented from owning land, voting, or holding public office and were held in contempt by their English landlords. In spite of the serious political, social, and economic drawbacks of being Catholic, few Irish Catholics were willing to give up their faith.

Although many Irish families did not want to leave their homeland, emigrating was their only hope of survival, especially after a plant disease called blight killed off the one crop they depended on, potatoes, two years in a row. The famine that followed cost more than a million lives and left many Irish peasants destitute. Landlords and government officials agreed to pay the fares of some of the poor just to get them out of sight and off their hands. In other cases relatives pooled their resources and sent one person to America. That person worked hard and saved enough money to bring another family member over, who, in turn, financed the passage of someone else. Irish families often held wakes for those going to America, just as they held wakes for loved ones that died. They doubted that they would ever see them again.

The Irish did not come to Illinois to farm. They had no money to spend on land, and their past experiences had made them wary of depending on agriculture for a living. Instead, they went to Galena to work in the mines, found jobs as laborers in the cities, or worked on large transportation projects such as the Illinois and Michigan Canal and the Illinois Central Railroad.

Circumstances connected with the building of the canal did turn some Irish laborers into farmers, however. Canal workers were paid in scrip, a substitute for money with which they could buy food, clothing, and other necessities. During the Panic of 1837, scrip lost most of its purchasing power, but it could still be used to buy land. A number of Irish families purchased acreage along the Illinois River or along the route of the canal and became successful farmers.

The Struggle for Public Education

Before 1855, less than one-third of the children in Illinois attended school. Those families that could afford to sent their children to private schools. But the education of children from poor families was a hit-and-miss affair. A few communities established free elementary schools before any laws compelling them to do so were passed. Chicago may have been the first when it opened an elementary school in 1834.

During the 1840s education conventions attended by teachers, school and government officials, and parents kept pressure on the General

Assembly. Laws passed in 1841 and 1845 permitted but did not require local school districts to levy taxes for education. Many chose not to. At last, in 1855, the General Assembly passed a law based on the principle that the state could use its taxing power to support local schools. Now that they were assured of state funds, dozens of rural communities built one-room schools, and some of the larger cities developed graded schools.

Education beyond the elementary level was another matter. A number of private academies and seminaries existed, but free public high schools were unheard of. The West Jacksonville District organized the state's first public high school in 1851, and Chicago started one in 1856. A year later the state legislature passed a law encouraging the building of public high schools, but another ten years went by before any downstate community did so. Many rural areas simply did not have enough people to provide a tax base large enough to support a high school.

By 1850 close to twenty private colleges sponsored by various religious denominations existed, but there was still no state-funded institution of higher learning. Charles Hovey, who organized the Illinois State Teachers' Association in 1853, kept insisting that elementary education would not improve until teachers received better training. Finally, in 1857, the General Assembly passed a bill creating the Illinois State Normal School. Located near Bloomington, the new institution was the first tax-supported college in the state and the first teachers' college in the Mississippi Valley. It later became Illinois State University.

By 1900 the building of four more normal schools had been authorized: Southern Illinois Normal at Carbondale (1869), Eastern at Charleston (1895), Northern at DeKalb (1895), and Western at Macomb (1899). All five state normal schools started out as teacher-training institutions and eventually became full-fledged universities.

Another Try at Railroad Building

In 1850 U.S. Senator Stephen Douglas of Illinois steered a bill through Congress that granted the state land to build a railroad. Illinoisans were jubilant when the news reached them and greeted their homecoming congressmen like conquering heroes.

Early in the new year, the General Assembly decided that this time they would allow private businessmen to build and run the railroad. Bids were let, and the best offer came from a group of eastern financiers led by Robert Rantoul. Rantoul and his associates were willing to pay the state 7 percent of their gross operating income as soon as the railroad began functioning. On February 10, 1851, Governor Augustus French signed the bill that gave the Rantoul group a charter to build the railroad and turned over to it the federal land that had been granted for the project.

The Rantoul group incorporated as the Illinois Central Railroad Company and chose Colonel Roswell B. Mason as its chief construction engineer. Mason had been one of the builders of the Erie Canal and had directed the construction of several eastern railroads. Arriving in Chicago with thirty assistants in May 1851, Mason sent teams to survey various sections of the route. By September all of the surveys were complete, the exact route was decided upon, and work had begun.

Sections of the railroad were built by different teams and then joined. Teams often competed to see which would be the first to reach a point where two sections met. "Big Bill" Mattoon, a contractor for a company that was building a line from Terre Haute to St. Louis, offered to bet Mason that his crew would beat Mason's to the place where the two railroads were to cross. Mason replied that he was not a betting man, but that the one whose team won should have the privilege of naming the station. Exuberantly the crews set out to prove themselves. Although Mason's men won, he was so grateful to Mattoon for having stirred the workers to such an effort that he named the station Mattoon.

Alcoholism was one of the worst labor problems connected with the building of the railroad. Drinking caused so many brawls and work stoppages that Colonel Mason prohibited whiskey from being trans-

"Locomotive No. 1," first of the Illinois Central Railroad's fleet. Courtesy of the Illinois State Historical Library.

ported on any section of the railroad. Illness also caused delays. Ague and other fevers constantly attacked workers, and the dreaded cholera struck in 1854 and 1855. Some laborers fled to avoid getting it.

When the main line from Cairo to Dunleith (near Galena) was completed in 1855, dignitaries aboard a special excursion train made the first complete trip, steaming into Cairo on May 8. In less than five years 705.5 miles of track had been laid through the wilderness. At the time of its completion, the Illinois Central was the longest railroad in the world.

Illinois moved from a time of great financial distress into a period of prosperity. Governor Ford's plan to pay off the state's debt was adopted, the economy stabilized, and Illinoisans were able to get on with the modernization of their state. In 1839 the state government moved to Springfield, the new capital. Delegates to the second constitutional convention created a new constitution in 1848. By 1850 a second attempt to build the Illinois Central Railroad was underway.

New accents were heard in the streets of the cities and towns and in the remaining wilderness as waves of immigrants arrived from Europe. Political unrest and hunger had driven them from their homes to Illinois, which they saw as the "promised land." Among them were wealthy people and poor; farmers, laborers, and intellectuals; and a rich array of ethnic groups. They had much to offer their new homeland.

Unfortunately, undercurrents of trouble rose to the surface during the next decade. The unsolved problem of slavery dovetailed into the states' rights question and pitted the South against the North. In Part 3 we will see the pivotal role Illinois played in the Civil War.

For Further Exploration

Daniel Harmon Brush. *Growing up with Southern Illinois, 1820–1861.* Edited by Milo Milton Quaife. Chicago: Lakeside Press, R. R. Donnelley, 1944.

The founder of Carbondale tells how he planned its location by figuring out where the Illinois Central would be likely to put a station. His description of the arrival of the first locomotive on July 4, 1854, captures the excitement of people seeing a train for the first time, some of whom realized that the railroad would soon become their economic lifeline.

Carlton J. Corliss. *Main Line of Mid-America: The Story of the Illinois Central.* New York: Creative Age Press, 1950.

Politicians, financiers, engineers, and rough-and-ready-laborers struggled to build a railroad through the Illinois wilderness. Early passengers traveled in rickety coaches with coal-burning stoves to heat them. One station telegraphed ahead to the next so that hot meals could be ready when the train arrived. People living in the towns and villages through which the locomotives chugged gathered along the tracks to witness the great new travel adventure of their fellow countrymen.

Mark Wyman. *Immigrants in the Valley: Irish, Germans, and Americans in the Upper Mississippi Country*. Chicago: Nelson-Hall, 1984.

Wyman discusses the reasons for the large-scale migrations of Germans and Irish to the Mississippi Valley and explains the interactions of these diverse groups with each other and with their English-speaking neighbors.

PART THREE

The Civil War Era

In the 1850s the North and the South were like two trains speeding toward each other on the same track. Attempts at compromise slowed the trains down only a little. Strongly held opinions on slavery and states' rights divided Illinoisans, but they rallied to the call to preserve the Union. And out of their midst came the man who was to guide the nation through these perilous years, Abraham Lincoln.

11

Prelude to War

Illinois, a "House Divided"

The seeds of the Civil War had been sown long before the war broke out. The architects of the Constitution had dodged the question of slavery because any solution would have taken a long time and may not have even been possible. They needed to form a solid union as quickly as possible so that the fragile new nation would be able to survive. But slavery did not go away, as some people had hoped. The problem intensified as it became tangled with the struggle to maintain a balance of power between the North and the South. Compromises provided temporary solutions, but it took the Civil War to decide such questions as: Should slavery be abolished? Who has the power to declare slavery legal or illegal—the federal government or the separate states? Can a dissatisfied state leave the Union?

If Illinoisans had been asked in 1861 to go to war to free the slaves, many would not have responded with enthusiasm. Although nominally a free state, Illinois had a history of slavery that extended back to the French occupation. During territorial days the indentured servant system was used to sidestep the prohibition of slavery in the Northwest Ordinance. The first state constitution prohibited the extension of slavery but did nothing to put an end to existing slavery. And the infamous Black Laws passed by the first General Assembly were still on the books when the war broke out. As late as 1853 the General Assembly was still passing laws that prevented blacks from permanently settling in the state and slave owners from bringing slaves to Illinois for the purpose of freeing them.

This is not to say that all Illinoisans sanctioned slavery. The state courts had ruled in favor of blacks even while the state legislature was passing laws against them. After one decision in 1838, black men and women could no longer be required to prove that they were free. In 1841 the selling of indentured servants was stopped. And in 1845 the state supreme court ruled that all slaves who had been held after the passage of the Northwest Ordinance and the Illinois Constitution of 1818 had been detained illegally and those who were still alive, as well as their descendants, were freed.

Illinois also had a nucleus of fearless and articulate abolitionists, one of whom was a young Presbyterian minister and journalist named Elijah Lovejoy. Lovejoy believed that allowing others to own slaves was as reprehensible as owning slaves oneself. The editorials he wrote and the sermons he preached angered many people. When he spoke out against the lynching of a free black man in St. Louis, a mob broke into his office and wrecked his printing press. At that point he moved to Alton, Illinois.

Lovejoy did not fare much better there. His press was dumped into the river by antiabolitionists. He replaced it with a new press, but in 1837 that press was wrecked, too, and Lovejoy was told to leave Alton. He refused, insisting that freedom of speech and of the press were guaranteed to him by the Constitution.

That November, the arrival of his fourth press caused an uneasy excitement among the townspeople. The press had been unloaded, and Lovejoy and his friends were standing guard over it when violence broke out. Shots were fired, and in minutes several people were dead, including Lovejoy himself. Lovejoy's courage in telling Illinoisans that slavery was wrong and his passionate insistence on freedom of the press earned him a place of honor in the history of journalism.

Lovejoy's brother Owen, together with other abolitionists, participated in the underground railway, hiding escaped slaves by day, then taking them to another safe place in the dark of the night. "Stops" are known to have existed in Quincy, Alton, Chester, Rockford, and Chicago. Some rural families also helped the brave runaways.

Nevertheless, Illinoisans in general were not ready to go to war to free the slaves. It was the call to defend and save the Union that became their rallying cry. Altogether, Illinois provided 259,092 soldiers. Only New York, Ohio, and Pennsylvania provided more. An Illinoisan, Abraham Lincoln, held the highest civilian office in the land during the war. Ulysses S. Grant, who was living in Galena, Illinois, when the war broke out, eventually filled the highest military post in the land.

Lincoln's Rise to the Presidency

Lincoln came of sturdy backwoods stock. His family was as poor as most other frontier families, so when it came time for him to earn his own living he took whatever jobs he could find. By the time he was in his late twenties he had worked as hired help on farms, manned flatboats on the Mississippi, clerked in a store in New Salem, gone into business for himself (unsuccessfully), worked as a surveyor, and served as postmaster for New Salem. It was up to him to educate himself, which he did by reading borrowed books and talking to people who knew more than he did. His everyday contacts with people were also valuable in preparing him for a future he could not yet envision.

Lincoln's First Experiences as a Public Servant

Lincoln ran for a seat in the state house of representatives for the first time in 1832 but lost. In 1834 he tried again, and this time succeeded. Meanwhile, he had been studying law on his own and in 1836 was admitted to the bar. That same year he was reelected and became one of the "Long Nine," a name journalists gave to a group of nine lawmakers from Sangamon County, each of whom was six feet tall or more. Altogether Lincoln served four terms in the state house of representatives, during which he rose from obscurity to a position of leadership.

Lincoln entered national politics when he was elected to the U.S. House of Representatives for the 1847–49 term. His opposition to the Mexican War made him so unpopular that he decided not to run for reelection. After an unsuccessful bid for a seat in the U.S. Senate in 1854, he returned to his private law practice in Springfield.

The Lincoln-Douglas Debates

Lincoln began his political career as a member of the Whigs, one of the two dominant parties in the country. (The other was the Democrat party.) Splintered by internal dissension, the Whigs found it increasingly difficult to field winning candidates. In 1854 the remnants of the Whig party, the Free Soilers (those who opposed the extension of slavery into western states), and the antislavery Democrats joined forces to create the Republican party. Lincoln did not want to be identified with uncompromising extremists, but when he saw that moderates were in control of the new party, he joined.

At the 1858 Republican National Convention, Lincoln was chosen to run against Stephen Douglas for a seat in the U.S. Senate. You may recall that Douglas was the Illinois senator who had worked so hard to get the land grant for the building of the Illinois Central Railroad. He, too, came from a background of poverty, but he had become rich by

Abraham Lincoln during his Springfield days. Courtesy of the Illinois State Historical Library.

Abraham Lincoln debated Stephen Douglas in the 1858 campaign for a seat in the U.S. Senate. Lincoln lost the election but gained public recognition. Douglas is seated to Lincoln's right. Courtesy of the Illinois State Historical Library.

making wise real estate investments in Chicago. Unlike Lincoln, Douglas was very short of stature, so much so that he became known as "the Little Giant." The "giant" referred to his intellectual and oratorical gifts.

In accepting the nomination, Lincoln made his famous "house divided" speech in which he said, "A house divided against itself cannot stand. I believe this government cannot endure permanently half slave and half free. I do not expect the Union to be dissolved; I do not expect the house to fall; but I do expect it will cease to be divided. It will become all one thing, or all the other."

After each candidate had spoken separately in a number of towns, Lincoln's advisors approached Douglas and asked if he would be willing to debate Lincoln during the rest of the campaign instead of making solo appearances. Douglas agreed to do so in the seven congressional districts in which he had not yet spoken. These debates took place at Ottawa, Freeport, Jonesboro, Charleston, Galesburg, Quincy, and Alton.

Lincoln accused Douglas of being willing to extend slavery, then maneuvered him into admitting that he cared little about the social and moral issues involved in slavery. Douglas charged that Lincoln's "house divided" speech was tainted with abolitionism and that Lincoln was fomenting discord and dividing the nation.

The Lincoln-Douglas debates made journalistic history. For the first time, newspaper correspondents were able to telegraph daily stories of the campaign to the nation's newspapers. Although he lost the election, Lincoln became known beyond the borders of Illinois.

The Presidential Election of 1860

Two years later Lincoln and Douglas faced each other again, only this time the stakes were higher. The two great politicians from Illinois were contending for the presidency of the United States.

The 1860 Republican National Convention in Chicago had all the razzle-dazzle of modern times. A frame building that could seat 10,000 people was quickly erected, but the "Wigwam," as it was called, could not contain the crowds that poured into the city. The only woman reporter covering the event was Illinoisan Mary Livermore.

Today it seems odd that a person likely to be nominated would not make an appearance at a convention, but at that time it was not unusual. Lincoln stayed in Springfield, waiting to hear the results. Even before the balloting began it became clear that Lincoln was very strong in the West. His supporters emphasized his western origins by referring to him as "Honest Abe" and the "Rail Splitter." He was against slavery but had distanced himself from those abolitionists who wanted the federal government to force the southern states to outlaw it. His moderate views made easterners and northerners believe that he was the only candidate who could carry Illinois and other pivotal states. With wild acclaim they chose Lincoln and notified him of his nomination by telegraph. A group of supporters serenaded him at his home that night.

The Democrats convened in Charleston, South Carolina, that year, but were unable to close ranks behind one candidate. Douglas had hoped to be nominated, but when the question of secession came up, he courageously and at some political cost to himself insisted that the Union must be preserved. The convention adjourned after voting to meet again in Baltimore on June 18, where Douglas was finally nominated after fifty-seven ballots. However, the southern Democrats then nominated their own candidate, John C. Breckenridge. Another group organized a new party, the Constitutional Union party, members of which were determined to take no stand on the issues dividing the North and the South. They chose John Bell as their nominee. Realizing that he could not win without the backing of the entire Democratic party, Douglas put aside his disappointment and traveled throughout the South, trying to stop the secession movement.

When the voters went to the polls on November 6, 1860, the Democrats divided their votes among three candidates: Douglas, Breckenridge, and Bell. That made it easier for Lincoln to win. He received 1,866,452 votes to Douglas's 1,376,957. Illinois voted for Lincoln as well as for all the Republicans running for state offices. Richard Yates became the next governor of Illinois.

The Inauguration

The famous detective, Allan Pinkerton, escorted Lincoln to Washington in mid-February 1861. Because of rumors that an attempt would be made on Lincoln's life in Baltimore, they slipped quietly through that city at night and arrived in the capital twelve days after leaving Illinois.

Early on the morning of March 4, Inauguration Day, clouds hung over a chilly Washington. But by noon the sun was shining brightly as President James Buchanan came in his carriage to take Lincoln to the ceremonies. Bands played as they passed under buntings and waving flags. However, in spite of the festivities, sadness and apprehension filled the air. In the preceding December South Carolina had made good its threat to secede from the Union if Lincoln were elected. In the months that followed, Mississippi, Alabama, Florida, Georgia, Louisiana, and Texas followed suit. On February 8, 1861, representatives from the seceding states met in Montgomery, Alabama, and established the Confederate States of America.

President Buchanan and Douglas, both of whom had been political opponents of Lincoln's, threw their support to him at this time of grave crisis. Douglas returned to Chicago and prepared for a speaking tour to plead the cause of the Union. But exhausted by the campaign, he contracted typhoid fever and died of complications shortly thereafter.

Fort Sumter and Faraway Cairo

The Confederate barrage of Fort Sumter in South Carolina officially began the war. President Lincoln issued a call for 75,000 volunteers. Up to this point, Virginia, North Carolina, Tennessee, and Arkansas had been hoping for a negotiated settlement, but now that war seemed inevitable, they, too, seceded. Less than two weeks later, Lincoln's Secretary of War, Simon Cameron, telegraphed Illinois Governor Yates and urged him to send troops to Cairo, Illinois.

Remote as it was from Fort Sumter, Cairo's strategic importance was already apparent. Illinois, shaped like an arrowhead, lay wedged into the South. At its tip, where the Mississippi and Ohio rivers meet, stood Cairo. Cairo was far enough north to make it a difficult target for an offensive attack by Confederate forces. At the same time, it was far enough south to make it a good staging area for Union expeditions into the Confederate States. Furthermore, of four north-south railroads that

Soldiers embarking at Cairo, which became the hub of the North's effort in the West during the Civil War. Courtesy of the Illinois State Historical Library.

served as gateways to the South, the westernmost passed through Cairo. Cairo, therefore, became the hub of the Union war effort in the West.

As the Civil War approached, Illinois was a "house divided" on the slavery issue. Elijah Lovejoy, like other militant abolitionists, considered slavery an injustice and a crime and said so in ways that enraged its supporters. The Lincoln-Douglas debates highlighted some of the issues. Douglas thought that the people living in a state should decide whether or not that state should have slavery. Lincoln insisted that the nation could not survive half-slave and half-free. Lincoln lost the election, and Douglas retained his seat in the U.S. Senate. However, when Douglas and Lincoln ran against each other for the presidency in 1860, Lincoln prevailed.

Even before Lincoln took office, some of the southern states had seceded from the Union and formed the Confederate States of America. The Confederate attack on Fort Sumter touched off the Civil War. In the next chapter we will see what an important role Illinois played in the long and bloody struggle.

For Further Exploration

Russell Freedman. *Lincoln: A Photobiography*. New York: Ticknor & Fields, a Houghton Mifflin Co., 1987.

Concentrating on Lincoln's years in public office and the issues he confronted, the author enhances the book with many fine photographs, a sampler of quotations from Lincoln, and a list of historic sites relating to Lincoln's life.

Paul Simon. *Lovejoy: Martyr to Freedom*. St. Louis: Concordia Publishing House, 1964.

This account of the issues surrounding the untimely death of Elijah Lovejoy ends with a thought-provoking discussion of who was responsible for the violence.

Mark E. Neely, Jr. *The Abraham Lincoln Encyclopedia*. New York: McGraw-Hill, 1982.

Filled with facts of all kinds that relate to Abraham Lincoln and his times, this book is an excellent reference work as well as good browsing.

12

Illinois Pitches In

Illinois Helps Build an Army

In 1861 the U.S. Army could not have launched much of an offensive against the South. It had only about 16,000 men thinly spread over the whole country. No draft laws were in effect, so the Union had to depend on volunteers. Each state was asked to supply a share of the men needed.

When the first call for volunteers went out, Illinois's quota was six regiments. Governor Yates called the General Assembly into session, and in a rush of patriotic fervor it authorized the formation of ten regiments and appropriated $3.5 million to cover the cost.

That summer, after the Union army in the East had suffered several serious losses, President Lincoln called for 500,000 more troops, and Illinois again had a quota to fill. Well aware of pro-southern sympathies in his home state, Lincoln asked John McClernand, an influential politician from southern Illinois, to "keep Egypt right side up." (Southern Illinois is said to have been nicknamed "Egypt" in the 1840s because it had supplied northern Illinois with food during poor harvests, just as ancient Egypt had supplied grain to neighboring areas in lean years.) McClernand had such a colorful and emotional style of public speaking that his campaigns yielded many converts to the Union cause and many recruits as well. He later became a general. Another politician from southern Illinois, John A. Logan, had opposed Lincoln before the war but then reversed his position and became a supporter. He, too, spoke at rallies and later served as a general, leading his men bravely in eight major battles. Other politicians and preachers crisscrossed the state, holding recruitment rallies made festive with marching, flag-waving, and singing. Young men left their jobs and farms and hurried to sign up. Some worried that the war would be over before they got there. They need not have worried, for the conflict lasted four long years. Altogether, Illinois provided 150 infantry regiments, 17 cavalry regiments, several artillery units, and 2,224 sailors and marines.

Instant Camps and Quick-Step Training

Like most other states, Illinois was unprepared to house, feed, and train all of the recruits who flocked to the cities to join up. In Chicago the Wigwam, the rambling wooden building in which Lincoln had been nominated for the presidency, was pressed into service as a barracks. Officials started construction of a new camp near the grave of Stephen Douglas. By the end of the war, Camp Douglas was one of the largest military bases in the North. In Springfield the fairgrounds were converted into a camp named for the governor, Camp Yates. Nearby, construction of a new camp, Camp Butler, got underway. Cairo, Peoria, Quincy, Carrollton, and Aurora also commandeered parks, fairgrounds, and large buildings to use as quarters for soldiers.

Camps were dirty and overcrowded, and everything from food to guns was in short supply. Some recruits foraged for bedding materials and food in the nearby countryside, while others bought overpriced items from city merchants who took advantage of the situation. At the same time many civilians brought gifts of food and clothing to the young soldiers. Spirits were high, and movement through the camps was usually rapid enough to forestall discontent.

Volunteers from similar ethnic backgrounds created several Illinois regiments, as did men of certain professions. James Mulligan recruited fellow countrymen for his Irish Brigade; Germans filled the Hecker and Koerner regiments and made up companies in other regiments; and men of Scottish descent formed the First and Second Scotch regiments. Railroad men put together a fighting unit, as did the lead miners of Galena; the ranks of the Rock River Rifles were filled with farmers, as was the regiment formed by the state agricultural society. So many ministers joined the Persimmon regiment that people referred to it as the Preachers' regiment. Charles Hovey, the president of Illinois State Normal School, resigned his position and recruited students for a fighting unit that became known as the Teachers' regiment.

The man who raised a regiment usually became its colonel, whether or not he had any military experience. Officers were often elected by the volunteers themselves. Mexican War veterans were prime candidates, but when no experienced soldiers were available, the election simply became a popularity contest.

Discipline was nothing like that in European armies where men had to obey orders unquestioningly and officers severely punished even the smallest infraction of the rules. Many of the Illinois soldiers were frontiersmen who felt they had a perfect right to question orders or to express their disapproval in strong language. Fist fights broke out between officers and privates, much to the wonderment and disgust of military men from the East. Companies sometimes got rid of an unpopular officer by making life miserable for him. On the other hand, western soldiers were able to spot competent and trustworthy officers and in many instances fought under them with great courage, loyalty, and endurance.

Guns were in such short supply that many recruits had to drill with sticks. In the early battles, some soldiers did not even know how to reload the guns they had hurriedly been issued. Raw recruits needed many hours of drill before they could respond rapidly and automatically to a series of commands, but in 1861 there was little time for such training, and few officers capable of providing it. Some companies drilled on an irregular schedule, if at all. Others wasted time on the impractical goose step or on parade formations.

The campaign to rid Missouri of Confederate soldiers involved only a few pitched battles, but the skirmishing there gave new recruits the training they sorely lacked. The Confederates in Missouri were too far from their supply lines to hold any territory they won, so they concentrated on guerrilla warfare. Illinois soldiers called them "bushwhackers" because they picked off sentries and killed or captured soldiers who had gotten separated from their units. One Illinois soldier said that his regiment had marched 350 miles in pursuit of the enemy only to find itself just 100 miles from where it had started. Another said he would rather be shot outright than kill himself marching aimlessly about with a heavy load of supplies and gear. Nevertheless, the long hours of marching conditioned and toughened the men. Occasional ambushes taught them vigilance and gave them experience with firearms.

Governor Yates sent agents to Washington to lobby for additional weapons and better equipment and later made several journeys there himself. His efforts paid off. Illinois troops were considered among the best equipped in the Union army.

Grant's Rise to Power

The Union armies in the East were committed to defending Washington, taking Richmond, and subduing General Robert E. Lee's Army of Northern Virginia. Almost 1,000 miles to the west, Union armies had two major tasks: to control the Mississippi River and to drive a wedge between the eastern and western portions of the Confederacy.

John C. Frémont, the famed western explorer who was appointed commander of the western armies in July 1861, took his appointment seriously. Without being ordered to do so, he tried to confiscate rebel property in Missouri, including slaves. He not only exceeded his legal powers but also aroused a storm of protest at a time when calm was needed. He was quickly reassigned to a less sensitive post in the East.

Henry Halleck, an easterner, was chosen as his replacement. Halleck had written several military textbooks and was known as "Old Brains," a nickname not meant as a compliment. It implied a rigidity and bookishness that both exasperated and amused the rough-and-ready men who served under him. His appointment to this post was probably not wise, as he found it difficult to understand the western soldier. But in the early days of the war, Lincoln and the War Department had little choice. They knew what they wanted to accomplish, but not how it could be done or who was capable of doing it.

Serving under Halleck was General Ulysses S. Grant, whom Frémont had appointed commander of the troops at Cairo. As great a general as Grant became, he had no love for warfare. As a young man, he had strenuously objected to entering his father's tanning business, yet was unable to decide on another occupation. He loved horses and became an expert trainer and rider. The drawings and watercolors he made as a young man show a surprising level of artistic competence. He also had considerable literary talent, as his memoirs were later to reveal. A vocational interest test would probably not have suggested a military career, but his father had obtained an appointment to West Point for him and insisted that he accept it.

It was at West Point that Hiram Ulysses Grant became U. S. Grant. The congressman who applied for his appointment knew him only as Ulysses. In filling out the necessary papers for the candidate, the senator was required to include his middle name. Speculating that Grant had been given his mother's maiden name, Simpson, as a middle name, he put down "Ulysses S. Grant." Grant was unable to get the army to correct its records, so he remained U. S. Grant.

Although his West Point record was not impressive, he showed himself to be a competent soldier during the Mexican War, a war of which he did not approve. After garrison duty in California, Grant left the army and tried his hand at farming on land his father-in-law provided near St. Louis. Next he went into business with a partner in St. Louis. After failing at that, he took his family to Galena, Illinois, where he worked as a clerk in his brother's leather store. When the war broke

U. S. Grant in camp. By the end of the Civil War, the highest political office and the highest military post in the United States were filled by men from Illinois (Lincoln and Grant). Courtesy of the Illinois State Historical Library.

Gunboats in Rear Admiral Andrew Foote's river fleet. Foote's flotilla assisted at the battles for Fort Henry and Fort Donelson. Courtesy of the Illinois State Historical Library.

out, Grant drilled his fellow townsmen and marched them to Springfield. After a few months at a military desk job, he was commissioned a general through the efforts of a Galena politician, Elihu Washburne.

Fort Henry and Fort Donelson

Grant first became a hero when his troops engaged in two battles at river forts in Kentucky: Fort Henry and Fort Donelson. Fort Henry was easily taken, with help from Admiral Andrew Foote's gunboats. Fort Donelson proved to be more formidable. After fierce fighting in which the outnumbered southern troops almost succeeded in breaking through the Union lines and escaping, all but two Confederate generals, Simon Buckner and Bushrod Johnson, slipped away with their men under cover of night. The next morning Buckner sent a message to Grant, asking him to state the terms of surrender. He and Grant had been friends before the war, so Buckner may have expected special treatment from Grant. But Grant sent the following reply: "No terms except an unconditional surrender can be accepted." Buckner surrendered.

The victories at Forts Henry and Donelson came at the right moment. Union forces in the East had suffered one defeat after another, and this pair of victories in the West revived flagging spirits. Illinoisans celebrated with bonfires, flags, speeches, and singing. At this rate the war would soon be over, they thought. They began calling U. S. Grant "Unconditional Surrender" Grant.

Shiloh

Confederate losses in the West continued to pile up. First, Nashville, Tennessee, fell to Union forces, then the river fortress at Columbus,

Kentucky, had to be abandoned because it was cut off from all outside support. A three-day battle at Pea Ridge, Arkansas, curtailed most Confederate activities in that state and in Missouri. After all these setbacks, the Confederates made a supreme effort to save their major base and railroad center at Corinth, Mississippi.

As it turned out, little fighting took place at Corinth. Instead, a country church named Shiloh, some fifteen miles east of Corinth, became the eye of the storm. Grant had disembarked 40,000 troops at nearby Pittsburg Landing and was waiting for General Don Carlos Buell to come up with an additional 35,000. Meanwhile, the Union soldiers set up camps in the woods and fields along the road to Shiloh.

Confederate General Albert Sidney Johnston knew he had to strike before Buell arrived, otherwise his 42,000 Confederate troops would be outnumbered by a Union force of 75,000. Early on the morning of April 6, 1862, he swooped down on the Union camps as the men were finishing breakfast. Confusion, panic, and terror scattered the Union forces. It took their officers a good part of the day to get them into battle formation. The southern forces had almost succeeded in driving Grant's troops all the way back to Pittsburg Landing, but word that Buell's men were arriving forced the Confederates to retreat.

The Union guns at Pittsburg Landing boomed all night. One Illinois soldier said the log cabin where the wounded were being treated was like a butcher shop doing a brisk business. There were no campfires that night, and the exhausted survivors sat about in a stupor. For miles around the roads and fields were littered with the dead of both armies. The once-peaceful little church stood in a grove of tattered trees and mangled corpses.

The Union armies prevailed, but 13,047 Union soldiers had been killed, wounded, or were missing. One-third of them were from Illinois. Grant's superior, General Halleck, reprimanded him for being unprepared and incautious and would not trust him to take Corinth. Northerners mourning their dead wondered if the victory had been worth the price.

Slavery Becomes the Main Issue

Lincoln had always opposed slavery and as a young lawyer had championed the rights of blacks in Illinois. But when he became president he was determined not to attack the institution in the South. From his point of view, nothing was more important than keeping the Union intact and slowing the momentum toward war. Lincoln's caution was not rewarded. War broke out, and by late 1862 the combatants had battled to a standstill.

At this point, Lyman Trumbull, an outstanding U.S. senator from Illinois, urged Lincoln to push forward with a definite plan for freeing the slaves. Trumbull had long been an abolitionist, and he felt that slavery had become a matter of conscience to many people and that freeing the slaves should be made the major objective of the war. He and other leaders also thought that foreign nations that had viewed the war as a family squabble when preservation of the Union was the main issue were likely to respond with greater understanding and support if the abolition of slavery became the principal goal.

Lincoln agreed but was concerned about timing. He realized that action on the slavery issue would be more readily accepted if it followed an important military victory. The battle at Antietam, Maryland (September 16–17, 1862), gave him the context he needed. On January 1, 1863, he issued the final version of the Emancipation Proclamation. It stated that all the slaves in the unconquered states were now free.

Vicksburg and Chattanooga

By 1863 Vicksburg, Mississippi, was the last Confederate stronghold on the Misssissippi River. Grant was ordered to move his armies up and take the city. At this point a cavalry colonel from Illinois, Benjamin Grierson, led a month-long raid south of Vicksburg to create a diversion and to inconvenience the enemy as much as possible. Grierson moved his swift and high-spirited horsemen deep into enemy territory, cutting telegraph lines, wrecking a railroad line, and capturing a train. The strange part of Grierson's story is that he had had a childhood riding accident that had left him with a fear of horses, a fear he apparently overcame when circumstances required.

Meanwhile, Grant moved on Vicksburg. Confederate General John Pemberton and his badly outnumbered forces tried valiantly to repulse the Union troops but were driven all the way back to their fortifications in the ravines and hills surrounding the city. Grant's forces alternated between almost suicidal thrusts forward into fierce gunfire and sitting around waiting for Vicksburg to starve. Unable to get supplies, the Confederate soldiers and the civilian population eventually found themselves in a desperate situation. Pemberton surrendered to Grant on July 4.

When news of the victory reached Illinois, people paraded, hung banners from buildings, and heaped praise on Grant, who once again became a national hero. After his next assignment at Chattanooga, Tennessee, he was made commander of all the Union armies, replacing his old superior, General Halleck.

The siege of Vicksburg, the last major action on the Mississippi, put the South out of contention in the West. Some Illinois troops went with Grant to Tennessee; others were dispatched to General William T. Sherman to take part in the March to the Sea; still others were sent to fight with regiments from other states. By the end of the war, soldiers from Illinois had engaged in every major battle in the East and the West.

Black Regiments in the Union Army

Before the Emancipation Proclamation, free blacks had tried to enlist in the Union army but had been refused. The proclamation made it possible for blacks to become soldiers and many did so, even though they were not offered equal pay and could not choose their own officers. The most famous black regiment in the country was the 54th Massachusetts Colored Infantry, made up of black soldiers from several states, including Illinois.

In October 1863 Governor Yates raised the first black regiment in Illinois, the 29th U.S. Colored Infantry. The next spring, the 29th left its camp in Quincy and proceeded to Washington, D.C. On April 25, as they were marching down 14th Avenue with other troops to board trains for the front, they happened to meet Lincoln. The new black soldiers raised their hats and gave three cheers for the president. They then boarded trains for Virginia, where they guarded strategic supply railroads, then took part in the fierce battles around Petersburg.

Official records show that more than 1,800 black Illinoisans served in the army. However, that total does not reflect the number of blacks who passed for white to become soldiers, nor does it include blacks who were attached to regiments in other capacities.

❧

Illinois was no better prepared for war than any other state. Recruits had little opportunity to drill and train in the quickly improvised camps, but the skirmishes in Missouri conditioned them and gave them some combat experience. Governor Yates, a strong Lincoln supporter, did everything he could to secure the best arms and supplies for his troops. Eventually the Illinois regiments became some of the best equipped in the Union army.

The most important tasks of the western armies were to gain control of the Mississippi River and its important tributaries and to isolate the westernmost of the southern states from those on the East Coast. Successes at Fort Donelson and Fort Henry made Ulysses S. Grant a popular hero in Illinois, but the costly battle at Shiloh sobered Illinoisans. The war was going to be longer and more ferocious than they had anticipated. But what was going on on the home front? The next chapter will concentrate on that and on the conclusion of the war.

For Further Exploration

Victor Hicken. *Illinois in the Civil War.* Urbana: University of Illinois Press, 1966.

For those particularly interested in the military aspects of the Civil War, this book details many of the battles and gives glimpses into the daily lives, thoughts, and feelings of the young soldiers who did the fighting.

Irene Hunt. *Across Five Aprils.* Chicago: Follett Publishing Co., 1964.

Like so many families living in southern Illinois at the time of the Civil War, the Creightons find themselves sharply divided in their attitudes toward southern slave owners, northern industrialists, and Abraham Lincoln. This novel covers many of the western battles as well as the tribulations of the farm families of rural Illinois.

Fletcher Pratt. *Civil War on Western Waters.* New York: Henry Holt & Co., 1956.

Naval historians tend to concentrate on the action of sea-going vessels along the East Coast during the Civil War, but Fletcher Pratt tells the story of the strange inland flotillas of hastily improvised rams, ironclads, turtles, and tinclads, many of which were built or refitted in Mounds, Illinois.

13

The Long Road to Peace

Illinois Women and the War Effort

Women were not allowed to join the army, but some dressed as men and enlisted anyway. An Illinois woman, Jennie Hodges, set the record for remaining undetected the longest. Her gender was only discovered in 1911 when she was sent to a veterans' hospital after a car accident. Another woman, Nadine Turchin, led her officer-husband's regiment in battle when he was ill. Chicagoan Frances Hook, alias Frank Miller, served in the army ten months before she was found out. After being mustered out she reenlisted. This time she was not exposed until she was captured by Confederate soldiers and shot in the leg while trying to escape.

Early in the war it became obvious that state and federal governments needed help if the armies were to be properly supplied and supported. Women of Illinois unhesitatingly stepped forward to offer their services. Some of them were members of women's groups devoted to civic and social progress and to gaining the right to vote. They put aside these goals to give their all to the war effort.

Volunteer groups sewed uniforms, made flags, and prepared bandages. They held sociables and arranged benefit concerts and performances to raise funds to defray the costs of meeting the soldiers' needs. Many joined the U.S. Sanitary Commission, which supplemented the limited medical care the government was able to provide for the sick and wounded. Illinois women solicited financial help from the wealthy and gifts of crops and firewood from farmers. Later they helped the families of soldiers left destitute when their men enlisted as well as the families of soldiers who were killed or disabled.

Known as the "cyclone in calico," Mary Ann Bickerdyke saved many lives by improving conditions in military hospitals. Courtesy of the Illinois State Historical Library.

Some women traveled to the camps and battlefields to nurse and comfort the wounded in the makeshift hospitals that sprung up near the scenes of action. Mary Livermore, whom we mentioned before as having been the only female reporter at the Republican convention of 1860, traveled tirelessly on behalf of the Sanitary Commission. Later she wrote about her experiences, giving many glimpses into life in the army camps and hospitals. She also became the trusted companion of Mother Mary Ann Bickerdyke.

Mary Ann Bickerdyke, a widow from Galesburg, was as famous in her day as Grant or Sherman. After hearing a sermon about the appalling camp conditions at Cairo, she went into action. A hearty, strong-willed woman with a knowledge of herbal medicine, she soon became known as the "cyclone in calico."

For injured soldiers, being sent to an army hospital was almost like receiving a death sentence, so filthy and poorly run were these institutions. Bickerdyke descended with spirited wrath on nineteen such hospitals during her four years of volunteer service and transformed them into models of what a military hospital should be. She soon became a beloved figure among the young soldiers, an angel of mercy whom they affectionately referred to as "Mother Bickerdyke." Some kept in touch with her long after the war had ended. Her reception among officers and army doctors was less enthusiastic. In general they resented the presence of women in the camps—and her commanding presence in particular. She was straightforward, brusque, and determined to have her way.

Mother Bickerdyke vigorously attacked the sordid conditions she found, ordering the scrubbing down of floors and beds and setting up the first laundries at army hospitals. Before this, soldiers simply lay in their dirty uniforms on dirty sheets until both clothing and bed linens were so filthy and tattered that they had to be discarded. Once the laundries were in place, the recuperating men could be made comfortable and safer from secondary infections.

She was uncompromising in her stand against the mean, low sneaks who stole from supplies meant for the sick and dying. Once she heard that men were stealing delicacies meant for her patients, so she added a strong emetic to some stewed peaches. The thieves were quickly discovered when they began throwing up and were told that next time it would be rat poison. Bickerdyke was also not reluctant to attack incompetent, high-ranking officers and physicians. Once a physician asked her on whose authority she was acting. She answered, "On the authority of the Lord God Almighty. Have you anything that outranks that?" One officer complained to General Sherman about Mother Bickerdyke. "If it was she, I can't help you," Sherman replied. "She has more power than I—she ranks me."

After some battles a strange light could be seen bobbing about on the battlefield after dark. When sentries investigated, they would find Mother Bickerdyke, lantern in hand, walking about making sure no wounded soldiers had mistakenly been left for dead.

When supplies ran low, she returned to Illinois to round more up. One wonders how her more sophisticated associates felt when she used the office of the Chicago Sanitary Commission as a depot for the one thousand hens she was collecting to take to a hospital in Memphis.

Few women volunteers were as colorful as Mary Ann Bickerdyke, but many others strained their physical and emotional resources to the limit as they ministered to the sick and wounded. Eventually their contributions were recognized by the government and some received pensions.

The Copperheads

Not everyone at home backed the war effort. People who committed violent acts to show their opposition to the war became known as Copperheads because they struck without warning like the deadly snake of the same name. Some identified themselves by cutting the heads out of copper Indian-head pennies to wear on their lapels.

During the winter of 1862–63, when discontent and discouragement were widespread, the Copperheads became increasingly active in Illinois. After every Union defeat they wrote articles and gave speeches encouraging tired and discontented soldiers to desert. Some organized themselves into quasi-military units and harassed Union supporters, beating them, wrecking their property, and spreading fear and insecurity. In some cases federal troops had to be called in to deal with the violence. The worst clash occurred at Charleston, where a riot between Union soldiers on furlough and armed Copperheads resulted in several deaths.

Most Illinois soldiers had no sympathy for either Copperheads or deserters. As the chaplain of one Illinois regiment put it: "Copperheads, yes Cowardly sneaks, Dirty Slippery Slimy nasty Copperheads, Pore pukes, the back of my hand to them."

An unfortunate effect of Copperhead activity was that it encouraged gangs of outlaws from Missouri and elsewhere to slip into the state and create further havoc. For example, the Clingman gang committed all manner of outrages before they were finally chased out of southern Illinois by angry vigilantes. Clingman was probably not associated with any pro-southern organization, but was simply trying to exploit the situation for his own ends. Rural families in southern Illinois suffered greatly at the hands of such hoodlums.

A Wartime Constitutional Convention

Illinois voters approved the calling of another constitutional convention, which got underway in 1862. Peace Democrats dominated the convention and tried to use it to promote their antiwar stand. They made much of the fact that Governor Yates had authorized agents to pay more for military supplies than the federal government had authorized, but in attacking his policies, they made a tactical error. Governor Yates had worked hard to see to it that Illinois soldiers were well provided for, and their families appreciated his efforts. He had visited the battlefields after some of the bloodiest confrontations and taken a personal interest in providing medical care and evacuation for the wounded.

After responding to numerous requests for more information, Governor Yates lost his patience and told the delegates they were in no position to tell him how to do his job. Sensing that the public was displeased, the delegates quickly changed their stance and voted to provide money for the care of the sick and wounded, something they had no authority to do. When they finally got down to the work of writing a new constitution, voters were so disgusted with their behavior that they voted to reject the document.

Lincoln's Reelection

By the time the 1864 presidential campaign got underway, the Union armies were locked in the fiercest and costliest campaign of the war. Rather than sending Union forces to take and occupy cities, Grant sent them in pursuit of the two Confederate armies still in fighting condition. For five months the Army of the Potomac engaged the Confederates in the Virginia wilderness where big guns and cavalry were almost useless, conventional battle lines were hard to maintain, and dense smoke turned battle zones into nightmare landscapes in which anyone could be the enemy. The Wilderness Campaign became a bloodbath for both sides.

Spirits flagged as the casualty lists grew longer and the northern armies seemed to be utterly stalled. Called a hero only a few months before, General Grant now became known as "the Butcher." Opponents of the war called Lincoln a widow-maker and said that his three greatest generals were general taxation, general conscription, and general corruption. Peace at any price was their motto, and they urged people to vote for a candidate who would be willing to compromise with the South. Republicans had been in power when the war began, so they were held responsible for all the suffering. Lincoln privately doubted that he could win reelection. Meanwhile, the Democrats chose General George B. McClellan as their candidate. Although McClellan was loyal to the Union cause, he allowed others to write a party platform that denounced the war.

At this low point in Lincoln's political affairs, General John A. Logan returned to Illinois to campaign for Lincoln. Logan's aid proved invaluable and made it possible for Lincoln to carry his home state. Fortunately, new victories on the battlefield also brought an upsurge of support for the president. The Republicans began saying that a vote for McClellan would be a vote for the rebellion when it was about to fail, a vote for slavery when it had been abolished, and a vote for disunion when reunion had almost been achieved. The Democrats had to abandon their peace platform at the last moment and try to find another issue around which to rally.

In spite of all the disillusionment over the war, Lincoln still had a deep core of support among the common people. Although they often criticized him, his steadfastness of purpose had strengthened them throughout the war years. Realizing how close victory lay, they returned

Lincoln to office, giving him 2,203,831 votes to McClellan's 1,797,019. Back in Illinois, other Republicans also won. Major General Richard J. Oglesby became governor of Illinois and war-time governor Richard Yates won a seat in the U.S. Senate.

The Last Tragedy of the War

Grant and Lee continued the struggle in Virginia until at last Lee realized that he would be needlessly sacrificing the lives of his men if he continued to resist. On the morning of April 9, 1865, he surrendered to Grant at the Appomattox Court House. Ely Parker, a full-blooded and gifted Seneca Indian who had been working as a government engineer in Galena before the war, had become Grant's military secretary. It was Parker who wrote the terms of surrender that Lee signed.

The news reached most of the troops by telegraph within the day. At Chattanooga, where the Fox River regiment from Illinois was stationed, the bugle had just sounded taps when the message came. As the news spread quickly from tent to tent, the soldiers ran out and fired their rifles into the air. Cannon were wheeled into place, and soon the buildings at Chattanooga were shaking with the continuous vibrations of the big guns. In North Carolina the chaplain of an Illinois regiment recorded that the men "raised the yell, burned their caps, and began to make merry." Union soldiers and civilians everywhere rejoiced.

In his hour of triumph Lincoln was already thinking about the future. He wanted to turn aside those who wished to punish the South and concentrate on healing and reunion instead. But he did not live to guide the nation through the years of recovery. On Good Friday evening, April 14, 1865, Lincoln and his wife went to Ford's Theatre in Washington, D.C. A crazed actor, John Wilkes Booth, stole into their box and shot Lincoln in the head. Lincoln died early the next morning. The whole nation went into mourning.

The death of the president had a deep, personal meaning for Illinois soldiers. They wept without shame. One young soldier wrote to his father, "You cannot imagine the depth of sorrow that weighed down the spirits of both officers and men."

Officials in Washington wanted Lincoln to be buried there, but a delegation from Illinois persuaded Mrs. Lincoln to have his body returned to Springfield. A train swathed in black carried Lincoln's body home along the same route by which he had first come to Washington. It stopped at some of the larger cities and moved through the towns at less than five miles an hour. Bells tolled, salutes were fired, and thousands of people lining the tracks stood in silence or wept as the train passed. When the

People mourning Abraham Lincoln as the train carrying his body makes its way to Springfield. Courtesy of the Illinois State Historical Library.

train reached Springfield, Lincoln's body lay in state in the capitol building. He was buried in Oak Ridge Cemetery on May 4.

Much later, an architect from Watseka, Illinois, Henry Bacon, designed the Lincoln Memorial in Washington, D.C. Begun in 1914, the monument was officially dedicated in 1922.

Going Home

Before being mustered out of the army, the Union regiments gathered in Washington, D.C., for a grand review. As one writer put it, the mingling of the soldiers from the eastern and western armies was like mixing oil and water. There was bragging, joking, and fisticuffs as "Sherman's Mules" (westerners) met the "Featherbed Soldiers" (easterners).

On the first day of the review, the eastern armies paraded through the streets in their best uniforms and were roundly applauded. The next day the western armies marched by the review stands, some of them proudly wearing the tattered uniforms they had worn in Georgia and Carolina rather than the new uniforms they had just been issued. Tall, strong, and jaunty, they had an air of the frontier about them. The crowds greeted them with wild cheers, waving, and clapping, and throwing wreaths of flowers.

Many of the Illinois regiments returned home by boat via New

Orleans, then up the Mississippi to Cairo. From there they took trains to the mustering out camps where parades, farewell speeches by politicians, and other celebrations took place. When these were over, the soldiers sat talking quietly as their last nights as comrades slowly passed. Having faced death together, they had become a special brotherhood. The shadow of separation mingled with the bright hopes of homecoming. Surely many of them sensed that nothing of this magnitude would ever happen to them again.

ᴿ

Illinois women served as nurses, social workers, suppliers, and fundraisers during the war. Some even dressed in men's clothes and engaged in combat.

By late 1862 the warring sides had reached a stalemate. The Copperheads in Illinois and elsewhere took every opportunity to discredit Lincoln and foment antiwar sentiment.

After the battle of Antietam, Lincoln issued the Emancipation Proclamation, which shifted the main focus of the war from saving the Union to ending slavery. Former slaves were then allowed to join the army, and one black regiment was raised in Illinois.

The people rallied around Lincoln once more and reelected him. However, before he could put any of his recovery programs in place, he was assassinated. After a period of public mourning, Lincoln was buried in Springfield on May 4, 1865.

In Part 4 we will explore the postwar years of rapid growth and modernization, during which Illinois became as important industrially as it was agriculturally.

For Further Exploration

Bob and Jan Young. *Reluctant Warrior: Ulysses S. Grant.* New York: Julian Messner, 1971.

Working in his brother's leather shop in Galena when the Civil War broke out, Grant gathered and drilled a regiment and marched it to Springfield. At first he was assigned desk duty, an inauspicious beginning for someone who would one day command all the Union forces. He was elected to the presidency in 1868 and reelected for a second term in 1872. Following that, he and his wife made a grand tour of the world that brought lasting good will to the United States. The closing chapter of the book deals with his determination to fight his last battle, against cancer, with courage and dignity.

PART FOUR

New Directions

The Civil War catapulted Illinois into the industrial age. New industries and businesses flourished, bringing huge fortunes to some and prosperity to many. Illinoisans now had the time and funds to bring high culture to their queen city. The glittering World's Columbian Exposition, held in Chicago in 1893, focused the eyes of the world on Illinois for a time. But in the shadows of the prosperous lived the impoverished workers, powerless and hopeless. When the economic system ran aground again, labor unrest in Illinois made national headlines. The remarkable experiment of social pioneer Jane Addams ushered in an age of reform.

14

The Winds of Change

The First Memorial Day

Illinoisans turned with relief from the bloodshed and destruction of war, but it was not easy to forget all of the sacrifices that had been made. On April 29, 1866, the citizens of Carbondale brought armfuls of flowers to decorate the graves of the Civil War soldiers buried in Woodlawn Cemetery. A clergyman and several other dignitaries, including General John A. Logan, participated in the ceremonies. This was the nation's first observance of Memorial Day.

Two years later General Logan became the national commander of the Grand Army of the Republic, the largest and most influential organization of Civil War veterans. (The GAR had been founded by another Illinoisan, an army doctor from Decatur named Benjamin Franklin Stephenson, shortly after the war ended.) In 1868 General Logan issued General Order 11 requesting all GAR posts to observe May 30 as a day of remembrance from then on. Eventually it became a national holiday.

The Postwar High

The end of the war brought an exuberant surge in industrial growth. Illinois factories that had been built to produce war goods rapidly converted to the production of consumer goods. Railroads carried waves of pioneers beyond the Mississippi, creating a huge market for building materials, farm implements, household goods, fencing, and clothing. Illinois industrialists had the advantage of being much closer to this new western market than their competitors in the eastern industrial cities. Entrepreneurs saw opportunities on every hand. One Illinois inventor reflected the upbeat mood of the times when he said he could build a bridge across the Atlantic Ocean if only he could find sponsors for such a project!

Richard Oglesby served as governor during this period of transition. A personal friend and early supporter of Abraham Lincoln, Oglesby had raised a regiment from Decatur and become its colonel. At Corinth a bullet had pierced his lung and brought his military career to an abrupt end. He was the first of three Civil War generals to become governor of Illinois.

A New University

In 1862 Senator Justin Morrill of Vermont had piloted a bill through Congress to help states finance the building of colleges and universities. The Morrill Act granted each loyal state 30,000 acres of public land for each senator and representative it had in Congress. The states could sell these lands, most of which lay west of the Mississippi, and use the proceeds to build state colleges and universities.

The General Assembly was too busy to take action during the war, but afterward it arranged to sell most of the 480,000 acres Illinois had received and chose Champaign County as the site for the new school. In 1868 110 male students attended the first classes offered at Illinois Industrial University. By 1871 a few women were also taking courses.

At first there was some confusion over the mission of the new school. Some thought only agricultural methods and industrial arts should be taught. But under the direction of the university's first president, John Milton Gregory, the curriculum was broadened to include languages, literature, science, and the arts. By 1885 Illinois Industrial University no longer seemed an appropriate name, so the institution was renamed the University of Illinois.

Another New Capitol

It seemed that nothing could stop the state's population growth. It had increased by leaps and bounds during the war, and that trend continued. The state government had to employ more people to do all it was expected to do, but office space in the capitol building was extremely limited. Officials and agencies had to share offices, and some even set up shop in alcoves and hallways. Clearly, a new capitol building was needed.

Once again other cities tried to lure the state government away from Springfield, but Springfielders were determined not to let that happen.

By the end of the Civil War Illinois was growing so rapidly that the state government needed a larger building. The present capitol, begun in 1868, took twenty years and $4.5 million to complete. Courtesy of the Illinois State Historical Library.

In answer to the complaint that there was a shortage of good overnight accommodations, they built an elegant new hotel, the Leland. They offered $200,000 toward the construction of a new capitol and a land trade in which the state would receive a seven-acre site on which to build. The General Assembly accepted the offer in 1867.

As for the fine old capitol building, Sangamon County officials bought it because they, too, needed more space. Much later, in 1961, the state bought the building back and restored it so visitors could see it as it looked in Lincoln's day.

Two Disappointed Minorities

Women and blacks had high hopes that their status would improve as a result of the war. Both were to be keenly disappointed.

Blacks in Illinois after the Civil War

Illinois—the Land of Lincoln—had the potential for becoming a leader in the civil rights movement. Early in 1865 U.S. Senator Lyman Trumbull of Illinois had telegraphed Governor Oglesby to tell him that Congress had approved the Thirteenth Amendment to the Constitution. Trumbull himself had drafted this amendment, which outlawed slavery. At Oglesby's urging, Illinois became the first state to ratify it. Within a few years the Fourteenth Amendment, conferring citizenship on former slaves, and the Fifteenth, giving them the right to vote, were also ratified. The Illinois law forbidding blacks to settle in the state was repealed, as were the harsh Black Laws that had existed in Illinois for almost half a century. The dawn of a new era of freedom and opportunity for blacks seemed to be at hand.

Cairo became an Ellis Island for hopeful blacks arriving from the South, but many did not find what they expected. Some came with nothing more than the clothes on their backs. The only kind of work many blacks knew was field labor. Their poverty was attributed to a lack of intelligence and initiative and an inability to govern themselves. Few whites took into consideration the fact that they had been forcibly kept from improving themselves.

Most blacks did not have enough money to buy farms. They hoped to work in the factories, but when new waves of European immigrants began flowing into Illinois after the war, employers hired them instead of blacks. Some black families were forced to return to the South and become sharecroppers. Those who stayed had to face discrimination, insecurity, and lack of economic opportunity.

The Status of Women

Earlville women are thought to have been the first in Illinois to organize a local woman suffrage association (1855). Others soon followed. Members supported the abolition of slavery, the prohibition of alcoholic beverages, improvements in education, and the development of better prisons and asylums. The right to vote was of major concern to these women because they wanted to be able to affect the law-making process directly to achieve their other goals. They realized that legislators were more likely to listen to people who could vote. But during the Civil War women put aside their drive for suffrage to concentrate on the war effort.

Afterward, women were shocked to discover that in spite of the willingness, competence, and energy they had shown, they were not to be rewarded with full citizenship. The Fourteenth Amendment, which made former slaves citizens, excluded women. Its second article, which

Myra Bradwell, founder of the Chicago *Legal News* and pioneer defender of women's right to enter the legal profession. Courtesy of the Illinois State Historical Library.

deals with the penalties for states that refuse male citizens their rights, says nothing about female citizens. The Fifteenth Amendment declares that the right to vote is not to be denied to citizens on account of race, color, or previous condition of servitude but says nothing about gender. That left states free to refuse women the right to vote.

The freedom of women to enter certain professions was also yet to be won, as Myra Bradwell's struggle shows. Bradwell had worked with the Sanitary Commission during the war. Shortly thereafter, she founded the Chicago *Legal News*, in which she published articles on court reform, reviews of prominent legal cases, information for professional lawyers, and a regular column on the status of women. Lawyers considered her newspaper the most important of its kind west of the Appalachian Mountains.

Bradwell passed the bar exam but was refused admission to the Illinois bar because of her gender. When she challenged this in the state supreme court, the court rejected her appeal saying that she could indeed be refused "by reason of the disability imposed by your condition"—that of being a woman. Next she appealed to the U.S. Supreme Court, which refused to hear the case.

Unable to pursue her own goal any further, Bradwell crusaded on behalf of a brilliant young woman named Alta Hulett, who was eventually admitted to the bar. Bradwell also successfully promoted a bill developed by Hulett that prohibited gender discrimination in employment. Although not very effective, this 1872 law was at least a beginning.

Women who wished to become physicians faced similar roadblocks. Even though they had served as medics during the war, medical schools refused to allow them to enroll. Undaunted, they opened their own medical schools, and when denied the right to practice in existing hospitals, they opened their own hospitals. One of the earliest of these was Women's Hospital and Medical College, founded in Evanston in 1870. It later became part of Northwestern University.

Trouble on the Farm

Illinois farmers realized that the federal government would no longer buy agricultural products from them once the war was over, but the prosperity they had achieved gave them the self-confidence to believe that they would be able to find new markets. Unfortunately, the industrial revolution brought new and complex economic problems.

During the war manufacturers had speeded up the development of labor-saving machinery. By 1865 so many farmers were producing bumper crops that the markets were flooded and prices fell. Farmers who had mortgaged their land to purchase more land or expensive equipment suddenly found themselves unable to pay their bills.

Even more distressing were their problems with the railroads. The railroads had grown so powerful that they were able to control rates and services. They gave large shippers better rates than small ones, charged less for long hauls than for short ones, and forced customers using small branch lines to pay more per mile. These practices worked to the disadvantage of small farmers. The farmers considered rate discrimination doubly unfair because in the 1850s they had helped finance the building of the railroads. Some had even mortgaged their farms to buy railroad bonds. Now they could not afford to ship their products to market.

The farmers' frustration reached an even higher level when they found that the railroads were extending their control to meat-processing plants, grain elevators, and warehouses. For example, in Chicago twenty-four giant grain elevators handled almost all of the Illinois grain marketed in eight states because the railroads had made deals with the elevator owners and refused to deliver grain to any others. Knowing that the farmers could not take their grain elsewhere, some operators graded the quality of the farmers' grain lower than it actually was so they could pay them less for it. Others boldly cheated when weighing it.

Farmers had traditionally steered clear of the union movement, but now they began feeling that to make themselves heard they would have to speak with one voice. In 1867 a young employee of the U.S. Department of Agriculture, O. H. Kelley, founded an organization for farmers that he called the Patrons of Husbandry. He wanted to end farmers' isolation and help them better their lives. Farmers all over the country formed local clubs called granges. Although the granges started out as social and educational organizations, their members soon became politically active.

Locked in a struggle with the railroads, Illinois farmers saw the value of forming granges. The first such organization in the state held its initial meeting in the Chicago office of the *Prairie Farmer* in 1868. Soon grange members began backing political candidates who would speak up for them. At last legislators realized that they could no longer afford to ignore the largest block of voters in the state, the farmers.

Hoping to satisfy the farmers without antagonizing the powerful railroad owners, the General Assembly passed a law requiring railroads to transport grain to independent elevators and to set "just and reasonable" rates. Predictably, this law was ineffective because the words "just" and "reasonable" were not defined. It took an article in the new state constitution to make effective regulation of the railroads possible.

The Constitution of 1870

Springfield hosted another constitutional convention in 1869–70. The delegates completed the new constitution in May, voters approved it that July, and it went into effect in August. This third state constitution lasted one hundred years.

Looking at older constitutions gives us glimpses of several practices we now find strange. For example, before 1870 Illinoisans could bring such issues as changing their names, adopting children, or starting a small business before the General Assembly for approval. During some legislative sessions more time was spent on these private bills than on public matters. This happened at the 1867 legislative session, when laws passed for the public good filled a 205-page booklet, while private bills filled 2,500 pages! The constitution of 1870 forbade the bringing of private bills before the state legislature.

In the new constitution the word "white" was deleted from the voting rights article. Elijah Haines, a member of the voting rights committee, asked that the word "male" also be struck so that women would be able to vote. His suggestion was not followed, but the delegates did consider giving voters a chance to vote on woman suffrage as a separate issue when they cast their votes for or against the new constitution. (Several issues were to be voted on separately, so that objections to a few items would not endanger the passage of the whole constitution.)

However, a small group of women activists, impatient with the traditional denial of their political rights, fired off speeches in which they said that men were out of place in legislative halls and on the judicial bench and should go back to the fields and workshops. Offended, the delegates pulled back and decided not to offer Illinois voters a chance to vote on the issue of woman suffrage.

The delegates broke new ground when they gave the General Assembly the power to pass laws regulating railroads. They reasoned that personal or corporate rights must not be allowed to override the public good.

New Railroad Laws

Shortly after the new constitution had been ratified, the General Assembly passed a law regulating the railroads and setting up a board of railroad and warehouse commissioners. This regulatory board was the first of its kind in the nation.

The railroad owners challenged the new law in court, claiming that railroads were private property and that the government could not regulate private property. They won their case in the Illinois Supreme Court when Chief Justice Charles Lawrence ruled that the law was unconstitutional because it prohibited any and all rate differences. Angered by his stand, which they perceived as thinly disguised support for the railroads, farmers campaigned against Lawrence, and he lost his bid for another term on the court.

The fight for regulation was then taken up by Shelby Cullom, an Illinois politician who had a long career. After serving in the state legislature, he was twice elected governor, then represented Illinois in the U.S. Senate for thirty years. At this time he was serving as speaker of the house in the state legislature.

Cullom drafted a new law that allowed railroads to charge higher rates only if they could prove it was necessary. For example, if a railroad could prove it was losing money on a branch line, it could increase the rate on that line. The law also gave the commissioners the power to license and oversee the operation of grain elevators. This provision led to a momentous battle in the U.S. Supreme Court.

The state railroad and warehouse commission took two men, Ira Munn and George Scott, to court because they were operating a grain elevator without a license. The state won the case, but Munn appealed, saying the new regulatory laws were unconstitutional. The Illinois Supreme Court ruled that the state could indeed regulate an industry whose operations so directly affected the public good. Munn then appealed to the U.S. Supreme Court and lost there too. After this landmark case, other states passed similar laws.

•&

After the Civil War, great opportunities coupled with enthusiastic entrepreneurship led to dynamic economic growth. But some groups were left behind. Blacks and women were disappointed when their hopes were not fulfilled. Farmers who had prospered during the war found themselves fighting to stay alive financially. Pitted against them were the powerful railroads. It was only by joining the grange movement that they managed to make themselves heard.

At the same time, many positive events took place. The General Assembly took advantage of the Morrill Act to create Illinois Industrial University (later renamed the University of Illinois). Work on a larger capitol building got underway in 1867. The third constitution went into effect in 1870, after which laws regulating the railroads were passed.

The next chapter begins with a disaster, from the ashes of which rose a new Chicago and a highly industrialized state.

For Further Exploration

Isabella Maud Rittenhouse. *Maud.* Edited by Richard Lee Strout. New York: Macmillan, 1939.

From the age of twelve until her marriage, Maud Rittenhouse kept a diary in which she recorded the joys and sorrows of growing up in Cairo, Illinois, in the post–Civil War years. Her account includes temperance teas and steamboat parties, floods and tornadoes, dating and courtship, and visits by celebrities.

15

The Pace of Industrial
Growth Picks Up

Industry Competes with Agriculture

From one point of view, the Civil War was a time out for industrial development. Factory owners had to turn their attention from manufacturing consumer goods to producing war goods, and an acute labor shortage put a ceiling on industrial growth. On the other hand, the war stimulated the development of larger and more efficient factories and made more money available for capital investment. Modernization might have taken much longer had there not been a war.

For many years agricultural products had dominated the state's economy, but during the 1860s capital investment in Illinois industries increased by 243 percent, the labor force increased by 261 percent, and total wages paid jumped 307 percent. By 1870 the value of industrial goods manufactured in Illinois almost equaled that of agricultural products. By 1880 manufacturing was contributing almost twice as much to the state's economy as agriculture.

The Great Chicago Fire

Chicago not only dominated the industrial scene but was also the heart of the state's transportation network. The disaster that befell it in 1871 threatened the economy of the whole state. On Sunday, October 9, a fire broke out in the barn behind Patrick O'Leary's cottage on Dekoven Street. (The popular story that it was caused by Mrs. O'Leary's cow kicking over a lantern is probably just a myth.) By the time firefighters arrived, flames were licking at nearby buildings. Chicago had

A sign advertising a grand opening at the Globe Theatre stands starkly amid the rubble of the Great Chicago Fire. The Chicago Public Library, Special Collections Division.

hundreds of wooden structures and even some wooden sidewalks and streets, all of them dry and ready to burn. Wind whipped through the city raining embers on roofs far from Dekoven Street.

By early Monday morning the conflagration had reached the courthouse district. Waves of fire swept outward, engulfing offices, banks, hotels, churches, stores, grain elevators, and factories. John Chapin, an artist who had just been sent to Chicago by *Harper's Magazine*, said that the fire devoured "the most stately and massive buildings as though they had been the cardboard playthings of a child . . . one after the other they dissolved like snow on a mountain."

Thousands of people fled to the prairie west of the city. Those trapped in the downtown area swarmed toward the beaches along Lake Michigan. Some buried themselves neck-deep in the sand or rushed into the water. Fire ran up the rigging of boats and turned masts into giant candles. Late Monday night, rain slowed the progress of the flames; by Tuesday the fire had burnt itself out. By then some three hundred people were dead and more than 100,000 homeless. Property losses came to hundreds of millions of dollars.

Word of the fire spread almost as fast as the fire had. By Tuesday fifty carloads of food donated by other cities had arrived. The next Sunday special trains began bringing tourists to view the ruins. In the weeks that followed, more than $5 million in contributions poured in from the rest of the nation and from twenty-nine foreign countries. Ulysses Grant, who had by then become president, sent a personal check for $1,000. A survey of the still usable structures made the picture less bleak. The stockyards had escaped, as had miles of docks along Lake Michigan. Railroad facilities were in good shape, and several hundred factories had survived. Civic and business leaders predicted that people who had the courage and imagination to invest in the new Chicago would make vast fortunes. They were right.

A Portfolio of Illinois Industries

Chicagoans rebuilt their city with stunning rapidity. It was not enough to replace what had been lost. Determined to make Chicago the queen city of the Midwest, industrialists and businessmen were open to new ideas and new technologies. Other Illinois communities watched what was happening in Chicago and were soon competing for factories themselves. By 1880 downstate cities had increased their industrial output so much that it equaled that of all of Indiana. The new prosperity resulted partly from a renaissance of older industries and partly from the development of more of the state's natural resources.

The Meat-Packing Industry

Already in the 1830s drovers could be heard shouting commands as they moved herds of pigs and beef cattle along the dirt roads to Chicago. In his autobiography, Gurdon Saltonstall Hubbard, a fur trader who turned to other pursuits when the fur trade died out in Illinois, tells how he built a huge warehouse in Chicago to store meat from the livestock he drove to market. People called it "Hubbard's Folly," never believing that he would be able to collect, process, and store enough

Incorporated by the General Assembly in 1865, the Union Stock Yards and Transit Company became the center of Chicago's huge meat-packing industry. The Chicago Public Library, Special Collections Division.

meat to make such a large building worth owning. He surprised them by succeeding.

At first Chicago's meat-packing industry was somewhat haphazard. Stockyards were scattered about the city, and drovers herded their animals through the streets. Sometimes slaughtered animals were stacked in piles outdoors for the duration of winter. Quick to recognize the economic importance of the industry, the General Assembly created the Union Stock Yard and Transit Company in 1865. The company included a system of branch railroads, a bank, a hotel, and hundreds of chutes and pens for the livestock. The new stockyard gave Chicago a competitive edge over other midwestern cities.

In 1870 Illinois produced meat products worth $19 million; just a decade later that figure soared to $98 million. Chicago had become the largest meat-processing center in the country, supplying about one-third of the nation's demand. Three entrepreneurs, Nelson Morris, Gustavus Swift, and Philip Armour, were responsible for much of the growth.

Morris, a German immigrant, came to Chicago in 1852. He took a job in a packinghouse, then began dealing in sick and dead stock on the side. Soon he was able to start his own company. He became a millionaire by supplying meat to the government during the Civil War.

Swift arrived in Chicago in 1874. He started out as a butcher, then became an independent meat dealer and cattle wholesaler. He revolutionized the meat-packing industry by developing the disassembly line for processing beef and pork. In 1877 he became the first packer to ship dressed beef to eastern markets in refrigerated cars.

Armour began by speculating in grain, buying and holding it until he could make a good profit. He and a partner then started a packinghouse in Chicago in 1875 and soon owned plants in Omaha and Kansas City.

These canny businessmen were said to have used all the parts of an animal but its squeal. They marketed margarine, lard, tallow for candles, grease for soap, buttons, glue, and fertilizer. Leather companies bought the hides, and the hair was sold to mattress and felt makers.

During the last decades of the century the National Stock Yards in East St. Louis grew, too. Meat-packers there were able to take advantage of the large market and shipping facilities of the city directly across the Mississippi River, St. Louis, Missouri.

Continuing the John Deere Tradition

John Deere, who began manufacturing plows in Grand Detour in 1837, moved to Moline where he had better access to steel. His company thrived and expanded its line of products. His success brought other entrepreneurs, and by the late 1800s Moline became one of the major centers for the manufacturing of corn planters, disks, harrows, and farm wagons. Rock Island and Peoria followed close behind.

Cyrus McCormick, a Virginian who invented a mechanical reaper in 1831, had trouble marketing his new machine in the East. By 1844 he was offering his Virginia reaper to farmers as far west as Missouri, but they complained that the big, clumsy reaper moved through the fields like an elephant and that men could harvest the grain just as fast without it. However, when the Mexican War and the California gold rush siphoned off significant numbers of laborers, McCormick's idea took off. The demand for mechanical farm equipment became so great that McCormick moved to Chicago and built the largest factory in the city. In 1876 the Chicago *Post and Mail* reported that McCormick's factory was producing a complete harvester every twelve minutes.

Inventor Joseph Glidden of DeKalb began manufacturing a new kind of fencing material in 1874. Made of metal wire with sharp barbs every few inches, it became known as barbed wire. Western farmers bought enormous quantities of the wire to keep free-ranging stock out of pastures and fields. Glidden became a millionaire and later donated land for the campus of Northern Illinois University.

Iron and Steel

Illinois needed iron and steel for its industrial boom to continue, but among its rich natural resources there were no deposits of iron ore. Once again, Chicago's superb geographical location made the difference. One of the largest iron deposits in the world, the newly discovered Mesabi Range in upper Minnesota, began producing ore about this time. Chicago was a natural port for the freighters that carried the ore through the Great Lakes.

The Chicago Iron Company built the first blast furnace in Illinois in 1868. Three years later the Joliet Iron and Steel Company installed one. Downstate, furnaces were built at East St. Louis and Grand Tower. Eventually a downstate industrial complex, which included East St. Louis, Belleville, Granite City, Alton, and Edwardsville, became a center for making iron and steel.

Iron extracted from the ore was poured into stubby molds that resembled a row of suckling pigs. The resulting ingots were called "pig iron." To make steel, pig iron had to be remelted and combined with carbon and other additives in a complicated and time-consuming process. Then, in 1855, an Englishman named Henry Bessemer invented a new type of furnace that eliminated many of the steps and produced a higher quality steel at a much lower cost. The state's steel industry rapidly expanded as companies converted to the Bessemer process. By 1880 Illinois had become the fourth largest steel-producing state in the nation.

Broadening the Economic Base

The widening range of successful industries in Illinois included printing and publishing, furniture making, the manufacture of men's and women's clothing and shoes, watch making, the processing of dairy products, and glass making.

By the late 1800s about one-fourth of the nation's supply of liquor was being distilled in Peoria, and many other Illinois cities had distilleries and breweries. Nine-tenths of the total national production of wagons and carriages took place within a 250-mile radius of Chicago. The Spalding Company in Chicago was making more baseball bats than any company in the country.

Weyerhauser, one of the giant lumber companies of the Pacific Northwest today, was originally an Illinois company. Frederick Weyerhauser and C. A. Denkman began operations in Rock Island in 1869 and later moved to Minnesota and Washington, harvesting the forests that became available as the nation expanded westward.

Hidden Riches

At first the great agricultural resources of Illinois overshadowed its mineral resources. Mineral deposits in the bedrock lay deep under layers of soil and ground rock that had been left behind by retreating glaciers. Before the modernization of mining technology, looking for them was like looking for the proverbial needle in a haystack. Galena's lead deposits were an exception because that corner of the state had not been glaciated.

As early as 1673 Marquette and Jolliet reported finding superficial deposits of coal in Illinois, and early settlers used lumps of coal they found lying on the ground for fuel. Commercial coal mining began in Jackson County about 1810 near Murphysboro. By the 1820s miners were at work in the Peoria area, St. Clair County, and the upper Illinois River Valley.

At first Illinois industrialists imported most of the coal they needed from Pennsylvania, Ohio, and Indiana, states that already had well-established mines. The opening of iron mines in Missouri created the first large-scale demand for Illinois coal. Factory owners in Illinois then realized that they could buy their coal much closer to home and save transportation costs. By that time enough railroads existed to carry coal from almost any part of the state to the industrial centers.

Illinois clay supplied the raw materials for brick manufacturers. As the supply of wood dwindled, the use of bricks increased. The ever-present danger of fire also prompted builders to choose brick for urban construction. By the 1870s Illinois was producing enough bricks to supply its own needs and exporting large quantities as well. Bricks made in Murphysboro were used in the building of the Panama Canal.

Illinois also had a wide belt of high quality clay that could be used for making dishes. In the early days some thirty pottery centers (known as "jug towns") did a brisk business supplying dishes, jugs, and other containers for frontier families. By the late 1800s large-scale factory production had replaced the small family-owned workshops, and Illinois began producing more pottery than any other state except Ohio.

Illinois limestone proved to be inferior to Indiana limestone as a building material, but many other uses were found for it. As was the case with coal, it was known about long before it was quarried commercially. There was no point in quarrying limestone for export when adequate transportation was not available, but railroads finally solved the transportation problem—and provided a market as well. Large quantities of broken limestone served as ballast on which to lay ties and track. The building and maintenance of roads required crushed limestone as did the steel industry. During this period of rapid industrial growth, Illinoisans also began to draw upon the rich deposits of sand and gravel in the state.

Prospectors struck oil in several counties of southern Illinois as early as 1865, but drilling techniques were primitive and investors few. The production of oil and natural gas would have to wait until after the turn of the century.

Fluorspar, a beautiful crystalized mineral that comes in various shades—green, blue, violet, yellow, and brown—was mined in small quantities in Hardin County before the Civil War. Eventually (in 1965) it became the official state mineral. In the early days it was used in the making of steel and glass. Since then, many other uses have been found for it: fluorspar (sometimes called fluorite) is used in the manufacturing of fiberglass and welding rods; it yields a fluorine compound that is sometimes added to drinking water and toothpaste to prevent tooth decay; and fluorite is also a component of artificial blood. The federal government now stockpiles Illinois fluorite for use in uranium enrichment.

"Give the Lady What She Wants!"

Entrepreneurs in Illinois grew rich during the years of industrialization and had plenty of money with which to make their lives more luxurious. But how to spend it was a problem. The affluent wanted more than the ordinary goods offered in shops that were so far from the stylish eastern cities. Items could be ordered from stores in eastern cities, but that was not the same as choosing a hat, drapes, or furniture in a store that offered many alternatives. Here was another great opportunity for ambitious businessmen with a flare for fashion and an understanding of social mobility.

Potter Palmer, Marshall Field, and Levi Leiter were such men. In 1852 Palmer built the first department store in Chicago, then entered into partnership with Field and Leiter. Realizing that women were an increasingly important body of consumers, these three men were eager to please them.

At first they used the upper stories of their building as a wholesale warehouse where shopkeepers from small Illinois towns could come and buy stock for their stores. The first floor was reserved for retail sales. Wealthy Chicago women could not resist the artistic and dramatic displays of exotic goods there. At last they felt they could keep in step with the fashionable women of the East.

Palmer became more interested in real estate than merchandising and sold out to Field and Leiter. Their very successful partnership carried them through several catastrophes, including the Chicago fire, after which they built a magnificent new store. But over the years personality differences led to the dissolution of the partnership. By the time Leiter rather unwillingly sold out to Field in 1881, sales were totaling over $25 million a year. Field purchased goods cheaply abroad, bought up several small factories, and even oversaw the production of some items on the premises. The store's success always remained tied to the motto, "Give the lady what she wants!"

After working as a clerk at Marshall Field's for a few years, Aaron Montgomery Ward recognized the importance of another large group of consumers: isolated farm families. In 1872 he and George Thorne teamed up to form their own company. They warehoused large quantities of items they thought would be of interest to their potential customers and developed a mail-order catalog. By eliminating the increases resulting from mark-ups by retailers, they were able to offer goods at reduced prices. All items carried a money-back guarantee, a policy that won the hearts of farmers who had often felt victimized by unscrupulous city slickers.

Later, another mail order company, Sears and Roebuck, moved to Chicago. Western farm families soon began calling the Sears Catalog the "Wish Book." Sears sold everything from clothes to furniture to farm equipment, and eventually it even offered cars and houses by mail.

❧

Between 1870 and the end of the century, Illinois industry caught up with and surpassed Illinois agriculture. Meat processing, iron and steel production, and the manufacture of agricultural equipment contributed heavily to the state's economy, and a wide range of smaller industries provided a healthy diversity. Mining and quarrying operations also increased.

The new wealth created by the industrial revolution gave successful

Illinoisans more money to spend on luxuries. The age of the department store began with a flourish as merchants competed to "give the lady what she wants."

But there was a darker side to all this progress. The working classes were for the most part left behind, and periodic downturns in the economy made life even more precarious for them. As we shall see, unrest and turmoil resulted.

For Further Exploration

Herman Kogan and Robert Cromie. *The Great Chicago Fire: Chicago 1871.* New York: G. P. Putnam's Sons, 1971.

This account of the great Chicago fire includes a wide selection of photographs and drawings that capture the panic, horror, and devastation of the event.

Lloyd Wendt and Herman Kogan. *Give the Lady What She Wants! The Story of Marshall Field and Company.* Chicago: Rand McNally and Co., 1952.

A lively study of American entrepreneurship, this book emphasizes the business sense, vision, resilience, and creativity of the founders. The authors also make interesting connections between the women's movement and innovations in merchandising.

16

Trouble in the Factory

Riches and Rags

For the entrepreneurs who launched the industrial revolution, the late 1800s was the golden age. The rich lived in sumptuous mansions, employed dozens of servants, and entertained on a lavish scale. Wealth gave them social status and political power. At the other extreme were the men, women, and children who labored in the factories. They lived in tenements and slums and felt fortunate when they had enough food to eat. Surely they must have wondered why they were singled out to suffer while others had everything. At the same time, they felt powerless to change their lives.

Most employers thought only about how much their workers could produce, not about the workers themselves. Factories were often drab, unhealthy, and unsafe. People were required to work twelve or fourteen hours a day, six or even seven days a week. With no minimum wage laws, employers were free to pay their employees as little as possible. Unskilled laborers were plentiful, so anyone who complained could easily be replaced. And few workers complained, at least not aloud.

Neither state nor federal officials were anxious to do battle on behalf of the workers, and public opinion was generally harsh toward the poor. Many people believed that poverty was the fault of the individual, not the system. They credited the economic success of the nation to the people who put up the money to build the industries, not to the millions who worked in them. Politicians were reluctant to help the workers if it meant interfering with big business and possibly causing an economic slowdown. Most were opposed to any attempt by the workers to organize themselves into unions and work for change.

The Labor Movement in Illinois

The first national coal miners union met in West Belleville in 1861. Soon railroad workers began forming brotherhoods in Illinois cities. Workers in the building trades, iron moulders, shoemakers, tailors, and cigar manufacturers organized locals, some of which affiliated with national trade unions. In 1864 the General Trades Assembly, which represented workers in many different trades, held its first meeting in Chicago. The Knights of Labor, a union organized in Philadelphia in 1869, was operating in Illinois by 1877. Its motto was "an injury to one is the concern of all."

Union-backed Eight-Hour Leagues formed for the purpose of persuading the General Assembly to limit the number of hours employers could require employees to work. On March 5, 1867, Illinois became the first state to draft an eight-hour law. Unfortunately, enforcement of the law proved almost impossible. Although forbidden to fire workers who refused to work more than eight hours, employers simply invented other reasons for getting rid of such troublesome employees.

In 1884 delegates to the Chicago Trades and Labor Association voted to form a new statewide organization, the Illinois State Federation of Labor. This union developed an ambitious sixteen-point program that included measures to ensure mine safety, employer liability for injuries, the prohibition of child labor, mine and factory inspection, stricter eight-hour-day laws, and the creation of an arbitration board. Although the founders did not live to see adequate laws covering all of these points enacted, their agenda provided guidelines for the union movement in Illinois well into the twentieth century.

Unions had to face not only hostility from politicians and the press but also apathy from the workers themselves. The movement gained momentum in troubled times, but at other times the workers seemed willing to accept their fate. They had come to think of their situation as utterly hopeless.

The Panic of 1873

In 1873 the worst financial panic the nation had yet suffered swept over the land. Companies tried to control their losses by lowering wages and cutting back production. Then they began laying off large numbers of workers. At first people held on as best they could, thinking the crisis would pass. Instead, conditions worsened. Forty percent of Chicago's workers were soon jobless, and many more suffered cuts in pay ranging from eight to 50 percent.

When more than three years had passed and the situation had not improved, workers became desperate. In Chicago and other Illinois cities, agitators took to the streets, offering drastic remedies for the plight of the workers. Socialists and anarchists, many of whom were European immigrants, started newspapers, distributed leaflets, and staged demonstrations to get out their message: capitalism must be replaced.

The socialists wanted a planned economy in which the state would regulate production and distribution and everyone would share the wealth. The anarchists were even more radical. They believed that all forms of government should be done away with and insisted that workers were justified in committing acts of violence if that was the only way they could free themselves from the bondage of the rich factory owners and financiers whom, they claimed, governments invariably favored.

In ordinary times most workers would not have paid much attention to such rhetoric, but now they were more willing to listen. However, the wild and inflammatory language the anarchists used frightened many citizens. They became distrustful of the workers and of any organization that tried to help them. The shadow of violence fell across the glitter of the Gilded Age, as the late 1800s came to be known.

The Long Hot Summer of 1877

In 1877 Illinois had more miles of railroad than any other state, and Chicago had become the railroad hub of the nation. Industrialists and officials were understandably jittery about what dissatisfied railroad workers might do. Wage cuts had brought violence in West Virginia and Pennsylvania, and authorities in Illinois feared the trouble would spread. In May the General Assembly prepared for such an emergency by modernizing the state militia and renaming it the Illinois National Guard. Then, on July 1, the legislators made it illegal for anyone to obstruct railroad traffic.

Railroad workers were too desperate to be deterred by the new law. Those in East St. Louis voted to strike at midnight July 21. Freight traffic was stopped, but mail and passenger service was not. Railroad workers in Aurora, Carbondale, Effingham, Peoria, and other cities also walked off the job, and coal miners organized sympathy strikes. Governor Shelby Cullom acknowledged the right of workers to assemble peacefully but said that disruption of the railroads would not be tolerated and acts of violence would be met with armed force.

Striking railroad workers in Chicago were in no mood to listen. Helped by mobs that had been organized by agitators, they closed down depots, attacked roundhouses and freight yards, and battled with the police. Nineteen people were killed and more than one hundred injured.

Governor Cullom sent in the Illinois National Guard, and the crowds quickly melted away. When similar violence threatened to break out in other cities, he requested federal troops. Soon trains were again running on all Illinois lines, and the frightened public felt relieved.

Meanwhile, violence had broken out in Braidwood, a coal-mining town southwest of Chicago. Miners' earnings there had dropped from $1.20 per ton of coal mined when the depression started to $0.80 per ton in 1877. Asking for an increase to $1.05, fifteen hundred miners struck. The mine operators countered by bringing in black strikebreakers. On July 27 the strikers tried to force the new workers to leave town, but the Illinois National Guard was sent in to prevent that. The strike dragged on until November, at which time a few miners went back to work on company terms while others left to find work elsewhere. Their union collapsed.

The Haymarket Tragedy

By 1879 conditions had improved, and many of the unemployed were back at work. But 1883 brought another panic, and workers who were struggling to stay afloat again became militant. In 1885 a strike at the McCormick Harvester Plant resulted in the owners grudgingly agreeing to a 15 percent wage increase. However, in February of the next year they retaliated by locking out workers who had struck and bringing in nonunion replacements. After that there were almost daily confrontations between union and nonunion workers. On May 3, when the locked-out workers hassled nonunion workers as they left the factory, riot squads were called in, and two unionists were shot and killed.

August Spies, a prominent Chicago anarchist who had been speaking nearby, rushed to the office of the *Arbeiter-Zeitung* newspaper and wrote an inflammatory article calling for revenge. He announced that a protest meeting would be held the next evening in Haymarket Square. A handbill appeared on the streets, the last line of which read, "Workingmen arm yourselves and appear in full force," but Spies had not written that line. Unfortunately, he and other anarchists had on so many occasions punctuated their speeches with threats and dire predictions that many citizens had come to fear and hate them.

Perhaps as many as three thousand people came to the rally on May 4, but by nine o'clock only about two hundred remained. Carter Harrison, the mayor of Chicago, stopped by and found the situation well under control. On his way home he went to the police station to tell Inspector John Bonfield that all was quiet and no action would be necessary. Bonfield, who despised anarchists and their followers and

Confusion reigns at the scene of the Haymarket tragedy. Courtesy of the Illinois State Historical Library.

believed in clubbing them into submission, disregarded what the mayor said and ordered 180 policemen to march to the meeting place. They moved up on the gathering and told the crowd to disperse. Suddenly a bomb flew through the air and landed in the middle of the policemen, killing seven and wounding many more. As people ran in panic from the square, the police gave chase and fired into the fleeing crowd, killing one person.

In the days that followed, newspaper journalists whipped up fear by suggesting that the incident was part of a foreign conspiracy and that Chicago was in immediate danger of being taken over by anarchists. Anarchists were rounded up and brought in for questioning. Eight were put on trial, even though no evidence was found linking any of them to the throwing of the bomb. Some of the accused had not even been present, and others had left before the violence began. Nevertheless, they were convicted, and Judge Joseph Gary sentenced seven of them to death and one to fifteen years in prison. He reasoned that because they were anarchists, they had to share responsibility for any violence committed by anarchists. In spite of the irrationality of this argument, the public was relieved that the government was taking such strong action to protect their streets from bomb-wielding foreigners.

The death sentences were appealed, but the Illinois Supreme Court upheld Gary's decision. Later, the U.S. Supreme Court refused to consider the case saying that it was an internal matter for the state to decide. Richard Oglesby, who was again serving as governor, commuted two of the death sentences to life imprisonment. One man killed himself in his cell, and four were hanged in November 1887.

Afterward, some thoughtful people realized that justice had not been done. The men had not been proven guilty of murder, the crime for which they were supposedly being tried. Instead, they were being punished for their political beliefs, which the Constitution forbids. George Schilling, a leader of the Trades and Labor Assembly, organized an amnesty drive and began circulating petitions on behalf of the three men still in prison. Schilling, who had consistently opposed the Chicago anarchists, could now come to their rescue without being called an anarchist sympathizer. Because of their concern about the erosion of constitutional freedoms, more than one hundred thousand people joined the amnesty movement.

One man who did not sign any of the petitions was John Peter Altgeld. Born in Germany, Altgeld had been brought to the United States as an infant. After years of deprivation and hard work, he managed to educate himself and become a lawyer. Like several other self-made men of that period, he made a fortune in real estate. He was the first foreign-born citizen to be elected governor of Illinois, taking office in January 1893.

During his first months as governor, Altgeld agreed to review the Haymarket trial records and was dismayed by what he found. Improper procedures had been followed in selecting a jury. There was indisputable evidence that the inspector, the prosecutor, and the judge had conspired to produce a guilty verdict. In their desire to make an example of the anarchists, they had violated the rights of the accused.

Governor Altgeld found himself caught in a struggle between his political ambitions and his conscience. After many hours of soul-searching he issued a statement criticizing the judge and inspector and on June 26 pardoned the three men still in prison. Altgeld was condemned as a pardoner of criminals and friend of anarchists, a dangerous politician who might use the Democratic party for purposes of revolution. His stand on this issue cost him a second term as governor.

The Pullman Strike

Governor Altgeld had another crisis to face in the spring of 1894. Trouble broke out in the model factory town that George Pullman had

George Pullman's carefully planned industrial town. Courtesy of the Illinois State Historical Library.

built and named after himself. Pullman had invented the sleeping car and began producing luxury versions of it at his Palace Car Company, which he had built in Chicago in 1867. He soon became one of the richest men in the state.

Pullman believed that if workers were offered a decent way of life in a decent community they would not join unions or strike. He decided to build such a place. His carefully planned town included modern factories, neat apartment buildings for the workers, paved and tree-lined streets, stores, churches, and recreational facilities. He was proud of his creation and expected his workers to be happy and appreciative.

Well intentioned though he was, Pullman saw himself as a strict but kindly father who knew what was good for his workers better than they did. And as generous as he wished to appear, he was first and foremost concerned with his own financial welfare. He arranged to earn a profit of at least 6 percent on all investments he made in the town. Rents were 25 percent higher in Pullman than in Chicago. Pullman owned all of the utilities and stores and controlled the prices. He even charged each religious denomination that wanted to use the church he had had built an annual rent of $1,200.

When another financial crisis rocked the nation in 1893, Pullman cut his workers' wages, some by as much as 25 percent, but refused to lower rents, utility charges, or the price of merchandise in the company stores. After a dreadful winter, Pullman employees began joining the American Railroad Union (ARU). Lead by Eugene V. Debs, this new union had recently had its first major success. It had gotten the powerful Great Northern Railway to restore full wages to its workers.

The Pullman employees wanted to strike, but Debs tried to persuade them not to. He doubted that the ARU was strong enough to take on another big company so soon. However, in May 1894, 90 percent of the Pullman work force walked off the job anyway. After visiting the town and seeing the conditions for himself, Debs was convinced that the strikers deserved help. When several attempts to get Pullman to negotiate failed, Debs ordered the ARU switchmen to refuse to switch any Pullman cars onto trains beginning June 26. He also ordered his men not to engage in any violence or to interfere with the mail trains, acts for which there were federal penalties.

Within a few days, ten railroads were tied up. The Railroad Managers Association fought back by adding mail cars to all trains with Pullman cars, in effect making them all mail trains. Then they got a court injunction to stop Debs and his men from interfering with the mails. Some managers said railroad property was in danger and asked for the protection of troops. The newspapers again sounded a hysterical note when reporting the events.

During the next few months, confrontations continued in and around Chicago. When a disturbance erupted in Blue Lake, President Grover Cleveland sent federal troops. Governor Altgeld strongly protested, saying that the responsibility for keeping order in Illinois was his and that federal troops should be sent only when a state requested help. Actually, the increasing use of troops in labor disputes had many people worried. They feared that the country would become a police state if it continued. Cleveland defended his decision by saying he had had to send in federal troops to keep the mail trains running.

On July 10 Debs was arrested on charges of conspiring to violate a court injunction. Convicted and sentenced to six months in jail, Debs spent his time reading books on socialism. Later he became a three-time presidential candidate on the Socialist ticket.

The ARU was ruined by the strike, and the Pullman workers lost their bid for higher wages. More than one thousand employees lost their jobs and were left destitute. When Governor Altgeld called upon the public to set up a relief fund, even the Chicago *Tribune*, a paper that did not generally support labor, agreed to help.

Four years later, the Illinois Supreme Court ruled that Pullman's charter for the company had not included the right to build the town in the first place and that company towns were not compatible with the American way of life. Pullman was ordered to sell all the property in the town that was not being used for industrial purposes. With that, his vision of a village of happy and obedient workers died.

As industry expanded, the contrast between the rich and the poor grew greater. Financial panics brought such misery that workers were more open to the arguments of the socialists and anarchists who urged them to get rid of capitalism and institute a government that would put their welfare before all else. Their doctrines appealed to the out-of-work and hungry, but their militant rhetoric frightened the general population. The Haymarket affair convinced many that foreign agents were about to overthrow the government and take over Chicago. The Haymarket trial made it clear how quickly constitutional liberties could be eroded in a time of fear.

George Pullman tried to head off discontent and strikes by building a town in which his workers could live in comfort and security. However, the town of Pullman turned out to be an Eden more in theory than in practice.

Even with all these troubles, Illinois continued to prosper. The wealthy wanted Chicago to become as sophisticated as any East Coast city. In the next chapter we shall see how they went about creating a new image for the city and for the state.

For Further Exploration

Ray Ginger. *Altgeld's America.* New York: Franklin Watts, 1973.

Although he served only one term, Governor Altgeld's devotion to freedom and justice and his determination to seek remedies for the social ills that beset his state set high standards for future governors and legislators.

Corinne J. Naden. *The Haymarket Affair: Chicago, 1886.* New York: Franklin Watts, Inc., 1968.

In this short book we meet the principal players in the Haymarket drama and come to realize that fear and panic are an inadequate basis for action.

17

A New Image for Illinois

The Pursuit of High Culture

Proud of all they had accomplished, Illinoisans nevertheless felt self-conscious. Illinois was catching up with the eastern states in terms of productivity and wealth, but it still had a frontier image. Easterners thought of Chicago as a brash and brawling place, rich in money and energy, but poverty-stricken when it came to high culture. Where were the museums, theaters, libraries, opera, and symphony orchestra that every leading city was expected to have? Illinoisans had to admit that they had few such resources. During the last three decades of the nineteenth century they moved to correct this shortcoming, creating a new and more sophisticated image for their state.

The Art Institute of Chicago

The Chicago art museum, founded shortly after the great fire of 1871, first rented space in a downtown building. It later moved into a building of its own, which it soon outgrew. When Chicago was chosen as the site of the 1893 world's fair, Charles Hutchinson, a Chicago banker, was appointed chairman of the Committee of Fine Arts. He put in motion a plan to fund the building of an exhibit and meeting hall that would be used during the fair and turned over to the Art Institute afterward. That building is a part of the Art Institute's permanent home today.

Public funds paid for most of the day-to-day expenses of the museum, but there was little money for the purchase of expensive works of art. Fortunately, Chicago's millionaires came to the rescue. Some contributed large sums of money to the acquisitions fund, and others donated paintings and sculptures. Among the most treasured gifts were the Impressionist paintings that Bertha (Mrs. Potter) Palmer willed to the museum. A collection given by steel magnate Martin A. Ryerson and his wife included textiles, prints, paintings, sculpture, and decorative arts from many periods of Western art history. It is one of the greatest gifts ever received by a museum.

In the early years of the twentieth century many museum directors were reluctant to show the work of controversial new artists, but the Art Institute showcased contemporary work. In 1913 it hosted an exhibition of paintings by artists whose work had almost caused riots when it was shown at the New York Armory earlier that year. The Art Institute became a place for enjoying the old masters and for confronting the new.

Libraries

The Chicago Public Library lost virtually everything in the great fire of 1871. The next year the General Assembly passed a law that made it possible for communities to use tax money to build and maintain libraries. While other states used this law as a model, the Chicago Public Library used it to start rebuilding.

Once again, public moneys were supplemented by private donations. After the fire Queen Victoria and a group of English writers gave seven thousand books; people in other countries also responded generously. Many of the donated books were in European languages, making it possible for Chicago immigrants to read books in their own tongues.

In 1884 the staff of the Chicago Public Library pioneered a special outreach program for readers who found it difficult to get to the downtown location. People could request books and pick them up at designated points around the city. These stops were the forerunners of branch libraries.

Libraries became the cultural centerpieces of many Illinois communities. Some were built with help from Andrew Carnegie, a Scottish immigrant who had grown up in poverty, then made millions in the steel industry in the East. To him, libraries were a lifelong resource for people who wanted to educate themselves as he had done.

Illinois Makes Music

Before 1890 Illinoisans who wanted to hear classical music had to wait for traveling orchestras to come to town. Then a group of leading citizens asked the conductor of one of these orchestras, Theodore Thomas, if he would be interested in forming a permanent orchestra in Chicago. Thomas, who had been waiting for just such an opportunity,

Mary Garden, Chicago's first opera star. Courtesy of the Illinois State Historical Library.

responded with an enthusiastic "Yes!" The committee rounded up donations of $1,000 from each of fifty wealthy persons and got the project underway.

At first the orchestra played in the elegant Auditorium Theater, but Thomas insisted that it was too large for the size of the orchestra—and too expensive. (The orchestra had to pay a steep rental fee for rehearsal time as well as for the hours it performed for the public.) The board of trustees decided to raise funds for a building that would have just the kind of performance space Thomas wanted. At the same time they saw a way to provide perpetual funding for the orchestra: the concert hall would be topped by several stories of office space that could be rented out. Orchestra Hall was completed in 1904, but Thomas did not conduct many concerts there. He died shortly after the dedication. Today the hundred-year-old Chicago Symphony Orchestra ranks as one of the leading orchestras of the world.

The Chicago Opera Company took shape during the first decade of the new century. Mary Garden, a beautiful and flamboyant soprano from Chicago who had been trained in Paris, created a stir when she became the first prima donna of the Chicago Grand Opera Company in 1910. Her sensuous performances on stage won her many ardent admirers—and brought vociferous outcries from others, who thought them indiscreet and indecent. Not one to care much what other people thought, she lived her private life with a dramatic flare, as if it were another stage role. In the 1920s the opera got its own building and was renamed the Chicago Civic Opera. Forced to close down during the Great Depression, it was revived by Carol Fox in the 1950s.

Opera houses sprang up in many downstate towns and cities, but they had little to do with grand opera. Traveling theater troupes, magicians, famous poets and authors reading from their works, lecturers, and musical groups made the circuit, stopping at these community halls. With the advent of radio, moving pictures, and television, many small-town opera houses fell into disuse. Now some of them are being rediscovered and renovated.

Smaller cities that could not afford to maintain an opera company or a symphony orchestra organized bands, choruses, and music clubs that relied heavily on local talent. Germans, Italians, Scandanavians, and other European immigrants often settled near people of their own ethnic background and the musical groups they formed reflected their particular heritage.

A Truly American Architecture

In 1870 Chicago did not seem a likely place for a uniquely American style of architecture to be born. For the previous fifty years builders and their clients had been quite satisfied to copy the styles that were popular in East Coast cities. Most of those styles were derived from classical Greek and Roman architecture. Illinois courthouses, city halls, and banks looked like Greek temples; some churches were scaled-down versions of European cathedrals; and details of Greek and Roman buildings were adapted for use in private dwellings. For the most part, this was true all across America. Very few architects looked to the American landscape or the American experience for inspiration.

The Chicago fire cleared the ground for a new architecture. Filled with optimism, businessmen and investors rushed to engage architects to design buildings suitable for the sophisticated metropolis they hoped to create out of the ashes. The challenges and opportunities Chicago had to offer attracted scores of talented engineers and architects.

The First Skyscraper

So great was the commercial promise of the city that real estate prices soared and downtown building space became scarce. The solution was to build up rather than out. However, the technology for constructing tall buildings was still somewhat primitive. The main problem was weight. The use of heavy stone as the chief building material resulted in extreme pressure on the bottom floors. Walls could be made thicker at the bottom, but that greatly decreased the interior space of the lower floors and allowed only small amounts of light to enter through small, tunnel-like windows. Eleven or twelve stories was the upper limit for this type of construction.

In 1885 an engineer named William LeBaron Jenney received a commission to build an office building for the Home Insurance Company. During the Civil War Jenney had been assigned to General William Sherman's troops as they swung through the South on their destructive March to the Sea. He had learned a great deal about building construction by demolishing buildings. For the Home Insurance project Jenney designed the first tall structure based on an iron skeleton. When Carnegie Steel Company officials informed Jenney that they could supply him with steel rather than iron, he was delighted. He knew that steel would provide even stronger support and would not buckle under the heat of a fire as easily as iron would.

The steel skeleton of Jenney's skyscraper was able to carry the weight of the whole structure without putting excessive strain on the foundation. The walls were much thinner than those of masonry buildings, thereby increasing the amount of interior space. The steel framing also permitted larger windows, allowing more light and air to enter.

Jenney's steel frame construction became known as "Chicago construction" and the windows as "Chicago windows." Chicago architects followed up his pioneer efforts with many more innovations, such as the use of caissons (cylindrical concrete foundation supports), fireproofing, wind-bracing, and reinforced concrete. Chicago architectural of-

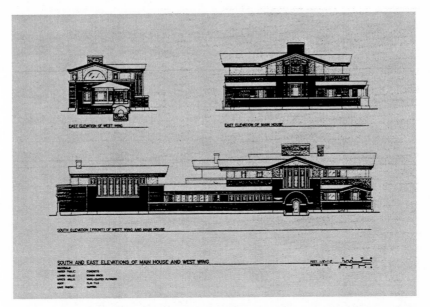

Architectural drawings of the Dana/Thomas house in Springfield, one of the many houses designed by Frank Lloyd Wright. Recently restored, this building is now open to the public. Courtesy of the Illinois State Historical Library.

fices began to resemble department stores in which clients could purchase the services of experts in all areas related to building. Best known of these firms were two partnerships: Daniel Burnham and John Wellborn Root, and Dankmar Adler and Louis Sullivan.

Sullivan, a temperamental artist of Irish extraction, is often considered the father of modern American architecture. Frank Lloyd Wright, one of the greatest architects of the twentieth century, began his professional career by working for Adler and Sullivan. All his life Wright referred to Sullivan as "Lieber Meister," beloved master.

Frank Lloyd Wright

Wright's mother claimed that she knew her son was going to be a great builder even before he was born. To make sure, she provided him with carefully selected toys that developed his sense of design. During his teen years he spent summers working on his uncle's farm in a lovely valley in Wisconsin, near where he had been born in 1867. Wright later credited his great physical and mental stamina to the self-discipline he had learned as a farmhand and said that those summers had brought him into a living relationship with nature. He observed the colors, textures, cycles, and patterns of the natural world that later helped him develop the idea of the "natural" house.

While working for Sullivan, Wright pondered Sullivan's theories: the form of a building must fit its function; imitation results in buildings unsuitable for the purpose, time, and place for which they were intended; decoration must be integrated with the purpose of a building, not applied like icing on a cake. Wright enlarged upon these ideas and added many of his own. While some builders voiced concerns that machines would standardize architecture, Wright thought that well-designed, machine-made products would enhance architectural design.

To Wright, the tall Victorian-style house with its turrets and gables was out of place on the Illinois prairie. Instead, he built houses whose low horizontal planes harmonized with the low, rolling plains. Rather than breaking up the interior space into many little rooms, he let it flow freely, using a minimum of walls and dividers. Windows, skylights, and doors brought the natural world of the outdoors into the home. Coordinated decorative motifs throughout the structure added both elegance and continuity.

During the seventy-two years of his professional life, Wright designed more than one thousand buildings, six hundred of which were built. His commissions included houses, churches, university buildings, shops, museums, hotels, and office buildings. The "Chicago School," which developed the skyscraper, and Wright's "Prairie School," which revolutionized residential architecture, became the heart of a truly American architecture.

Newspapers and Novels

During these decades of cultural ferment, the newspapers on which Illinoisans had long relied for information and entertainment recruited gifted young writers as columnists. The most famous humorist of the day, Finley Peter Dunne, created a character to speak for him in his column in the Chicago *Evening Post*. Saloonkeeper Martin Dooley amused readers as he expressed his opinions in Irish dialect, covering just about everything and everybody, including prominent socialites and politicians. Cloaked in the humor of the column were Dunne's serious concerns about the shortcomings of American society.

When you were a child perhaps someone read you, "The Duel," a poem about the gingham dog and the calico cat who ate each other up during a fight. The poet who wrote it, Eugene Field, became a household favorite in many families after his column, "Sharps and Flats," began appearing in the Chicago *Daily News* in 1882. His clever, humorous, and sometimes satiric poems and essays appealed to a wide audience and were often quoted. Field was deeply mourned when he died at the age of forty-five.

Another young journalist, George Ade, moved to Chicago in 1890 and began working as a reporter. Roaming the streets, he found the varied and dynamic spectacle of city life endlessly fascinating. The idea that literature could be made out of the lives of everyday people was relatively new then, but Ade felt very comfortable with it. His column "Stories of the Streets and of the Town" began appearing in the *Morning News* in 1893. Much of his work was later published in book form, as was the work of Dunne and Field.

Most young midwesterners who aspired to be writers felt that New York and Boston were where the action was. Hoping to give the Midwest a literary center, novelists Hamlin Garland and Henry Fuller joined with other writers to form elite clubs whose members were committed to encouraging each other and stopping the drain of talent to the East. Other, less genteel, writers formed clubs that met in taverns where they argued, sometimes vociferously, about the new movements in literature and about life itself.

The Great White City

With the four-hundredth anniversary of Columbus's voyage to the New World approaching, Congress authorized a world's fair. Chicago competed for the honor of hosting the event and won. Frederick Law Olmsted, the gifted landscape architect who designed Central Park in New York City, was hired to convert a two-mile swamp along the lake front into fairgrounds. His plan included a lagoon along which the exhibit halls would be built and a basin in which replicas of Columbus's three ships would float.

The architectural director of the fair, Daniel Burnham, commissioned many well-known architects to build the more than 150 buildings that were needed. They were not meant to be permanent; most were iron frameworks covered with plaster mixed with a fiber called jute. The finished buildings, which gleamed like white marble in the sun, were illuminated at night by hundreds of electric lights. Visitors who had never seen such an elaborate display of this relatively new kind of lighting found it stunning. The fairgrounds became known as the "Great White City."

Sullivan and Wright were disappointed that so few of the participating architects tried to introduce people to the new architecture. Sullivan's Transportation Building was the only really modern building.

Commemorating the four hundredth anniversary of Columbus's discovery of America, the World's Columbian Exposition brought millions of visitors to Chicago's "Great White City." The Chicago Public Library, Special Collections Division.

In other respects, however, the World's Columbian Exposition developed into a stunning display of new technology. Between May 1, 1893, when President Grover Cleveland officially opened the fair, and October 30, 1893, when it closed, more than twenty-seven million people were shown the wonders of the industrial age and treated to a preview of the twentieth century. They saw their first steam turbines, marveled at the newly invented refrigeration equipment, traveled by moving sidewalk, and rode the "third-rail" electric train.

Most of the states and forty-six foreign nations prepared exhibits. The center of attention in Canada's building was a ten-ton cheese, the largest in the world. The California exhibit featured a large knight on horseback made completely of California prunes. The Illinois Building, the largest of the state buildings, had a huge relief map based on a recent geological survey of the state.

Before the fair opened, Bertha Honore (Mrs. Potter) Palmer, a wealthy Chicago socialite, started Columbian Clubs, whose members planned the women's exhibits for the fair. One committee collected and displayed five hundred books written by Illinois women, and another

Advances in science and technology were an important component of the fair. This display featured an automatic electric engine. The Chicago Public Library, Special Collections Division.

obtained models of 249 inventions on which Illinois women had taken out patents. Other women's groups exhibited woodworking, weaving, photography, sculpture, painting, leatherwork, ceramics, and decorative needlework. Professional women organized a hospital on the fairgrounds where female doctors and nurses offered free medical aid to fairgoers. Women educators set up a model kindergarten in which people could observe children being taught by the newest methods.

When fairgoers needed a change of pace, they headed for the Midway, a pleasure park of colorful villages of South Sea Islanders, Eskimos, Arabs, Lapplanders, and other ethnic groups. Everyone wanted to see "Little Egypt," a belly dancer in the "Streets of Cairo" exhibit. As the fairgoers walked along, many of them munched a new treat invented by a German immigrant, F. W. Rueckheim. He coated popcorn with molasses and put a little prize in each package of it. A salesman tasting some for the first time exclaimed, "That's a Cracker Jack!" So "Cracker Jack" became the name of the new confection.

Wanting to have a structure that would dominate the fairgrounds as the Eiffel Tower had dominated the Paris Exhibition of 1889, Burnham had commissioned George Washington Gale Ferris, an engineer from

Built by George Washington Ferris of Galesburg, this giant wheel could carry more than two thousand people at a time. The Chicago Public Library, Special Collections Division.

Galesburg, to come up with an idea. Ferris was attending a club dinner when suddenly he knew exactly what he wanted to build. Based on some quick notes he made on the spot, he designed the first Ferris wheel.

The giant wheel carried thirty-six cars, each of which could hold up to sixty people. In order to insure passenger safety, Ferris made the axle six times stronger than calculations indicated it needed to be. The axle alone weighed seventy tons. Slowly and gently the wheel lifted as many as two thousand people at a time far above the fairgrounds. One car was reserved for a band that played as the wheel turned.

After the fair, the Ferris wheel was dismantled and stored until the planners of the St. Louis World's Fair of 1904 asked to use it. It took 175 freight cars to transport it there. The next scheduled move—to Coney Island in New York—fell through, and the giant wheel was blown up with dynamite as newspaper reporters and others snapped photographs of the dramatic explosion. The scrap metal was sold for $1,800. But the Ferris wheel lived on, and smaller versions of it still provide pleasure and thrills for people at fairs, carnivals, and city amusement parks.

If you walk through Chicago's Jackson Park today, you are walking across the site where the Great White City once stood. When the fair ended, the only large building left standing on the fairgrounds was the one that had served as the Palace of Arts. It was later replaced with a sturdier building in the same style and became the Museum of Science and Industry. (The Art Institute was designed as a permanent building and of course survived, but it was not located on the fairgrounds.) Marshall Field, the department store tycoon, donated money for a museum to house the valuable artifacts left behind by various exhibitors. We know it as the Field Museum of Natural History.

✎

Industrialization brought great fortunes to many Illinoisans and prosperity to many more, but the state's most important city remained a cultural outpost. In the late 1800s wealthy Chicagoans led the drive to change that. Their generous donations greatly increased the permanent collection of the Art Institute, provided for the establishment of a symphony orchestra, and supported other institutions devoted to learning and the fine arts.

During these years of hectic growth Illinois architects revolutionized architecture and created a uniquely American style of building. Gifted artists and writers began to find Chicago a congenial place to work.

People all over the state worked hard to put together the World's Columbian Exposition, creating a sophisticated new image for Illinois. Unfortunately, the prosperity that had made cultural progress possible had bypassed a large segment of the population. To the poor, the Great White City might as well have been castles in the sky. In the next chapter we shall learn more about their plight.

For Further Exploration

Perry Duis. *Chicago: Creating New Traditions*. Chicago: Chicago Historical Society, 1976.

Concentrating on the cultural flowering that took place in the closing decades of the nineteenth century, Duis, in this richly illustrated book, explores topics not generally covered in conventional history books.

John E. Hallwas, editor. *Illinois Literature: The Nineteenth Century*. Macomb: Illinois Heritage Press, 1986.

This literary sampler includes excerpts from pioneer diaries, letters of Civil War soldiers, and selections from most of the writers mentioned in this chapter, along with short biographical notes.

Frederick Koeper. *Illinois Architecture from Territorial Times to the Present: A Selective Guide*. Chicago: University of Chicago Press, 1968.

Published in celebration of Illinois's first 150 years of statehood, this handbook with its photographs and descriptions of 150 significant buildings gives an idea of the rich mixture of styles, materials, and building techniques to be found in the towns, cities, and rural areas of Illinois.

Frank Lloyd Wright. *An American Architecture*. Edited by Edgar Kaufmann. New York: Horizon Press, 1955.

Wright spoke and wrote about his work with clarity and passion. In this book he discusses many of his best buildings, showing how he solved the engineering and aesthetic problems they presented. Many fine photographs and architectural drawings illustrate his comments and are a pleasure to look at.

18

A Different Perspective

Life in the Shadows

Just blocks from the gleaming halls and beautiful lagoon of the Great White City, Chicago's poor struggled to exist in the dark and dangerous streets of the city's worst slums. Chicagoans who were better off tried to isolate themselves from those who lived in the shadows. But one visitor to the fair, English journalist William Stead, wandered beyond the bright lights. Sickened by the terrible conditions he saw, he wrote a book entitled *If Christ Came to Chicago*. In it he catalogued the physical hardships of the poor and described the prostitution, alcoholism, gambling, and street crimes that were part of their everyday life.

Chicagoans were outraged that someone had strayed into the back streets—and then told the world about it. The Chicago *Tribune* called Stead's book a directory of sin and said it should be banned. The *Dispatch* suggested that readers should spurn the author as a "mangy dog." But those who went to see for themselves could not call Stead a liar.

Bosses and Boodlers

The poor had no place to turn for help. True, charitable people did sometimes bring food and clothing, but poor families could not depend on occasional handouts. The General Assembly was beginning to develop labor laws that would help, but that was a slow, trial-and-error process. However, some politicians were more effective, namely, the bosses and boodlers (corrupt officials who worked out elaborate schemes for obtaining graft).

The chaotic growth of Chicago made it an ideal place for "machine" or "boss" politics to take root. The underlying ideas were simple. The voters in each of the thirty-four wards elected a representative to the Board of Aldermen. "Elect me," a candidate would tell them, "and I will take care of you." Generally he kept his promise.

A big factor in the success of the boss politician was that he lived among his people and was constantly accessible to them. He handed out food and clothing to the needy, got jobs for the unemployed, kept the police from raiding illegal businesses, and obtained city contracts and other favors for his constituents. The poor often knew, liked, and appreciated their alderman. For example, Chicago's first ward was run by an "odd couple" nicknamed Bathhouse John (John Coughlin) and Hinky Dink (Michael Kenna). They ran an illegal gambling house, which was popular because no cheating was allowed. When times were bad, they served free hot meals and allowed people to sleep in their tavern. Johnny Powers, the boss of the 19th ward and vice king of Chicago, was said never to have missed a funeral in his ward. By contrast, most of the people never saw or heard from those who supposedly represented them at the state and federal levels.

Where did the ward bosses get the power and the money to take care of their people? They cooperated with the big boss, the mayor. He depended on the aldermen to get the voters in their wards to vote for him. To make sure this happened, he gave the ward bosses city jobs to hand out and did them other favors. City council meetings became bargaining sessions in which aldermen approved each other's shady deals. City politics worked like a machine: each cog and wheel meshed to produce some city services, some relief for the poor, and considerable gain for the bosses.

All kinds of shenanigans went on. Powers bribed tax assessors to undervalue the property of a rich friend. It was assessed at only $1,336, even though the man owned a luxurious mansion, a stable of racing horses, a private museum and library, and an art collection that sold for over $700,000 at the time of his death. The millionaire rewarded Powers for having helped him avoid paying high taxes. A baker who had been giving his stale products to a farmer to feed to his hogs arranged through the boss of his ward to sell them to the city for use as human food in a public institution. Of course, he gave the boss a cut of the profits.

As well as the machine sometimes worked, in the long run it cost taxpayers millions of dollars. In addition to what the bosses and boodlers stole, the city lost money every time a wealthy businessman bought his way out of paying taxes or contracted to run a public utility at a rate that allowed him to make excessive profits. After a long decline in the quality and quantity of city services, Chicagoans had had enough. They prodded the city council into refusing to grant a transportation franchise to a man they regarded as a wealthy crook. At last Chicago reformers felt that they might be able to uproot the bosses and boodlers. In 1895 at least fifty-seven of the sixty-eight alderman in Chicago were said to have been involved in graft. By 1900 only seven members of the old boodle gang were left.

A New Profession

The favors that the bosses and boodlers did for the poor came nowhere near solving the problem of poverty. In fact, they were not meant to. The bosses needed a large number of dependent poor in their wards to be able to muster enough votes when election day rolled around. True social reform would have to come from other quarters. Jane Addams was one of the first Americans to realize that.

Addams was born in Cedarville, Illinois, in 1860, the year Lincoln was elected president for the first time. Her father, John, a Quaker and an abolitionist, served in the Illinois senate for sixteen tumultuous years (1854–70). He and Lincoln were friends. When Lincoln wrote to Addams, he addressed him as "My dear Double-D'ed Addams."

Sadness fell over the Addams household when Mrs. Addams died shortly after the youngest daughter, Jane, was born. The four little girls had only their father to look to for guidance and support. Fortunately, he was equal to the task of raising them by himself. He enjoyed spending time with his daughters and carefully supervised their education. Social problems, politics, and philosophy were common topics of conversation around their dinner table. All of them attended nearby Rockford Seminary.

Jane wanted to become a physician, but the stress was too much for her, and she had to drop out of medical school. Complicating her life was the fact that since childhood she had been afflicted with a serious curvature of the spine. Operations to correct this condition were primitive, very painful, and often ineffective. She endured four such surgeries during her lifetime.

At her father's suggestion, she rounded out her education by making two excursions to Europe. On her second trip, she and her friend, Ellen Gates Starr, visited the first settlement house in the world. In trying to come up with solutions to the problem of poverty, a group of Oxford University students had become convinced that the usual practice of dropping in on the poor from time to time to offer a little food or clothing and an uplifting message accomplished very little. If we went to live among the poor, they reasoned, we would get to know them and could develop programs that would be more effective. They rented Toynbee Hall, a building deep in the slums of London, and went to live side by side with the people they were trying to help. The Americans were most impressed by what they saw.

By the time they returned to Illinois, Addams and Starr had decided to start a settlement house in Chicago. They had some misgivings, as the project they were about to undertake was unheard of for women of their social class and they both realized how much effort would have to go into it. Nevertheless, they bought an old mansion that had once been the country home of the Hull family but was now surrounded by factories and run-down tenements.

Their neighbors were mostly poor immigrants. After the Civil War, large numbers of unskilled laborers from Poland, Italy, Russia, Slovakia, Serbia, and Greece came to live in Chicago. They had left overpopulated areas or had been displaced by the industrial revolution. Unfortunately, new labor-saving machines had eliminated a large number of unskilled jobs in America, too, and many of the newcomers could not find work.

Immigrant families crowded together in dark, dirty hovels that lacked toilets and bathtubs, sanitary waste and garbage disposal, and adequate heating and lighting. Landlords charged exorbitant rents and made few repairs or improvements. Slum children were constantly exposed to crime and violence, diseases and drunkenness. In its way, life in the 19th ward was as harsh and uncivilized as anything that frontier families had experienced in the early days of settlement.

In 1890 Hull-House began operations by opening a kindergarten and day-care center. Addams and Starr quickly expanded their program to include nutrition and cooking classes and basic instruction in speaking, reading, and writing English. Both men and women came to Hull-House to learn trades, and eventually adult high school classes and even college extension courses were offered. The Hull-House employment bureau helped newly trained workers find jobs. Recognizing the importance of shared good times, Addams organized teas, dances, and parties for young and old.

When more space was needed, Jane Addams arranged to purchase adjoining structures until at last the Hull-House complex included thirteen buildings. But Addams's influence reached far beyond that. Hull-House became a training ground for some of the first professional social workers in the nation. Addams lectured and served as a consultant in many other cities and influenced thousands of people with the books and pamphlets

Jane Addams, whose work at Hull-House spanned forty years, entertaining a group of children. University of Illinois at Chicago, The University Library, Jane Addams Memorial Collection.

she wrote. She participated in various reform movements, was politically active, and became a peace advocate during World War I.

Many gifted women who were drawn to Hull-House later made contributions of their own. Among them was Julia Lathrop, through whose efforts the first juvenile court in the world was established in Chicago in 1899. President William Howard Taft appointed her chief of the newly organized federal Children's Bureau in 1912. Florence Kelley made the first comprehensive sociological survey of an American urban center when she studied Chicago's sweatshop system. Her report led to the Sweatshop Act of 1893, which limited a woman's work day to eight hours, forbade the employment of children under fourteen in factories, and provided for the inspection of workplaces. Governor John Peter Altgeld appointed her the first chief inspector. Alice Hamilton, a research physician specializing in bacteriology and pathology (the study of disease), was hired to teach at Northwestern University. She heard Jane Addams speak and decided she wanted to help at Hull-House. Venturing out into the neighborhood, she became well acquainted with the medical problems of the poor and took a special interest in work-related illnesses. She pioneered in industrial medicine and later became a professor at Harvard Medical School.

As successful as they were, Jane Addams and her associates realized that privately run foundations could not cope with the overwhelming need for social welfare programs. They hoped that the best of their programs would someday be taken over by government agencies. Addams and her colleagues strongly influenced public opinion by showing that people living in poverty could improve their lives if given a helping hand. By the end of the century many people were taking a new attitude toward the poor.

꘏

The poor who lived in the shadows of the prosperous were easy for most people to ignore. But bosses and boodlers soon saw that the poor constituted a base of power. These crooked politicians did favors for the impoverished people living in their wards to receive their votes. Having established themselves in office, the boodlers grew rich on public moneys. This was no way to solve the problem of poverty, but for a while dishonest politicians were almost the only people the poor could depend upon.

Jane Addams and her colleagues had other ideas. By living among the people they were trying to help, they were better able to plan programs suited to their needs. They also used political avenues to bring about much needed change. Their efforts touched off an era of reform, which, as we shall see, lasted thirty years.

For Further Exploration

Jane Addams. *Twenty Years at Hull-House.* New York: Macmillan, 1910. Reprinted in 1990, with original illustrations by Norah Hamilton and an introduction by James Hurt, by the University of Illinois Press.

The founder of Hull-House describes the first activities she and her colleagues were able to offer and shows how their mission expanded to include a wide variety of services for people of all ages. It is also her political autobiography, showing how she arrived at her conclusions about government involvement in social problems.

PART FIVE

Illinois in the Modern World

The twentieth century opened with a period of optimism and reform, but soon bitter conflict enveloped the world. After World War I came the carefree days of the Roaring Twenties and the Depression of the 1930s. The prosperous years that followed World War II were marred by the uneasy atmosphere of the cold war and domestic conflict. Vietnam divided the nation as it had not been divided since the Civil War. Illinoisans were full participants in all these events and by 1970 were engaged in another round of reforms that culminated in a new state constitution.

19

The Reform Era

Making Progress Work

Illinois became industrialized so rapidly that by the 1890s it ranked fourth among all states in manufacturing. But progress was not without its price. In the rush for success and wealth the problems of the less fortunate had been overlooked. Legislation to protect workers had been spotty, and troublesome warning signs in race relations had been ignored. What we now call the infrastructure—the facilities, services, and administrative apparatus a modern state needs to function properly—was far from complete.

Illinois needed a time out to look at where it had been and where it was headed. Fortunately, both the leadership and the public will to do so existed. The spirit of reform took fire during the late 1800s and carried forward into the new century.

Improving Physical Conditions

During the years of hectic growth, Illinoisans had been annoyed by inconveniences in their daily lives, but not enough to demand change. When these inconveniences became too troublesome—or even dangerous—they let their voices be heard.

Cleaning up the Water

In the late 1800s Chicagoans living in even the best of houses sometimes turned on their faucets only to get cloudy brown water with a foul smell. And no wonder: for years the city had dumped sewage, garbage, and industrial wastes into the Chicago River, which emptied

The Sanitary and Ship Canal under construction. When completed in 1900, it was the world's second largest artificial waterway. The Chicago Public Library, Special Collections Division.

into Lake Michigan about a mile southwest of the city. Although drinking water was pumped from farther out in the lake, every so often some of the sewage mixed with the drinking water. Generally people considered this more of an unpleasant inconvenience than a danger. But in 1885 a six-inch, two-day rain flooded the river, and the river's polluted discharge swirled far out into the lake. Chicago's water supply became so badly contaminated that it was dangerous to drink.

Engineers finally came up with a radical solution to the problem. Why not build a canal that would *reverse* the flow of the Chicago River so that the waste-laden water would be carried southward rather than into Lake Michigan? The General Assembly approved the plan in 1889. Eleven years later Chicago celebrated the beginning of the new century by opening the control gates of the Sanitary and Ship Canal.

The channel followed the twenty-eight-mile route of the old Illinois and Michigan Canal and was cut deep enough to accommodate ocean-going vessels. The new canal solved not only the waste-water problem (at least from Chicago's point of view) but also became the last link in a modern commercial waterway running from the East Coast, through the Great Lakes, and down to the Gulf of Mexico. At the time of its completion, the Sanitary and Ship Canal was the largest artificial waterway in the world, except for the Suez Canal.

Cleaning up the Beef

During the Spanish-American War (1898), three large Chicago meatpacking companies, Armour, Swift, and Morris, made huge profits shipping canned meat to the troops. The meat was apparently tainted with chemicals that had been added as preservatives, and many soldiers got sick from eating it. Soon it was being called "embalmed beef."

An investigation brought charges that the packers had used bribery to obtain Army contracts and had failed to provide a safe and appetizing product. The packers claimed that the illnesses resulted from poor handling of the meat in the field kitchens, not from the way it was processed in the packing plants. Although the companies were not penalized, many people were convinced that the meatpackers were guilty.

When Upton Sinclair's novel, *The Jungle*, came out in 1906, people had not forgotten the embalmed-beef scandal. In *The Jungle* Sinclair described the plight of the poor immigrants who worked in Chicago's packinghouse district and also gave his readers a graphic picture of the unsanitary conditions under which the meat they ate was prepared. Sick animals were processed along with the healthy ones; workers with tuberculosis and other infectious diseases handled the meat; and tools and surfaces were not sterilized. Although Sinclair was trying to arouse public indignation about the poor conditions under which the packinghouse workers labored, his readers were more disturbed by the filthy conditions he described. As he later said, "I aimed at the public's heart and by accident hit it in the stomach." After angry citizens demanded action, Congress passed the first pure food laws.

Pulling up out of the Mud

The craze for cars swept Illinois when the automobile industry was still in its infancy. Between 1899 and 1919 ten Chicago companies built electric automobiles, and four others tried unsuccessfully to market steam-powered vehicles. The farm machinery companies in Moline developed nine models of cars; a car assembled in Joliet became the model for the Checker Taxi; and until 1928 John Hertz made cars in Illinois for use in his auto-leasing firm. However, Illinois manufacturers could not compete with Henry Ford's Detroit-based assembly line factories. But not becoming the motor capital of the United States did not dampen the enthusiasm of Illinoisans for cars. By 1910 thousands of new owners could be seen weaving in and out of the horse-drawn

The John Deere Company of Moline, one of the earliest farm equipment manufacturers in Illinois, also produced cars in the early days of the automobile. Courtesy of the Illinois State Historical Library.

traffic on city and country roads. Owning a car—now that was a goal worth working for!

Automobile owners reveled in the possibilities of this newest form of transportation. They looked forward to traveling about on their own and being able to get where they were going faster and more comfortably than before. What held them back was the condition of the roads. Very few roads had hard surfaces, and dirt roads turned to axle-deep mud in winter thaws or spring and summer rains. Car owners all too often felt like people all dressed up with no place to go.

The public demand for better roads began early in the twentieth century. Fortunately, Illinois had three reform governors in a row: Charles S. Deneen (1905–13), Edward F. Dunne (1913–17), and Frank O. Lowden (1917–21). Deneen set the road-building movement in motion by creating a highway commission headed by a trained engineer. At the same time, the General Assembly passed a law requiring motorists to register their cars and pay two dollars for license plates, the revenue from which was put directly into a road fund.

Progress continued during Dunne's time in office, and Lowden finally completed arrangements for the financing of new roads. The next governor, Len Small, was not a reformer and scoffed at the political reforms his predecessors had made. But he enthusiastically carried forward the plans to pull Illinois up out of the mud. By the time he left office, Illinois had one of the finest hard-road systems in the nation with more than seven thousand miles of paved highways.

Reforms in Business and Industry

For a long time, public opinion was against the regulation of big business. However, it became increasingly clear that unregulated free enterprise could actually bury competition and subvert the democratic ideal of a free market economy. Also, the public's trust in industrialists and financiers to guide the economy and keep it healthy was shaken by the repeated financial panics that had occurred in the previous half-century. Furthermore, the apparent disregard of management for the health and safety of workers surfaced again during the reform era.

Antitrust Legislation

By the late 1800s industrialists had discovered that cooperation and consolidation paid greater dividends than ruthless competition. By merging two or more companies into a larger one, corporations amassed an alarming amount of power. The Illinois steel industry provides a good example.

In 1889 two Chicago steel plants merged with the Joliet Steel Company to become the Illinois Steel Company. In 1898 Illinois Steel merged with plants in Minnesota, Ohio, and Pennsylvania, thereby creating the Federal Steel Company. In 1901 officials of Federal Steel persuaded Andrew Carnegie to sell out to them. The resulting merger, and the purchase of eight more companies, created the United States Steel Corporation. Its holdings included ore, coal, and limestone lands, 112 steamships, and more than 1,000 miles of railroads. It had everything it needed to control all phases of the steel industry.

Such giant corporations eliminated competition by forcing smaller, independent companies out of business. That put them in the position of being able to set prices and production figures and to deal with their employees however they chose. Some steel workers worked as many as eighty-four hours a week at substandard wages under very dangerous conditions. There was no compensation for on-the-job injuries or help for the families of workers killed on the job. Furthermore, these corporations had huge financial resources with which to fight unionization and government regulation.

As the negative effects of mergers became more obvious, a cry for reform was raised. In 1890 Congress passed the Sherman Antitrust Act, which made illegal any merger or combination entered into for the purpose of controlling a whole industry. The next year the Illinois General Assembly passed a similar law. Some corporations were quick to spot loopholes in the laws, but the idea that regulation was necessary had gained a foothold.

The Most Dangerous Job in the State

Although the General Assembly had begun work on coal-mining legislation as early as 1870, coal mines remained the most dangerous workplaces in Illinois. Floods, fires, explosions, and the collapse of scaffolds and props took many lives; miners also faced long-term health risks from inhaling fumes and lethal coal dust. Miners' unions tried to get action, but most mine owners were not very receptive. It seemed that only disasters could get the General Assembly to act.

The worst mine disaster in Illinois history happened in 1910. At that time, Cherry Mine No. 2 in Bureau County still used animals to pull coal cars. The animals were stabled underground, and the hay with which they were fed was kept below ground, too. One day a spark ignited a pile of hay lying in a coal car. A miner tried to shove the cart away, but mistakenly pushed it nearer a ventilation opening. The flames were sucked into the ventilation system, and within minutes the supporting timbers burst into flame and the mine became a cave of fire. For 259 miners there was no escape.

The General Assembly met in special session and appointed a commission to sift through all the old mining laws and to evaluate and organize them. New regulations were added, and a much improved set of mine safety laws emerged.

Changes in the Political System

Reformers reached out in many directions to correct specific problems. At the same time, they made important changes in the political system itself.

Women and the Vote

Illinois women made important gains during the closing decades of the nineteenth century. Increasing numbers of women were being admitted to universities and colleges, and a few even became faculty members. Women began entering professions that had traditionally been closed to them. More women, both married and single, were employed outside their homes in a wider array of occupations than ever before. Some ran successful businesses of their own. Women had spearheaded many of the reform movements, and yet, at the turn of the century, they still did not have the right to vote.

Although pride and self-respect were important considerations, the desire to vote was not simply a matter of wanting to prove that women were as competent as men. Women wanted to vote for the very practical reason that politicians are more responsive to people who can vote them in or out of office than they are to those who cannot. Being able to vote also carried with it the promise of eventually being able to hold public office.

The many woman suffrage organizations in the state became more effective when they united under the banner of the Woman's Christian Temperance Union. The WCTU, headquartered in Evanston, Illinois, had a large national membership. Originally organized for the purpose of stopping the sale and consumption of alcoholic beverages, its members soon saw that without the right to vote they would not be able to accomplish their goal. Therefore, they took over leadership of the woman suffrage movement, speaking to groups, lobbying legislators, organizing parades, and writing articles and pamphlets. Tireless workers, the suffragettes publicized their cause and won many supporters, both male and female. Lawmakers found it increasingly difficult to ignore the issues they raised.

Finally, in 1913, Illinois became the first state east of the Mississippi to pass a law allowing women to vote in municipal and presidential elections. Known as the "Illinois Law," it became the model for suffrage laws in other states. Some opponents of the woman suffrage movement had maintained that most women would not want to vote even if they could. They were wrong. Over 200,000 Illinois women turned out to vote in the 1916 presidential election.

The Illinois Law preceded the Nineteenth Amendment to the Constitution by seven years. Ratified in 1920, the Nineteenth Amendment gave women in all states the right to vote.

Dumping the "Spoils" System

"To the victors belong the spoils," the old adage reads. Sometimes it was applied to victorious candidates for public office. Newly elected presidents, governors, and mayors felt free to fire government employees who had been hired by their predecessors. That made it possible for them to reward their friends and campaign workers with the vacated jobs. Politicians recognized the unfairness of the spoils system, but at the same time shrugged it all off by saying, "Well, life isn't fair anyway." Sometimes they claimed that government was more efficient when leaders chose their own staff members.

But what happened when incompetent and inexperienced people replaced those who were better qualified? What did creating jobs expressly for the purpose of paying off political debts cost the taxpayers? And how could government agencies suffer such major disruptions after each election and still be efficient and cost-effective? These are the kinds of questions the reformers were asking when Governor Deneen took office.

Deneen laid the groundwork for a civil service system under which potential employees would be required to take tests to prove they were qualified. Once hired, they could be fired for wrong-doing or incompetence, but not to make room for party favorites. Unnecessary jobs were to be eliminated, and state agencies were reorganized so they would operate more efficiently. The governor ran into stiff opposition when he tried to put his plan into effect, but he did reorganize the welfare agencies, putting all 2,200 employees of state institutions under the supervision of a five-member board. It replaced the seventeen local boards that had previously supervised these workers.

The next governor, Edward Dunne, continued the drive for total reorganization of the state government by creating a commission on efficiency and economy with Professor John Fairlie of the University of Illinois in charge. Fairlie made many valuable suggestions, one of which was to consolidate the dozens of separate agencies into many fewer departments. Although this was not done during Dunne's term in office, the next governor, Frank Lowden, made use of Fairlie's work.

The Civil Administrative Code of 1917 was Lowden's greatest accomplishment as governor. The code, which incorporated many of Fairlie's suggestions, abolished 125 state agencies and reorganized the others into nine departments: finance, agriculture, labor, mines and minerals, public works and buildings, public welfare, public health, trade and commerce, and registration and education. Each department was to be headed by a director who reported to the governor. All budgeting and accounting matters were to be funneled through one office. Fourteen other states that were undergoing similar reforms thought the Illinois plan so good they copied it.

Facing up to Racial Problems

During Governor Deneen's administration, a racially motivated riot broke out in Springfield. It happened at a time when there was a nationwide epidemic of lynchings of blacks, and the riot attracted national attention because it took place in the city where Abraham

Lincoln had lived. In separate episodes two black men had been jailed on serious charges. When angry crowds gathered, Springfield police decided to move the two men to another location to keep them safe from would-be lynchers. They created a diversion, then transported the men in a borrowed car.

When the mob realized the men were gone, they wrecked the car and the cafe run by the car's owner, then stormed into the black section of the city and burned a large area of it. For no apparent reason they dragged a black barber out of his house, killed him, and mutilated his body. Later they hung an eighty-year-old black man, probably because he was married to a white woman. That morning the governor called out the National Guard. The city quieted down, but sporadic acts of violence continued.

A grand jury indicted 117 people, but no one was convicted of murder, and only a few participants received any punishment at all. William Walling, a southerner and socialist, happened to be in Springfield at the time. He thought it a shameful affair and wrote about it in the Springfield *Independent*. Mary Ovington, who had given up her status in high society to become an activist, contacted him. Working with New Yorker Henry Moskowitz, they got in touch with others who agreed with their point of view and founded the National Association for the Advancement of Colored People. They were able to persuade W. E. B. Du Bois and other prominent black leaders to join.

By the time Governor Lowden took office, Chicago's black population was rising dramatically. Just as white pioneers had set out from the East Coast in search of a better life in the West, so large numbers of enterprising blacks began moving to northern cities about 1915. Known as the Great Migration, this movement profoundly influenced urban development.

Black immigrants to Chicago were directed to the Black Belt, a long, narrow strip of housing on the south side. The area was overcrowded, and much of the housing was substandard, but it was better than the plantation shacks the newcomers had left behind. Unfortunately, many black immigrants were not able to get jobs. Some unions would not admit them, and white employers gave jobs to white immigrants in preference to black people. Black workers often had to take menial jobs much below the level of their skills.

Segregation was not as harsh and visible in the North as it had been in the South, but it existed nonetheless. There were certain neighborhoods into which blacks wandered at their own peril. Although schools and public recreation facilities were not officially segregated, in practice they were. In 1919 this led to a bloody riot in Chicago.

A black teenager floating on a raft had gotten caught in a current and floated too close to a "white" beach. He was killed by a white man who threw a rock that struck his head. Although witnesses were able to identify the attacker, he was not arrested. During the next few days angry blacks clashed repeatedly with whites. Before the violence was over, twenty-three blacks and sixty-five whites were dead, and 537 people were injured.

In spite of all the problems they faced in northern cities, most blacks still felt they were better off than they had been in the South. In Chicago they could sit anywhere they wanted on public buses and were not expected to step off the sidewalk to make way for whites as they had been in the South. The Chicago riot had been bloody and frightening, but it was a rare occasion; in the South beatings and lynchings were almost routine. In their new home poll taxes and literacy tests were not used to prevent them from voting.

In 1915 Oscar De Priest became the first black alderman to be elected to the Chicago City Council. De Priest, the son of a former slave, came to Chicago when he was seventeen, started a real estate business, and helped organize the Negro Business League. In 1928 he became the first black Illinoisan to be elected to the U.S. Congress.

☙

During the years of rapid industrialization lawmakers as well as most of the voters thought that big business ought to be left to operate as it pleased. After all, they reasoned, big business is the very heart and core of our economic well-being. But soon it became apparent that not all industrialists and financiers were high-minded people who kept the best interests of the workers and the general public in mind. An era of reform followed.

The building of the Sanitary and Ship Canal corrected Chicago's sewage problem and at the same time expanded the transportation system. Illinoisans embraced the age of the automobile with enthusiasm and built one of the best hard-road systems in the nation.

Laws were passed prohibiting corporations from forming monopolies. Illinois became the first state east of the Mississippi to pass a law giving women the right to vote in presidential elections. Three consecutive governors worked to eliminate the spoils system and streamline the state government. Racial incidents reminded people of the need to improve relationships between blacks and whites, but progress was slow in this sensitive area.

The reform era lost momentum as attention turned to winning

World War I. In the next chapter we shall see how that catastrophe affected Illinois.

For Further Exploration

James R. Grossman. *Land of Hope: Chicago, Black Southerners, and the Great Migration*. Chicago: University of Chicago Press, 1989.

The author explains the incentives that brought many black southerners to Chicago during and after World War I and discusses to what extent their hopes were realized. He also deals with the complex class structures they encountered in both the black and the white communities.

Robert P. Howard. *Mostly Good and Competent Men: Illinois Governors, 1818 to 1988*. Springfield: Illinois State Historical Society, 1988.

Howard's collection of short biographical essays includes many interesting details about Illinois governors as well as outlining their major accomplishments. He rates Deneen, Dunne, and Lowden as good and competent. Governor Small does not quite make the cut.

Herman R. Lantz. *People of Coal Town*. With the assistance of J. S. McCrary. N.p., 1958. Reprint. Carbondale: Southern Illinois University Press, 1971.

A sociological study of a coal town in southern Illinois, this book uses records, newspapers, and interviews to cover the history of the community from preindustrial days until the two mines there closed in the 1950s. We are shown the work habits, family patterns, separation of ethnic groups, lawlessness and violence, attempts at reform, and relationship of miners to the company, to their co-workers, and to the neighboring farmers.

20

Illinois in World War I

The Call to Arms

Until the twentieth century it had been the policy of the United States not to participate in European wars. Americans were glad to be free from the old conflicts that ravaged Europe. When World War I broke out in 1914, they were in no hurry to get involved. In 1916 President Woodrow Wilson ran for reelection. "He kept us out of war," said his supporters. Not only had he refused to send troops to Europe; he had tried repeatedly to bring the warring nations to the conference table. He was reelected.

During Wilson's second term freedom of the seas became a critical issue. In 1915 a German submarine sank an unarmed British passenger ship, the *Lusitania*. More than a thousand people died, including 128 Americans. Wilson persuaded the Germans to pay reparations and to promise not to sink any more nonmilitary ships. But in 1917 Germany proclaimed all the seas around Great Britian and Western Europe a war zone subject to unrestricted submarine warfare. Any merchant or passenger vessel that entered that zone was fair game.

By 1917 the combatants had fought to a standstill, and the nations allied against Germany pleaded with the United States to send troops and equipment so the war could be brought to a conclusion. Their urgent request, coupled with the fact that American vessels no longer enjoyed the freedom of the seas, changed President Wilson's mind about the war. He now felt that we should participate to make the world "safe for democracy." A reluctant Congress declared war on Germany on April 6, 1917.

Inspection of a crashed airplane at Chanute Field, World War I. Courtesy of the Illinois State Historical Library.

When President Wilson called for troops, Governor Frank Lowden mobilized the Illinois National Guard and set up recruitment facilities. Old camps were reactivated, and a large new camp near Rockford, Fort Grant, was quickly built. The airplane had never been used in combat before, so few facilities for the training of pilots existed. The University of Illinois set up an aviation program in which young pilots received their first course of instruction. After completing that, they received in-flight training at the new Chanute Air Field at Rantoul or at Scott Air Field near Belleville. The Great Lakes Naval Training Station, built in Chicago in 1904, received funds for expansion and more than 50,000 sailors trained there. A total of 314,504 soldiers, sailors, and marines from Illinois took part in the war.

The Farmers Mobilize

One of the first slogans to come out of Washington after the United States declared war on Germany was, "Food will win the war." That had special meaning for a state as agriculturally rich as Illinois. Farmers saw their chance both to be patriotic and to improve their financial situation. But there was one catch: as young farmers and farmhands were drafted, the shortage of farm labor became acute.

Farm wives did their best to fill in for the men who had been called to active duty, but they could not continue to do the tasks they had done before and keep up with the field and stock work as well. A "land army" made up of city volunteers willing to work on farms had only limited success because it was too small and most of the recruits did not know much about farming. Government officials then set up a program for high school students that allowed them to take classes in agriculture and receive school credits for farm labor. Although about 21,000 trainees were placed on farms, their efforts did not increase the output enough. Officials finally began giving farmers deferments so they could stay home and grow crops.

Patriotic Illinoisans agreed to conserve food. More than 850,000 families signed pledge cards promising to eat less. Restaurants and hotels cut down on their use of food and threw less away so that more could go to the war effort.

Illinois Industry during the War Years

Even before the United States entered the war, Illinois factories had geared up to meet the overseas demand for war goods and supplies. After Congress declared war on Germany, Illinois manufacturers tried even harder to increase their output, and they had the cooperation of the unions. Historically, labor leaders had almost always opposed war because they felt that the working classes did most of the fighting and dying while the corporations and financiers profited by producing military goods. However, in this case American union leaders generally backed the war effort because they saw the German kaiser (emperor) as a dictator, and dictators had seldom been good to the working class.

A shortage of workers proved to be as much of a problem for industry as it was for agriculture. Women and high school students filled some of the vacancies, and blacks came from the South to work in the factories of Chicago and other Illinois cities.

As important as their labor was to the war effort, blacks were not home free. Factory owners still gave preference to white immigrants from Europe. Friction developed between black and white workers because blacks were willing to work for lower wages. Many unions refused to admit them. In 1917 serious racial violence broke out in East St. Louis. When workers at an aluminum ore plant there went on strike, the company brought in black strikebreakers. The strikers never got their jobs back and took out their anger and frustration on the blacks. A rumor that a black man had shot a white man during a holdup brought spasms of violence as whites pulled blacks off streetcars and out of their workplaces and beat them up. The National Guard was called in, but as soon as the troops left the harassment of blacks intensified. On July 2 whites met at the Labor Temple and armed themselves, then went on a rampage of beatings and house burnings. The National Guard came back, but did little to stop the violence; some of its members may even have contributed to it. More than fifty people were killed, hundreds more were injured, and sixteen acres of property were burned, including 250 buildings.

Finally the violence died down, but Governor Lowden kept troops on hand to protect the blacks still living in East St. Louis. He then set up a commission to study the economic and industrial aspects of the racial problem, naming several important leaders, black and white, as members. The war had highlighted the need for civil rights legislation, but it would be decades before much progress was made in this sensitive area.

Civilian Efforts

Samuel Insull, head of the Defense Council, thought Germany might be able to wipe out the democratic nations of Europe unless the United States intervened. Of special concern to him was England, the land of his birth. After coming to Illinois, Insull had made a fortune in utilities. When Governor Lowden asked for his help, he furnished a six-story office building and a staff to run the Defense Council at his own expense. From these headquarters he directed the work of thousands of civilian volunteers.

The peace movement was strong in Illinois, so Insull's first task was to convince people that the war was necessary and should be supported. He quickly trained a group of volunteer speakers known as "Four-Minute Men." They traveled about making four-minute speeches preceding theatrical performances and other community events in which they explained why the United States had entered the war.

Other volunteers conducted drives to sell war bonds. Eventually Illinoisans bought $1.3 billion worth of bonds and gave more than $40 million to the Red Cross and other relief agencies. More than 300,000 volunteers knitted sweaters, prepared medical supplies, worked in government offices without pay, and performed other auxiliary tasks.

Resistance to the War

In 1917 Illinois had a larger German-speaking population than any other state. While not in sympathy with the German government's political and military goals, German-born Americans felt a kinship with and concern for their friends and relatives still living in Germany. Shortly before Congress declared war on Germany, a committee of German-Americans from Illinois had gone to Washington to plead with

President Wilson not to enter the war. However, when the United States finally entered the conflict, many young men of German descent served in the armed forces. German-American civilians contributed money to the war effort and served in support organizations. Nevertheless, they often lived under a cloud of suspicion.

A large number of Illinois women initially opposed the war, but after the United States entered it, they rallied to the cause. However, Jane Addams, the founder of Hull-House, refused to be swayed by appeals to patriotism. She explained her position in these words: "I do not see why people who believe in peace and who believe that killing is wrong should not speak out in time of war the same as at any other time. . . . Opposition to the war is not necessarily cowardice." Before this she had been regarded as an American saint. Now she was labeled "the most dangerous American." Nevertheless, she stood firm against the pressure of public opinion during several difficult years. A few years before her death in 1931, she became a co-recipient of the Nobel Peace Prize.

At first Governor Lowden attempted to suppress large meetings of peace groups. In one case he sent troops to prevent pacifists from meeting in Chicago, but by the time the troops arrived the speakers had already completed their speeches. The leaders of the organization instructed the participants to offer no resistance and to disband. They did so and no blood was shed.

Other groups had more serious problems with the authorities. The International Workers of the World (IWW) had its headquarters in Chicago, even though it had few active members in Illinois. Because some of its members were thought to be working up antiwar sentiment in the western farming centers and encouraging people to dodge the draft, they were placed under surveillance and harassed at their public meetings. Eventually more than a hundred IWW leaders were tried in Chicago for obstructing the war effort and sentenced to twenty-year prison terms and large fines. In the light of such events, people began to express concern that some of the basic freedoms guaranteed by the Constitution—the freedom to assemble for peaceful purposes, freedom of speech, freedom of belief, and freedom of the press—were being eroded.

Acts of violence against pacifists reached a crisis in Illinois early in 1918 when a socialist named Robert Prager was lynched by a mob in Collinsville. Prager, a good citizen of German descent, had at first opposed the war. However, when the United States finally entered it, he had tried to enlist but had been rejected for medical reasons. Nevertheless, miners who lived near him continued to suspect him of being a German spy. The community resentment they worked up against him got out of hand and resulted in his being hung without a trial. Governor Lowden was outraged and spoke out strongly against such acts of violence. Although he continued to keep dissidents under surveillance, he also began sending troops to protect their meetings when necessary.

President Wilson, too, was dismayed by such acts of violence. He said, "There have been many lynchings and every one of them has been a blow at the heart of ordered law and humane justice. I can never accept any man as a champion of liberty either for ourselves or for the world who does not reverence and obey the laws of our own beloved land, whose laws we ourselves have made. He has adopted the standards of the enemies of his country whom he affects to despise."

The War Ends on a Downbeat

In the spring of 1918 the Germans mounted their last great offensive in France, and American troops went into action for the first time. The French, British, Belgians, and Americans halted the German advance and brought the war to an end. At 5:00 A.M. on November 11, German and allied officials met at Compiegne, France, and signed an armistice. The fighting ended six hours later.

The following year a treaty conference was held at Versailles, France. Although President Wilson had prepared and publicized a fourteen-point program for a lasting peace, the other Allies were not willing to follow it. Instead, they vindictively laid heavy war debts on Germany and divided its foreign colonies among themselves. They showed little interest in working together to prevent such devastating conflicts from happening in the future.

To Wilson, the most important of his fourteen points was the last one—the setting up of a League of Nations. To get cooperation on that point, he compromised on some of the others. The League of Nations was formed, but to Wilson's profound disappointment the U.S. Congress voted not to join it.

Americans celebrated the armistice with parades, parties, and fireworks. But when the sobering facts came in, it turned out that more than 37 million soldiers worldwide were dead, wounded, or missing in action. A staggering 10 million civilians had lost their lives. And although the war had been fought "to make the world safe for democracy," the seeds for an even more deadly conflict had been sown.

Just as one great threat to international stability was eliminated, another frightening development spread fear and panic to America. The ancient monarchy of Russia had been overthrown, and in 1917 Communists took over the Russian government. The leaders of the Reds, as the Communists were called, had succeeded in getting the workers and peasants to revolt and were promising that Communism would one day take over the world. The "Red scare" made Americans wary of labor unions and nervous about any unrest. Some thought that the Communists were sending spies and agents to the United States to foment a revolution. People who expressed any interest in Communism were considered suspect, as were socialists and other dissidents. Although some of the fear was well founded, the quandary of what to do about civil liberties at such a time would persist well into this century. In fact, it is still with us today.

❦

When the United States entered World War I, the federal government looked to the great agricultural states to step up food production. Illinois contributed heavily in this area, in spite of a shortage of farm workers. Illinois industries trained new workers and produced large quantities of war goods. Civilian volunteers undertook tasks ranging from knitting sweaters for the troops to selling war bonds.

However, some Illinoisans opposed the war. Pacifists ran the risk of being ostracized or even attacked because of their anti-war stand. The lynching of Robert Prager brought the issue to a head.

People celebrated the end of the war with great fanfare, but in the long run, a lasting peace was not achieved. War-weary people did not want to think about the future. Instead, they tried to turn the 1920s into one long party. In chapter 21 we shall look at Illinois in the Roaring Twenties.

For Further Exploration

William T. Hutchinson. *Lowden of Illinois: The Life of Frank O. Lowden.* Vol. 1, *City and State.* Chicago: University of Chicago Press, 1957.

Lowden's biography, a "rags to riches" story, includes his marriage to George Pullman's daughter, Florence, his experiments at his model farm, Sinissippi, and many other interesting sidelights. It also covers Lowden's four years as governor—a troubled time in which he was nevertheless able to accomplish his goals.

21

The Wild and Reckless Twenties

Breaking Loose

After World War I, many Illinoisans found themselves better off financially than they had ever been. They rushed out to purchase homes,
cars, and appliances, then began looking for more ways to spend their
leisure time. A search for pleasure and excitement replaced the hard
work and sobriety of the reform decades and the war years.

The New Woman

The Nineteenth Amendment, ratified in 1920, gave women in all
the states the right to vote. Avant-garde women celebrated the opening
of a new era by having their hair cut in sleek, short bobs, throwing off
the tyranny of corsets, and wearing knee-length dresses and skirts. Some
began smoking and drinking in public. Known as flappers, these stylish
young women danced the charleston and the shimmy with young men
they had met on their own instead of through family connections.
Prewar morals and social conventions seemed quaint and outdated to
them.

The Barnstormers

Illinoisans had a long-lasting love affair with the flying machine. As
early as 1890 Octave Chanute, a railroad and bridge engineer, had
begun experimenting with gliders. His aeronautic experiments led him
to design a biplane glider whose wings were arched surfaces held
together by vertical posts. Chanute corresponded with the Wright
brothers, who used some of his ideas in building their first successful
plane. Chanute Field at Rantoul is named for him.

As soon as the war ended, some of the surplus war planes were converted into mail planes. Regular mail runs between Chicago and New York began in 1918, and two years later people could send letters by airmail between Chicago and the West Coast. Other surplus planes were sold to individuals who became the daredevils of their day. They traveled around the country, stopping to perform daring aerial acrobatics wherever they could assemble a paying audience. Many Illinoisans saw their first flying machines while standing in a farmer's field watching one of these dashing young barnstormers. Some barnstormers also offered flying lessons and limited passenger service.

Illinois manufacturers, hoping to cash in on the demand for aircraft, started more than 130 small airplane plants during the 1920s. Most were run by enthusiastic amateurs. Barnstormers bought some of these new planes, as did wealthy sportsmen who wanted to add the thrill of flying to their weekend pleasure trips.

Movie Madness

Thomas Edison's kinetoscope had drawn large crowds at the World's Columbian Exposition of 1893. The kinetoscope consisted of a small cabinet in which a fifty-foot length of motion picture film was shown to one person at a time. Edison continued to work on his motion picture machine, and other inventors also brought out improved versions of it. Working separately, Chicagoans George Spoor and William Selig developed movie projectors that cast images onto a screen so that many people could watch at once.

Spoor and Selig soon branched out into making films as well as projectors. Spoor, teaming up with actor G. M. Anderson, formed the Essanay Film Manufacturing Company, the largest in Illinois. The great Charlie Chaplin made movies at Essanay between 1914 and 1916.

Selig made some of the first westerns, including the Tom Mix movies, which became immensely popular. Luther Pollard started what was probably the first black-owned and -operated film company in the nation, Ebony Film Corporation. Other Illinois companies made training and promotional films for various industries and thousands of short films for the nickel theaters that sprang up. But movie-making in Illinois was a flash in the pan. Before the 1920s were over, all the Chicago studios had closed. The filmmakers moved to California where the sun shone almost every day and movies could be shot outdoors the year around.

Another great movie entrepreneur, Walt Disney, was born in Chicago in 1901. After studying briefly at art schools in Chicago and Kansas City, he made his way to Hollywood in 1923. He and his brother Roy

Bronco Billy, one of the first western movies ever made, being shot at Essanay Studios in Chicago. Chicago Historical Society.

opened a studio and made a specialty of producing animated films. Mickey Mouse was "born" in 1928, followed by Snow White, Pinocchio, Bambi, and a host of other popular cartoon characters.

Waukegan was the hometown of comedian Jack Benny, who began in vaudeville and later became a radio and movie star. The popular "Jack Benny Show" was broadcast each week for twenty-three years. When television came along, the versatile comedian starred in a weekly show that continued into the 1960s.

Chicago Blues and Jazz

In New Orleans small black bands had been part of communal ceremonies for years. They played at weddings and funerals and took part in seasonal festivities. Their strongly rhythmic and emotional music had its roots in the Afro-American culture, expressing both the heartache of the black experience and the energy and joy of the black spirit.

The same black musicians who played at these events began playing blues and jazz in the cabarets of a section of New Orleans known as Storyville. But because Storyville's gambling joints and saloons were near naval training facilities, the Navy closed Storyville down during

Louis Armstrong, one of the many black musicians who brought jazz to Chicago in the 1920s. Courtesy of the Illinois State Historical Library.

World War I. Black musicians then headed north in search of a new place to play their music. Cornet player "King" Oliver, one of the first to move, arrived in Chicago about 1918 and two years later formed his own jazz band.

Few of the early jazz musicians had any formal training, and many did not know how to read notes. Improvising together, they created new combinations of sounds and rhythms in an ever-changing display of virtuosity. Young musicians, both black and white, hung around to listen and learn.

King Oliver encouraged other black musicians to migrate from New Orleans to Chicago, among whom was a young trumpet player named Louis Armstrong. A gifted musician and great innovator, Armstrong played, sang, composed, and eventually became one of the giants of jazz. He took the new music to New York, Europe, and many other parts of the world.

Benny Goodman, born in the Jewish ghetto of Chicago, began his musical career by playing in the Hull-House Boys' Band. His father then arranged for him to have private clarinet lessons with a member of the Chicago Symphony Orchestra. But when Goodman heard jazz, he knew that it was the kind of music he wanted to make. After serving apprenticeships with dance orchestras in Chicago and New York, he started an orchestra of his own. Black jazz musicians generally played only in black bands, but Goodman broke the color line when he invited black musicians to play with him.

The Chicago clubs in which the jazz musicians first played were not luxurious, nor were the neighborhoods in which these places were located. But people loved the beats and moods of the new music and came streaming in to hear more of it. During the 1920s Chicago became one of the jazz centers of the world.

Sporting Events

The 1920s were big years in the development of collegiate and professional sports in Illinois. New sports stars and stadiums attracted thousands, and with the advent of radio even isolated farm families could follow the fortunes of their favorite teams.

Amos Alonzo Stagg, a top baseball and football player during his student years at the University of Chicago, stayed on to become an outstanding coach. By the time he retired in 1931, his teams had won seven championships, and a new stadium had been named for him.

The University of Illinois was also fortunate to have a great coach during this period, a German immigrant named Robert Zuppke. He had never played varsity ball himself, but under his leadership the

University of Illinois won seven Big Ten championships. He recruited many outstanding players, the most famous of whom was Red Grange. Grange played in 237 games and scored 531 touchdowns. When the University of Illinois Memorial Stadium was dedicated in October 1924, more than 67,000 fans watched Grange run for five touchdowns to defeat Michigan.

Another player on Zuppke's team, George Halas, heard Zuppke say that it was too bad that just when players really began learning how to play football they graduated and were lost to the game. Halas took the remark seriously. Sponsored by the A. E. Staley Company of Decatur, he started a team called the Staleys in 1920. After the first year, Staley was unable to continue to support the team, so Halas formed a partnership with another player, Dutch Sternaman, and moved the club to Chicago. In 1922 they renamed their team the Chicago Bears and joined the newly organized National Football League. Halas later became known as "Papa Bear."

For a few years they had to squeak by on a very tight budget, but in 1925 Halas persuaded Red Grange to join the Bears. Red Grange drew huge crowds and helped popularize the game. Halas contributed to the sport by inventing plays, helping to refine the rules, and taking an active part in the administrative aspects of professional football. Some credit him with having exerted a stronger influence on the game than anyone else during the fifty years he spent as player, coach, and owner.

The National Association of Baseball Players, formed in Chicago in 1871, had been beset with gambling irregularities and financial difficulties. When Chicago businessman William Hulbert, owner of the Chicago Cubs, persuaded a young pitcher, Albert Spalding, to join the team as player-manager, he had several objectives in mind. In 1875 Spalding had pitched fifty-seven of the seventy-one games the Boston Red Stockings had won. He also had a deeper grasp of the potential of baseball as a spectator sport than most of his peers. Hulbert wanted to draw upon Spalding's managerial skills as well as his pitching ability.

When Spalding joined the Cubs in 1876, Hulbert asked him to draw up rules for an improved baseball league, which they named the National Baseball League. Eastern teams consented to join it because for many of them it was the only way they could stay afloat financially. When the American League was organized in 1900, it also had a Chicago team, the White Sox. In 1906 the White Sox beat the Cubs in the only World Series they have played against each other.

Scandal rocked the world of baseball in 1919 when the supposedly unbeatable White Sox lost the World Series to the Cincinnati Reds. Rumors circulated that gamblers had paid the Sox to lose. Eight players were indicted, but jurors acquitted them because they felt it was unfair to penalize the players when the gamblers had gone free. Hoping to restore public confidence in the game, the team owners hired Kenesaw Mountain Landis, a former federal judge, as commissioner of baseball. Landis banished the eight players from baseball for life.

The Wide Open Years of Prohibition

For many years, the Woman's Christian Temperance Union (WCTU) tried with only modest success to persuade people to give up the drinking of alcoholic beverages voluntarily. Frances Willard, one of the outstanding women in Illinois history and the only one to be represented in the statuary hall of the National Capitol in Washington, D.C., served as president of the WCTU for twenty years. She introduced a new approach that emphasized the harmful physical and mental consequences of alcohol consumption rather than considering alcoholism as a purely moral issue.

About 1900 the Anti-Saloon League took over the drive to get a law passed that would force people to stop drinking. Pressured to take action, Congress passed the Eighteenth Amendment to the Constitution. Ratified in 1919, it prohibited the manufacture, sale, and transportion of intoxicating beverages. However, reformers did not anticipate the strong reactions against prohibition that came in the wake of the new law they had worked so hard to get.

Gangster City

Within hours after the Eighteenth Amendment went into effect, violations were reported all across the country. Those opposing prohibition believed the new law infringed on individual freedom and would be impossible to enforce. Immigrants who considered the drinking of wine and beer a part of their culture felt discriminated against. The stage was set for bootleggers, opportunists who quickly saw that they could make millions by supplying illegal liquor. Rival gangs competing for control of the undercover alcohol trade made newspaper headlines with their highjackings, shootouts, and murders. Chicago, one of the centers of these activities, became known as "Gangster City."

"Big Jim" Colosimo, a gangster who had gained control of the criminal elements in the city, was murdered by rivals in 1920. Even city officials who were supposed to be fighting crime attended his elaborate funeral. When Colosimo's nephew, Johnny "The Fox" Torrio, took over, he divided Chicago into territories and forced each gang to operate only within its assigned boundaries.

For several years Chicagoans tolerated organized crime because gang violence generally did not affect them directly and many people were anxious to buy alcohol. Mayor "Big Bill" Thompson allowed and even encouraged bootlegging and other illegal activities. But, in time, Chicagoans became alarmed and elected a new mayor, William Dever, who refused to cooperate with the criminals. Torrio was forced to move his base of operations out of Chicago. However, that only left a vacuum to be filled by other gangsters struggling for control. Between 1923 and 1926, more than 200 mobsters died in gang warfare, and the police killed another 160.

Al "Scar Face" Capone took over the mobs in 1926. Capone used fear, torture, reward, and murder to shore up the crumbling crime empire he inherited. A rival gangster on Chicago's north side, "Bugs" Moran, proved hard to intimidate, so on Valentine's Day, February 14, 1929, Capone's hoods ambushed Moran's headquarters, killing seven men. After the Valentine's Day massacre Moran fled, leaving Capone completely in charge. Eventually Capone went to jail, not for the violent crimes he had committed, but for income tax evasion. He died of syphilis after having spent seven years in federal penitentiaries.

Downstate Bootlegging

More violence resulted from clashes between the bootleggers in downstate rural counties and the vigilantes who tried to stop them. The Ku Klux Klan had always been against foreigners and Catholics. Because many of the bootleggers and their customers fell into these categories, klansmen in Williamson County saw an opportunity to further their own aims by appointing themselves defenders of the public morals. They hired a former government agent, S. Glen Young, to head up the fight against the bootleggers. He arranged to have a number of klansmen deputized by a prohibition agent, then led raids on suspected downstate manufacturers and suppliers, shooting up their places and engaging in gun fights with them. Young's career came to an abrupt end when he and three of his men were killed in a shoot-out in a Herrin drugstore.

The Herrin Massacre

While the postwar years were prosperous and rollicking for many Illinoisans, they were not for Illinois coal miners. In southern Illinois a labor dispute that ended in mob madness brought outcries from people all over the country.

When William Lester opened a strip mine near Herrin in September 1921, he hired fifty men, all of whom belonged to the United Mine

Workers. On April 1 of the following year, soft coal miners all over the country went on strike, so the Herrin miners struck, too. Lester, who had gone into debt to buy equipment, met with local union leaders who agreed that he could extract coal while the strike was in progress so long as he did not load or ship it.

Not satisfied with that arrangement, Lester fired the union miners and brought in fifty nonunion men, about half of whom were miners and the other half mine guards. The guards, already hated because of their reputation as strikebreakers, behaved like arrogant bullies. The union miners regarded Lester and his strikebreakers as a threat to all they had gained through unionism in the last twenty-five years. Merchants and bankers in nearby towns sided with their customers, the union miners.

Refusing to listen to warnings that there would be violence if any coal was shipped out, Lester arranged to have sixteen loaded railroad cars leave Herrin on June 16. Retaliation was swift. On June 21 union men ambushed a truck carrying another load of strikebreakers to Herrin. Three strikebreakers were hospitalized. Afterward several hundred angry miners met in the Herrin Cemetery, then marched to the mine.

At 3:30 the mine supervisor called the sheriff to say that the mine was surrounded and that more than five hundred shots had been exchanged. Lester, who had gone to Chicago, was called and agreed to close the mine. A truce was to be arranged, one provision of which was that the strikebreakers would be guaranteed safe conduct out of Herrin.

The next morning the strikebreakers surrendered. A mob of miners in an ugly mood marched them toward Herrin, taunting them and beating them with rifle butts. Then a burly roughneck spoke up and said, "The only way to free the county of strikebreakers is to kill them all off and stop the breed." Someone said that they should not kill anyone on a public road but should take them over to the woods and shoot them. A thirst for vengeance overwhelmed the mob as men who probably would never have done so on their own got caught up in the frenzy and chased and shot twenty of the unarmed prisoners. In some cases they mutilated the bodies. A temporary morgue was set up, and townspeople were allowed to view the bodies and commit further acts of disrespect.

When news of the Herrin massacre hit the front pages of newspapers all across the country, people were frightened and outraged and demanded that something be done. However, a coroner's jury concluded that all the dead had been killed by unknown assailants. After further public outcry, 214 men were indicted, but local juries failed to convict any of them. Williamson County became known as "Bloody Williamson," a title it is still trying to live down.

Illinois Writers of the Twenties

The flashiness of the 1920s was offset by a new generation of thoughtful and serious Illinois writers. Five of the most notable were Theodore Dreiser, Vachel Lindsay, Edgar Lee Masters, Carl Sandburg, and Harriet Monroe.

Although he wrote many of his novels in the 1920s, Dreiser was more in tune with the reformers that preceded the wild years. Having grown up in poverty, he made every effort to expose the social evils of the day. His novel, *An American Tragedy*, was based on a true story Dreiser had read in a newspaper. It follows the career of a poor boy who manages to scramble up the business and social ladder only to end up being tried for the murder of his girl friend. The book created an uproar because people were not used to realistic novels in which writers reported true experiences rather than developing romantic plots with happy endings.

Because he thought poetry should be available to everyone, Lindsay made long walking tours, earning his keep by reciting his work. His audiences loved the strong rhythms of such poems as "General Booth Enters Heaven" and "The Congo." Lindsay was the forerunner of a group of poets who later tied poetry to the beat of jazz and to the emotional appeal of the blues.

As a child, Masters lived with his grandparents on the outskirts of Petersburg, where he intently observed the life of small-town Illinois. Intending to create a novel about the kind of people he knew best, Masters found himself making a poetic experiment instead. The result was the *Spoon River Anthology*, a book of related poems in which people buried in the local cemetery come back to life long enough to tell their sometimes happy, sometimes grim stories.

The most beloved Illinois poet of all, Carl Sandburg, was born of Swedish immigrant parents in Galesburg in 1878. His book, *Chicago Poems*, includes the famous poem in which he called Chicago the "Hog Butcher for the World" and the "City of Big Shoulders." It was followed by *Cornhuskers*, *Smoke and Steel*, and *Good Morning, America*, all written in the 1920s. Sandburg later won the Pulitzer Prize for his six-volume biography of Abraham Lincoln.

Monroe made her literary debut by presenting her "Columbian Ode" at the 1893 world's fair. However, her lasting fame comes not from her poems, but from the magazine she started in 1912, *Poetry: A Magazine*

Carl Sandburg, poet laureate of Illinois, recited his own work as well as the folktales and songs he collected, accompanying himself on the guitar. Courtesy of the Illinois State Historical Library.

of American Verse. Monroe was gifted with the ability to pick out the best of the new poets, even when they wrote in strange and unfamiliar styles. During the 1920s she published nearly every major American poet, including Robert Frost, Amy Lowell, T. S. Eliot, and Ezra Pound.

On the lighter side, Illinois newspapers provided information and entertainment. The Chicago *Tribune* began putting out a voluminous Sunday edition, and other papers followed suit. The *Tribune* was also one of the first papers to begin carrying comic strips, several of which originated in Illinois. Frank Willard, a resident of Anna, created "Moon Mullins." Elzie Segar, the creator of "Popeye," lived in Chester. The popular detective comic strip, "Dick Tracy," was written by Chester

Gould, who lived in Woodstock. Each time one of Dick Tracy's enemies was killed, Gould put up a small grave marker in his backyard. After Gould died, his backyard cemetery was dismantled.

☙

In the 1920s Illinoisans concentrated on enjoying life. They enthusiastically embraced the new, whether it was a hair style, a dance, or a style of music. Cars, planes, and movies were part of the excitement.

Prohibition created more problems than it solved. Bootleggers and vice kings organized gangs, and the level of violence rose. Late in the 1920s Chicagoans began to think that things had gone far enough and elected a reform mayor. Surprisingly, while all this was going on Illinois writers were creating another literary renaissance.

For many Illinoisans the Roaring Twenties were wild and gay. But then the stock market crash, which triggered the Great Depression, brought the reckless years to an abrupt end.

For Further Exploration

Paul Angle. *Bloody Williamson: A Chapter in American Lawlessness*. New York: Alfred A. Knopf, 1952. Reprint. Urbana: University of Illinois Press, 1992

In the 1920s Williamson County, in the heart of the southern Illinois coal-mining district, was the scene of several violent episodes in the state's history. The author gives an impartial account of the Herrin massacre, making clear how people on opposing sides felt and why. He also covers Glen Young's exploits and the activities of a band of outlaws known as the Birger Gang.

Studs Terkel. *Giants of Jazz*. New York: Thomas Crowell, 1957.

Studs Terkel first heard the sounds of jazz in the Chicago clubs where black musicians from New Orleans played. His short biographical sketches show how they set the course of American popular music for decades to come.

22

The Lean Years

Black Thursday and Its Aftermath

The New York Stock Exchange was a lively place during the prosperous 1920s. Speculators made fortunes by buying stocks, holding them until their value had skyrocketed, and then quickly selling them. Some bought large blocks of stock on credit, paying the balance out of the profits they made when they sold them. For many, buying and selling stocks was both a business and an exhilarating game.

The feverish activity on the stock market seemed to suggest a booming national economy. Then, suddenly, the good days were over. For reasons that have still not been fully explained, the stock market crashed. On Thursday, October 24, 1929, the worst day in stock market history, 16.4 million shares were sold at a loss of $32 billion. Stock prices tumbled as investors rushed to sell their holdings before they lost everything. Soon there were more sellers than buyers, and the market was flooded with stocks that were worth only a small fraction of their previous value. By the end of the year, investors had lost over $40 billion, and a decade of business failures, unemployment, and poverty began.

The downward spiral of the Great Depression of the 1930s followed the pattern of the financial panics of the late 1800s, but it was so much more intensive that it made all previous economic crises seem insignificant. Businesses could no longer depend on funds from investors, so factory owners had to curtail plans for building new factories, updating machinery, and experimenting with new products. When they found that cutting back on growth was not enough to keep them solvent, they began producing less and laying off workers. Because the unemployed had no money to buy the manufactured goods, large inventories accumulated—which only triggered another round of cutbacks and layoffs. Distributors and retailers lost so many customers that many had to go out of business. Illinois coal mines closed down one after the other as industrial demands for coal fell. More than half the state's miners were idled, and those who remained on the payrolls worked an average of only six months out of the year.

Illinois farmers were in trouble even before the depression began. After the war they had continued to grow record crops, but this created surpluses that, in turn, brought lower prices. Some farmers could not sell their crops at all. With factories, farmers, and mine owners all in trouble, railroad operators found themselves taking in only about half their normal freight revenues. When the number of people who could afford to ride trains declined, passenger revenues fell off, too. The Illinois Central had to fire half of its 60,000 employees.

People began using their savings for daily expenses and withdrew their money from banks at an alarming rate. Banks that could not come up with enough cash to cover the demands of their depositors tried limiting how much an individual could withdraw at one time or simply locked their doors, hoping the panic would subside and they would be able to reopen later. Many were never able to.

"Brother, Can You Spare a Dime?"

These words, from a popular song of the time, echoed the desperation of the common people when the Depression hit bottom in 1932. One-fourth of all factory workers in Illinois were out of work. Others had had to accept reductions in wages or in the number of hours they worked. Rumors that a job was going to be available in a factory or store brought hundreds of applicants. Lawyers were willing to work as clerks or salespersons, and small business owners became door-to-door salesmen. People even sold apples or balloons on street corners. Some were reduced to begging.

Few families had enough savings to carry them for more than six months or a year. Some were in debt because during the prosperous years they had gotten into the habit of buying items on credit. Many had to sell their cars, then, sadly, their homes. Because so many houses were for sale, the prices fell far below what the houses were worth, and people had to accept whatever they could get.

Families that lost their homes or could not pay their rent had to look for other places to live. Sometimes relatives or friends took them in or loaned them enough money to move into a boardinghouse or small apartment. Soon, though, few people had anything left to lend. Homeless people took shelter under viaducts or bridges or made flimsy cabins out of cardboard cartons, pieces of linoleum or sheet metal, scraps of lumber—anything they could find.

Even in a state as agriculturally rich as Illinois, people went hungry. Neighborhood grocery store owners allowed old customers to buy food on credit until they found they could no longer afford to replenish their shelves. Many had to close down. Unemployed men, then whole families, began lining up at soup kitchens organized by charitable organizations and later by government agencies.

Poor families living in already depressed southern Illinois counties became even poorer during the 1930s. Farmers could not sell their crops, and some lost their land when they could not make payments on it. They did whatever they could to conserve the little money they had: burned less coal than usual, used electricity as infrequently as possible, stopped eating at their favorite restaurants, and canceled magazine and newspaper subscriptions. Young people headed to the cities, hoping the situation would be better there.

As the Great Depression worsened, men who had always provided for their families felt a deep sense of guilt, humiliation, and failure. Many never fully recovered their self-confidence. Some went on the road as hobos rather than face their hungry families. Some even took their own lives. Rich people who had lost fortunes were shattered by the experience and found it difficult to adjust to a life of uncertainty and want. By 1932 the Great Depression had severely affected the lives of millions of Americans, and no relief was in sight.

Bailing out the Sinking Ship

Many voters had voted Republican in the 1928 election because they believed the Republicans were responsible for the prosperity they were enjoying. Herbert Hoover won the presidency by a landslide. Illinoisans chose Republican Louis Lincoln Emmerson as their new governor.

Len Small, who had served as governor from 1921 to 1929, had revived the spoils system, firing government employees to give their jobs to his cronies. Governor Emmerson brought back some competent officials Small had fired and chose reputable people for new positions. He also saw to it that the last 2,000 miles of the hard-road system were completed. Unfortunately, Emmerson was totally unprepared to deal with a catastrophic depression, as were most other governors.

The Search for Solutions

In 1930 Emmerson set up the Governor's Commission on Unemployment and Relief and made its members responsible for coordinating the efforts of private charities. However, the number of unemployed was so great that private funds were soon exhausted.

At Emmerson's suggestion, the General Assembly passed a sales tax and at the same time reduced property taxes. Like many other Republicans, Emmerson opposed giving welfare payments to needy people, favoring instead state construction projects that would provide jobs and give people wages rather than handouts. However, the state could not finance enough projects to provide work for all the unemployed.

In 1932 the General Assembly created a seven-member Illinois Emergency Relief Commission with an appropriation of $20 million to be used during the next year. The money was gone in six months. The governor asked state employees to give up one day's pay a month during the worst two years of the Depression, which many did. Despite such noble efforts, the number of desperate Illinoisans kept rising. Other states faced similar crises. No state could bail itself out because each state's economy was intricately linked with the economy of the whole nation.

President Hoover, a brilliant mining engineer who had directed important projects all over the world, had shown himself to be an able administrator. During World War I President Wilson had asked him to take charge of the nation's food supply. After the war, Hoover headed up relief efforts that saved the lives of millions of Europeans. He would seem to have been the perfect man for the job of Depression president, but his organizational skills conflicted with his political beliefs.

Like Governor Emmerson, Hoover did not approve of giving people money without requiring them to work for it, not even as an emergency measure. He was willing to have the federal government back large public works projects, and he created the Reconstruction Finance Corporation to help farms, banks, and businesses avoid bankruptcy. But the nation's economy remained paralyzed, and no one seemed to know what to do next. People began blaming Hoover and the Republicans. The hastily constructed shantytowns that fringed most cities became known as "Hoovervilles." Hobo camps were known as "Hoover Hotels." In the 1932 election voters looked to the Democrats for help, electing Franklin Delano Roosevelt president. Illinois voters chose Democrat Henry Horner to be their next governor.

FDR and His Critics

Although Roosevelt came from a wealthy family, he did not hesitate to blame rich financiers and businessmen for the Depression. He said they had taken excessive profits and wrecked the stock market by wild speculation. Claiming that previous Republican administrations had usually sided with big business, Roosevelt promised the people a New Deal. During his administration, he said, the needs of the working class would come first.

In his first inaugural address, Roosevelt told Americans that they had nothing to fear but fear itself and followed these bold words with bold actions. He gave all the banks a holiday, closing them down to stop runs on banks by depositors trying to withdraw their savings. When the holiday was over, only banks that were in fairly good shape were allowed to reopen.

Many people were opposed to giving money to the poor without requiring anything in return, but Roosevelt saw the dole, as it was called, as the fastest and most efficient way to get relief to those most in need of it. He pumped hundreds of millions of dollars into the economy to help people buy food and clothing and pay their rent. With more money in the hands of consumers, the demand for goods and services slowly began to rise.

Roosevelt also authorized the formation of new programs designed to put people back to work. The Civilian Conservation Corps (CCC) sent young men who could not find jobs to work camps all over the country. Being part of the CCC was a little like being in the army except that the troops planted trees and worked on conservation projects rather than training for combat. The Works Progress Administration (WPA) put people to work building roads, bridges, facilities in state parks, sewer systems, sidewalks, schools, playgrounds, and airports. It also sponsored various educational and art-related projects.

New laws creating the Securities and Exchange Commission and the Social Security Administration were passed in 1934 and 1935. The Securities and Exchange Commission was charged with the task of overseeing the trading of stocks and bonds and protecting investors against stock market manipulation and fraud. The Social Security Act provided income for retired people and for families whose wage earners had died. That basic social security legislation has been expanded more than ten times and now includes disability payments, health insurance for retired people, welfare funds for mothers and children, and other special benefits.

Some businessmen resented that Roosevelt blamed them for the Depression and were unhappy about the steps he took to regulate the stock market. They also disliked his pro-union stand. Other critics opposed the rapid, sprawling growth of the federal government with its new commissions and agencies. They were concerned about the huge debt the federal government was taking on to fund New Deal programs. Some thought the dole was breaking down the traditional work ethic

During the Great Depression government agencies put some people back to work. Here a WPA street crew repairs a street in Aurora. Courtesy of the Illinois State Historical Library.

and creating a permanent class of dependent poor. Still others complained that WPA jobs were busy-work rather than useful labor. Nevertheless, Roosevelt's programs gave new hope to people in the darkest days of the Depression and created new confidence in the American economic system.

Governor Horner's Administration

Because he was almost seventy years old and had suffered a slight stroke while in office, Governor Emmerson chose not to run again in 1932. Much to his dismay, his party nominated Len Small, the governor who had preceded him and been involved in political corruption. Emmerson therefore threw his support to the Democratic candidate, Henry Horner. Horner won the election and became the first Jewish governor of Illinois.

When Governor Horner took office, federal officials told him that unless Illinois took more responsibility for its own recovery, federal relief would stop. Horner therefore urged the General Assembly to raise the sales tax, an unpopular step. The members finally agreed to do so and appropriated another $30 million for state relief funds, making Illinois eligible to continue participating in federal relief programs. Over 100,000 Illinois men joined the CCC, and more than 1 million were employed on WPA projects. Small though they were by today's standards, the wages these workers received kept many families together.

An aggressive leader and a strong Roosevelt supporter, Governor Horner literally worked himself to death before finishing his second term. He was the second Illinois governor to die while in office.

Other Events in the 1930s

The Great Depression dominated the news during the 1930s, but other developments also captured the public interest in Illinois. Chicago's mayoral election of 1931 was one such event.

Anton Cermak

Chicagoans finally had enough of "Big Bill" Thompson, the mayor who served throughout the 1920s and had cooperated with the crime syndicates. However, civic leaders knew Thompson was well entrenched and would be hard to beat, even though his political machine was weaker than it had been earlier in the decade. They finally settled on Anton Cermak as the candidate most likely to unseat Thompson.

Cermak had the backing of many of Chicago's ethnic groups. He had long been an outspoken critic of prohibition and could count on the votes of the rising number of people who opposed it. Cermak won the mayor's seat easily, becoming the first person of Czech descent to be elected to a major public office in the United States. He then proceeded to build a political machine of his own, much to the chagrin of the reformers who had helped him win.

In 1932 Cermak strongly opposed the nomination of Roosevelt. But after Roosevelt was elected, Cermak was anxious to make amends. In 1933, when he heard that Roosevelt was going to Miami, Florida, for a speaking engagement, Cermak went, too. On February 13 he was killed by an assassin's bullet that some historians think was meant for Roosevelt. Others think that a disgruntled Chicago gangster may have hired the gunman to kill Cermak.

"A Century of Progress"

In 1933 Chicago hosted another successful world's fair. Sleek modern buildings housed exhibits showing the social, scientific, and technological progress of the last hundred years. The Thomas A. Edison Memorial Building honored America's great inventor by exhibiting items from his laboratories as well as many of his inventions. The Transportation Building was filled with vehicles ranging from those used by the pioneers of the 1830s to the cars, trucks, trains, and airplanes being used

The Travel and Transportation Building, an example of the ultramodern architecture of the 1933 "A Century of Progress" Exhibition. University of Illinois at Chicago, University Library, A Century of Progress Records.

in the 1930s. The Hollywood Sound Stage gave many people their first chance to see a movie being shot. *The World a Million Years Ago* featured animated models of prehistoric animals and people. The building in which it was housed had a revolving floor that carried visitors from exhibit to exhibit.

The City of New York, a polar ship used by Admiral Richard Byrd on an expedition to the South Pole, floated in a lagoon. Replicas of Fort Dearborn and of several buildings that had been important in Lincoln's life drew many visitors. And almost everyone stopped at the 200-foot high outdoor thermometer, which had neon tubes electrically activated by a thermostat in the base instead of a mercury column.

The Midway offered rides on the Flying Turns, the Lindy Loop, and in hot-air balloons. The Sky Ride, whose twin towers were higher than any building in Chicago at that time, had cables strung between them on which "rocket" cars ran. Passengers saw the fairgrounds from more than 200 feet above the ground. From the enclosed observation platforms at the tops of the towers they could view parts of four states: Illinois, Indiana, Wisconsin, and Michigan.

The "Century of Progress" lasted two years and attracted more than

Skyride "rocket" cars gave visitors a view from 200 feet above the fairgrounds. University of Illinois at Chicago, University Library, A Century of Progress Records.

39 million visitors. President Roosevelt praised its organizers for emphasizing scientific and social progress at a time when the people of the nation needed to regain hope and self-confidence.

The Twenty-first Amendment

The Prohibition Amendment had proved extremely difficult to enforce and had led to so much corruption and crime that people felt the nation would be better off without it. In 1933 the Twenty-First Amendment to the Constitution repealed prohibition. However, individual states, counties, and cities had the option of remaining "dry" if they wanted to. Many Illinoisans did not want their communities to be dry but thought that the sale of liquor should be regulated by the government. In 1934 the General Assembly passed a law dividing the responsibility for controlling the sale of alcoholic beverages between state and local officials.

❦

The stock market crash brought long-term suffering to millions of Illinoisans in both rural and urban areas. So many people lost their jobs that there were not enough state funds to keep them going until the economy righted itself. Under Franklin Delano Roosevelt the federal government created programs to help the unemployed.

The "Century of Progress" Exhibition, held in Chicago in 1933, lifted people's spirits by making them see all that had been accomplished and giving them a glimpse of a better future. That same year, the Twenty-First Amendment repealed prohibition.

As the Depression decade neared its end, a new menace hovered over the world. A German soldier turned politician had guided his country back to prosperity by building a huge war machine. By the late 1930s he was moving to take over "living space" beyond Germany's borders.

For Further Exploration

Robert Hastings. *A Nickel's Worth of Skim Milk: A Boy's View of the Great Depression.* Carbondale: Southern Illinois University (University Graphics and Publications), 1972.

Warmth and humor lighten this short memoir of the Great Depression in the hard-hit farming and mining counties of southern Illinois.

Studs Terkel. *Hard Times: An Oral History of the Great Depression.* New York: Random House, 1970.

Chicago writer Studs Terkel interviewed people who lived through the Great Depression and collected their memories into a book that documents their sufferings as well as their courage, ingenuity, and perseverance.

23

A World Spinning out of Control

The United States Enters World War II

Another great conflict broke out in Europe when Adolf Hitler, the dictator of Germany, invaded Austria, Czechoslovakia, and Poland in the late 1930s. England and France joined forces to stop him, but they were hard-pressed to hold their own against the crack fighting troops that the Germans had developed. France soon surrendered, and English troops were forced to retreat to their island nation. Winston Churchill, the prime minister of England, tried to persuade President Franklin D. Roosevelt to enter the war and help save the free nations of Europe. However, Roosevelt knew that many Americans did not want to fight another war. He proposed instead that America become the "arsenal of democracy," supplying war materials rather than troops.

Meanwhile, Japan had also come under the control of aggressive military leaders. Intending to build a great empire, the Japanese invaded China, Southeast Asia, and islands in the South Pacific. Then Japan and Germany signed an agreement to aid and support each other for ten years, long enough for each to complete its military objectives.

The Japanese were determined to drive all Western powers out of the Pacific, keeping "Asia for Asians." Freedom of the seas was again at issue. While diplomats were working on a compromise with Japan that would make it possible for American merchant ships to travel safely in the Pacific, the Japanese made a devastating surprise attack on the American naval base at Pearl Harbor. On December 7, 1941, Japanese submarines and aircraft destroyed a major portion of the American Navy's Pacific Fleet and many airplanes on nearby airfields.

The next day President Roosevelt went before Congress and asked for a declaration of war against Japan, calling December 7, 1941, "a date which will live in infamy." Congress did as he requested. Honoring its treaty with Japan, Germany then declared war on the United States. Once again our country was caught up in a world-wide conflagration of proportions few could even imagine.

Military Preparations in Illinois

War preparations began on a rather curious note in Illinois. Shortly after taking office in January 1941, Governor Dwight Herbert Green called the General Assembly into special session. One of the members proposed that General Santa Anna's wooden leg be returned to Mexico! (The leg had been placed in the Illinois State Museum at the close of the Mexican War almost a century before.) Backers of the resolution must have hoped that such a goodwill gesture would improve the nation's relationship with Mexico, a neighbor whose cooperation might be needed in the coming crisis. This bizarre suggestion took up only a small part of the special session. The rest was devoted to the more practical issues of how to organize and finance the war effort in Illinois.

Recruitment and Training

After Pearl Harbor, Illinois quickly set up 361 local draft boards to handle the paperwork involved in recruitment. Of the 16 million Americans who served in the armed forces in World War II, almost 958,000 men and 14,000 women were from Illinois, and more than 24,000 of these were killed. Many more were wounded.

In previous wars many recruits received training in their home state, and their fighting units were identified with that state. This changed in World War II. Soldiers from many different states and cultures mixed in the training camps and fighting units. However, black soldiers were segregated from white and had little chance to work their way up in rank. Illinois made an attempt to remedy at least part of this problem by building an all-black training center, Camp Robert Smalls, on the Great Lakes Naval Air Base in Chicago. Named for a former slave and hero of the Civil War, Camp Smalls gave trainees opportunities to learn industrial arts that would help them both in the armed forces and when they returned home. And except for Tuskegee Institute in Alabama, Harlem Airport in Oaklawn, Illinois, was the only place a black man could earn his wings. The armed forces were not officially desegregated until 1948, three years after the war ended.

Many women joined the WACs (Women's Army Corps) or the WAFS (Women's Auxilliary Ferrying Squadron), both of which were created in 1942. The Marine Corps' Women's Reserve and the Navy's WAVES (Women Accepted for Volunteer Emergency Service) dated back to World War I and were now reactivated. No women were trained for or engaged in combat. Instead, they served as administrators, nurses, instructors, office workers, photographers, electronics and aviation specialists, transportation officers, and in many other positions.

Competent personnel were desperately needed, so crash training programs were quickly set up. The University of Illinois developed the largest officer training program in the country except for the military academies. World War I hero General John Pershing subsequently dubbed the university "the West Point of the West." Colleges and universities throughout the state devised tests for measuring aptitudes, worked on literacy programs so more men would be eligible for military service, and wrote pamphlets and textbooks to train people in specific fields. They contracted with the federal government to provide instructors and classroom space as well as access to laboratories and research facilities for the military and for industry.

Military Facilities

Built in 1886, Fort Sheridan was intended to supply rapid military protection in times of labor unrest. The only time it was used for that purpose was during the Pullman strike. When World War II broke out, new training facilities ranging from a bakers' school to a motor transport repair school were added to Fort Sheridan. Both men and women trained there, and later it served as a base camp for 15,000 prisoners of war.

Camp Grant, near Rockford, had the capacity to train 7,000 paramedics at a time. Camp Ellis in the Spoon River Valley, the newest and largest in the state, trained engineering and medical personnel. Chanute Field at Rantoul became one of the nation's top aeronautics training centers while Scott Field near Belleville became the chief air force communications school. One class of recruits at Scott and Chanute already knew all about flying, namely, the pigeons being trained to carry messages in combat zones. In spite of the fact that it was 1,000 miles from an ocean, the Great Lakes Naval Training Base at Chicago prepared over 1 million sailors for active duty—nearly one-third of all U.S. Navy personnel.

Radio operators and mechanics in training were stationed in the Stevens and Congress hotels in Chicago, a unique approach to the space

Workers at the Excelsior Motor Manufacturing and Supply Company in Chicago making airplane motors and parts during World War II. Courtesy of the Illinois State Historical Library.

problem. The federal government also leased administrative office space in several Chicago skyscrapers.

War Industries

As early as 1938 Illinois factories began making military equipment for the British and French. Production increased greatly after the United States entered the war. Seneca, on the Illinois River, became known as the "Prairie Shipyard" because landing craft were manufactured there and floated down the Illinois and Mississippi rivers to salt water. The Pullman Company built tanks and aircraft parts while International Harvester specialized in gun carriages. Employees of the biggest factory in the world, the Dodge Plant in Chicago, assembled engines for B-29 Superfortresses. C-54 Skymaster transport planes, popularly known as "Flying Boxcars," were also made in Illinois.

The old arsenal at Rock Island retooled to make modern weapons. Ordnance plants in Moline, Elwood/Kankakee, Savanna, and Crab Orchard worked around the clock to supply much of the firepower for

Top-secret atomic experiments took place at Stagg Field on the University of Chicago campus. Argonne National Laboratory.

allied bombers, battleships, long guns, and rifles. The Elgin Watch Company made bomb fuses, the Western Electric Company in Cicero worked on radar units, and other Illinois companies entered the rapidly growing field of electronics.

As in previous wars, workers were in short supply. Retired people went back to work, and many women took industrial jobs—260,000 in the Chicago area alone. Teenagers were allowed to quit school to work in war factories. More than 100,000 blacks came to the Chicago area to work in the war plants.

The Terrible Secret

For some time physicists had believed that atoms could be split, releasing energy in a powerful, self-sustaining chain reaction. A bomb based on such a reaction would be the most deadly weapon in any arsenal on earth. The Allies suspected that German physicists had either split atoms or were close to being able to do so. The thought that Germany might be the first to make an atomic bomb was a chilling one. The U.S. government quickly, and with the utmost secrecy, launched its own atomic research program.

People passing by the west grandstands of Stagg Field on the University of Chicago campus had no idea that they were near a top-secret and vitally important laboratory under the general direction of the University of Chicago's Nobel Prize–winning physicist, Arthur Compton. There Enrico Fermi, the brilliant Italian-born physicist, was busy testing atomic theory. Using bricks of graphite, slugs of uranium, and rods of cadmium, he and his assistants succeeded in splitting atoms and releasing nuclear energy.

After the Chicago experiments had been completed, plants for purifying uranium and making plutonium were built at Oak Ridge, Tennessee, and Hanford, Washington. Scientists sponsored by the University of Chicago worked at Oak Ridge and at testing grounds in New Mexico. The Stagg Field reactor was moved to the Argonne National Laboratory twenty-five miles southwest of Chicago, where research on atomic energy continued.

Illinois Volunteers

Millions of Illinoisans volunteered to help in the war effort. They signed up at special volunteer placement offices where their interests and abilities were recorded so they could be assigned to suitable tasks. There was plenty of work to go around!

Civil Defense

In the early years of the war, one major concern was the safety of American towns and cities. The Illinois State Council of Defense worked with two hundred local councils to organize civil defense teams. Volunteer spotters watched for enemy aircraft, air raid wardens supervised air raid drills, and other men and women served as auxiliary police and firemen, medical assistants, and on bomb demolition squads.

In the climate of apprehension created by Pearl Harbor, officials feared that Japanese-Americans living near the West Coast might serve as spies and saboteurs or cooperate with the Japanese in an invasion of the United States. Congress therefore decided to intern them for the duration of the war. Japanese-Americans were deeply shocked to find that their U.S. citizenship would not protect them. They had to sell their homes and businesses for a fraction of their actual value, pack as many of their belongings as they could, and report to special camps located far away from their homes and from population centers. In some cases, they were allowed to go to inland cities where sponsors were willing to take them in. Twenty thousand Japanese-Americans came to

Chicago under such arrangements. When the war was over, most had made new lives for themselves and stayed on.

War Bonds

Volunteers went from house to house urging people to buy war bonds. Movie stars including James Cagney, Victor Mature, Fred Astaire, Judy Garland, and Harpo Marx performed and spoke at bond rallies in Chicago and other Illinois cities. Organizations ranging from the Ringling Brothers and Barnum & Bailey Circus to the Chicago Symphony Orchestra gave benefit performances.

Illinoisans responded well. In the eight major war bond drives, Illinois exceeded its quotas by many percentage points. The largest single investment by an individual in Illinois, and perhaps in the United States, was that of Marshall Field III, heir to the Field department store fortune. He put up more than $10 million.

Victory Gardens

When crops raised on Illinois farms began going directly to the government, city dwellers were left without a reliable source of fresh vegetables. Even canned vegetables were hard to obtain because tin had to be saved for military use. The Victory Garden program encouraged people to start their own vegetable gardens. By 1943 more than 1.1 million Illinoisans were planting victory gardens each spring. They used whatever space they could find: their yards, empty lots, even containers set out on balconies and rooftops. In some cases city property was made available to people. Government agencies and private horticultural societies furnished helpful pamphlets. When green-thumbed enthusiasts began growing more vegetables than they could use, they set up community canning centers. Every county in Illinois eventually had one. Some victory gardeners also grew flowers to take to nearby army hospitals.

War-Time Recycling

In the early 1940s school playgrounds often looked like junk yards. Old lamps, car fenders, broken tools, pots and pans, and other metal objects lay where they had been piled by schoolchildren who collected scrap metal. Some communities turned Halloween into a scrap metal hunt. Businessmen lent trucks, and union members working on their own time transported odd assortments of junk to processing centers. The modest prices the federal government paid for scrap metal helped Illinois children raise part of the $60,000 needed to buy one of the original copies of Lincoln's Gettysburg Address for the state archives in Springfield.

Some high school students gave up their beloved jalopies, calling them "Hitler's Coffins." Paraphrasing a popular song, some scribbled on their car doors: "Praise the Lord, I'll soon be ammunition." Students at Chicago's Hirsch High School dismantled an old factory, thereby securing tons of scrap metal. People paid in aluminum items to attend street dances. Peoria constructed a "Mount Aluminum."

Women saved bacon grease, lard, and other fats and took them to their neighborhood meat markets. Butchers routed the fats to military processing plants where they were used in the making of explosives.

The USO and the Red Cross

Young soldiers and sailors on leave often felt lost and lonely in unfamiliar cities. The YMCA, YWCA, Salvation Army, Travelers Aid Society, National Jewish Welfare Board, and the National Catholic Community Service combined their efforts to create the United Service Organizations or USO.

Illinois had ninety USO centers in forty-two towns and cities. Housed in railroad stations, hotels, and community centers, USO canteens provided simple meals and sometimes overnight accommodations for soldiers on leave. Many had dance floors, game rooms, libraries, writing rooms, and craft shops. In downstate towns not large enough to support a USO, local women set up canteens in train stations and maintained a steady flow of coffee, sandwiches, pies, doughnuts, and cookies for soldiers passing through.

The eighty-eight Illinois chapters of the American Red Cross concentrated on the needs of soldiers who were on active duty, in transit, or convalescing. They helped the families of men in service, conducted blood drives, and recruited 3,598 nurses for the army. The Red Cross also trained nurse's aides to work in civilian hospitals whose staffs had been depleted.

Victory!

French, British, Russian, and American troops converged on Berlin early in 1945. Hitler committed suicide in the bunker where he had been hiding, and the remaining German generals had no alternative but to surrender. They did so on May 7, 1945. Allied efforts were then concentrated on the eastern theater of the war.

The Japanese had been forced to retreat from China, Southeast Asia, Burma, and the South Pacific but still refused to surrender, even after Allied planes began bombing their homeland. President Roosevelt died in April 1945, leaving the new president, Harry S Truman, with an agonizing decision: should the United States use the atomic bomb against Japan? If it did, many innocent civilians would die. But if the bomb were not used, Japan would have to be invaded and conquered town by town, with the loss of thousands of American and Japanese lives. President Truman's decision to use the bomb is still being debated, but it did bring the war to a quick end. The devastation brought about by the the atomic bombing of Hiroshima and Nagasaki was so terrible that the Japanese surrendered on September 2, 1945.

The news that the war was over brought wild celebrations all across the United States. People sang and danced in the streets, rode on fire engines, swam in public fountains and swimming pools with and without their clothes, set off fireworks, buzzed their towns in small planes, and continued partying throughout the night. In the weeks and months that followed, the euphoria died down, and people were again faced with the task of making the transition to peace-time living.

⟡

When the United States entered World War II, Illinois factories once again converted to military production, supplying military vehicles and parts, airplanes, munitions, clothing, guns, and other war goods.

Old military installations were modernized, and new training facilities were built. The Great Lakes Naval Air Station became one of the largest Navy training centers in the nation, while Chanute and Scott fields prepared pilots and aeronautical technicians. Large numbers of Army medics also got their training in Illinois.

Civilians raised funds, bought bonds, planted victory gardens, collected reusable materials, and served as air raid wardens and emergency personnel. They also ran service centers for the men and women in uniform and participated in Red Cross activities.

Many of the federal government's Depression programs were phased out during the war because they were no longer needed. In fact, there were more jobs than there were people to handle them. As we will see, the new prosperity continued into the postwar years as factories shifted back to the production of consumer goods.

For Further Exploration

Mary Watters. *Illinois in the Second World War*. Vol. 1, *Operation Home Front*. Vol. 2, *The Production Front*. Springfield: State of Illinois, Illinois State Historical Society, 1951.

Packed with facts and figures not easily available elsewhere, these volumes show how the war affected the people and communities of Illinois. You may not want to read both volumes cover to cover, but they provide an excellent research tool and good browsing.

24

Peace and Progress

"Happy Days Are Here Again"

Finding employment was not a problem for most veterans. Many returned to the jobs they had held before the war. Others had acquired work skills in the Army and were able to qualify for good jobs when they came home. More jobs became available when women who had worked in war plants left the work force and returned to their lives as homemakers.

Postwar Industries

Old industries made a comeback as people eagerly bought manufactured items they had been unable to obtain during the war. New industries thrived, too. Illinois became a leading producer of radios, television sets, and other electronic devices.

Illinois kept pace with advances in science during this period and even led in several areas. The first nuclear reactor designed to produce electricity was built at the Argonne National Laboratory. In 1951 a brilliant electrical engineer named John Bardeen came to the University of Illinois, where he spent the next forty years teaching and pursuing his scientific interests. While working for Bell Laboratories, he and two colleagues, Walter Brattain and William Shockley, ushered in the "information age" by developing the transistor. Later Professor Bardeen received two Nobel prizes, one for his role as co-inventor of the transistor and another for his work on superconductivity.

Although Illinois lost its aircraft industry to other competitors, Chicago retained its importance as an air transportation center. In 1946 the federal government declared the airport adjacent to the plant where

C-54 Skymaster transport planes had been assembled surplus property and gave it to the city. It was renamed for a Navy pilot and hero of aerial combat in the Pacific, Edward "Butch" O'Hare. Repeatedly expanded by federal and state grants, O'Hare International Airport is now one of the busiest air terminals in the world. In fact, it is so overcrowded that an additional airport is being planned for the Chicago area.

Illinois Agriculture after the War

Wartime research ushered in the age of hybrid seeds, chemical fertilizers, weed killers, insecticides, and complex machinery capable of doing the work of many farmhands. Production increased, but so did farmers' costs. It took more acreage to grow enough to pay for the expensive new chemicals and equipment. To stay competitive some farmers bought more land, but those who could not afford to went out of business. As a result, the number of small farms decreased, and the remaining farms increased in size.

On the whole, though, the postwar years were good years for Illinois agriculture. Of all the counties in the nation, McLean County took first place in corn production, and Henry County produced the most hogs. Imported from Manchuria between the two world wars, soybeans had become an important source of cooking oils when tropical oils became unavailable during the war. Growing conditions in Illinois were ideal for this new crop, and Decatur became the soybean capital of the nation. Chicken, dairy products, fruits, and vegetables accounted for another large segment of the state's economy.

The Postwar Spending Spree

Many civilians had built up savings accounts during the war because there had been so few consumer goods on which to spend their money. After the war, wages were higher than they had ever been, due partly to the activity of labor unions and partly to the demand for consumer goods. With more money to spend, Illinoisans, like people all over the country, went on a long spending spree.

Between 1945 and the early 1950s, the ownership of automobiles doubled in Illinois. Shoes had been rationed during the war, and women's stockings had been a luxury. Now they were again on the shelves of stores, along with mountains of other clothes, including some made of a new fabric called nylon. People no longer had to line up to buy canned goods, sugar, meat, and other foods. Instead they lined up to buy automatic washers, dryers, and television sets. But the primary goal of many young couples was to buy a new home in the suburbs. Many were able to do so.

Illinois Politics after the War

Illinois's wartime governor, Dwight Herbert Green, was reelected and served until 1949. Adlai Stevenson, running as a reform candidate, succeeded him. Stevenson came from a family of politicians; his grandfather had been vice-president of the United States under Grover Cleveland.

Stevenson instituted a new merit system of hiring and promotion. Under his direction law enforcement agencies broke up organized crime rings in Rock Island, Peoria, Joliet, Decatur, Springfield, and East St. Louis. Stevenson also was able to move ahead on public health, education, welfare, and highway construction projects because the state treasury still had surplus funds accumulated during the war years.

As had many of his predecessors, Stevenson insisted that Illinois needed a new constitution, but the General Assembly refused to take action. Stevenson then backed the Gateway Amendment, a measure designed to make amending the constitution less complicated. It stipulated that ratification of an amendment required the approval of two-thirds of those who voted on the amendment itself, rather than two-thirds of all those who voted in that particular election, as had been the case before. The Gateway Amendment of 1950 gave proposed amendments a better chance of passing, but changing one small part of the constitution at a time was still a piecemeal and unsatisfactory way of updating it.

During Stevenson's administration, the second worst mine disaster in the state's history took place at the New Orient Coal Mine #2 near West Frankfort. Sparks from electrical equipment touched off a pocket of methane gas, killing 119 miners. Only four years before, 111 men had lost their lives in a Centralia mine. Once again, disaster brought legislative action. The Coal Mine Safety Act of 1952 updated mine safety laws and provided for more stringent inspections.

In 1952 Stevenson was persuaded to become the Democratic candidate for president. His Republican opponent, General Dwight D. Eisenhower, was a popular war hero who had commanded the Allied forces in Europe during World War II. Stevenson lost to Eisenhower in 1952 and again in 1956. In 1960 Stevenson supporters tried once again to obtain the Democratic party's nomination for him, but delegates to the convention chose John F. Kennedy instead. When Kennedy became president, he appointed Stevenson U.S. ambassador to the United Nations. It was a position in which Stevenson had ample opportunity to use his wide knowledge of foreign affairs and his diplomatic skills. He served in that office until his sudden death from a heart attack in 1965.

Postwar Architecture

The postwar boom brought about a new period of growth and innovation in architecture and community development. The Chicago skyline changed again. With property at a premium, new office buildings and apartments began to tower over the existing skyscrapers.

Ludwig Mies van der Rohe and Urban Architecture

The German architect, Ludwig Mies van der Rohe, had developed a straightforward, unadorned style of design that contrasted sharply with the highly ornamented and monumental buildings of many European cities. In 1930 he was appointed director of one of the most influential schools of modern design, Germany's Bauhaus. However, Hitler did not approve of modern art and architecture, so he closed the Bauhaus. Ludwig Mies found the political and cultural situation in Germany so restrictive that he could not function freely as an artist. He came to Chicago in 1938.

Mies served as chairman of the architecture department at the Illinois Institute of Technology and in 1940 laid out a master plan for the development of the campus. It featured a grouping of low-slung, very plain, steel-framed buildings, elegant in their simplicity. During the twenty years he spent at the institute, Mies designed several buildings for downtown Chicago. The Lake Shore apartments, twin towers on the lakefront, startled people with their clean, uncluttered design. They had absolutely no ornamentation. The steel structure covered with glass walls was all that was needed, Mies insisted. His ideas spread quickly, and for several decades he was the leading figure in this austere school of modern architecture.

One of his students, Jacques Brownson, designed Chicago's Civic Center in the 1960s, paying tribute to his mentor's ideas with a steel-frame office building set apart from the surrounding commercial buildings by its scale and simplicity. Pablo Picasso, one of the great artists of this century, donated a striking sculpture for the plaza in front of the center.

After a while, however, clients and the general public grew tired of hard, clean lines and perfectly plain facades. They began to want more dramatic and decorative structures. The new John Hancock Building, the tallest building in Chicago until the Sears Tower was completed in 1970, featured diagonal steel beams crisscrossing its glass sides. Skyscraper design in general became more dynamic and individualistic. When Chicago held a competition for the design of a new public library, the winning entry was a throwback to the more ornate classical style of architecture.

Architects faced another challenge when corporate headquarters began moving to the suburbs. They realized that a skyscraper in the middle of a small, rural community would be altogether out of place and out of scale. When commissioned to design a new administrative center for the John Deere Company in Moline, architect Eero Saarinen designed a low-slung grouping with a reflecting pool that fit perfectly into the rural landscape. Other architects followed his lead, demonstrating that industrial expansion need not detract from the beauty of suburban environments.

Building Suburbia

The history of suburbs does not begin with the end of World War II. In Illinois suburbs became popular when commuter railway service expanded after the Civil War. With a fast and dependable way of getting to and from work, families could live beyond the city limits, an appealing idea to people concerned about crime, disease, and overcrowding.

One of the first suburbs in Illinois, Riverside, became a showpiece known all over the world. In the early 1870s Frederick Law Olmsted, the landscape architect who had laid out the plan for Central Park in New York City and designed the Columbian Exposition fairgrounds, worked with his partner, Calvert Vaux, to develop the plan for Riverside. They used graceful curved streets rather than the usual grid system and set aside almost half of the 1,600 acres for parks and tree-lined roadways.

During the 1920s the automobile brought another surge in suburban growth. But during World War II it was almost impossible to buy a car, and the flow of city dwellers to the suburbs slowed down. The migration picked up after the war when cars, gas, and tires became available once more.

While few of the quickly built postwar subdivisions could match Riverside in grace and beauty, everything in them was new, and new was what people wanted. Suburban houses and yards were generally larger than middle-class homes in the city, and property taxes were lower. Parents with small children as well as older people felt safer in communities where there were fewer traffic hazards and lower crime rates. In the suburbs children could go to new, modern schools, while in many city neighborhoods they would have had to attend older and sometimes poorly maintained schools. People bought suburban houses as rapidly as they could be built.

As the shift to the suburbs continued, people wanted to shop closer to home. This ushered in the age of the shopping mall. Old Orchard Shopping Center in Skokie, built in 1954, showed what a shopping mall could be. The landscape architects who laid out the space worked closely with the architects who designed the buildings to create a grouping of sleek new stores in a beautiful setting of ponds and gardens. They paid special attention to lighting because planners were aware that much shopping would be done at night after commuters had returned home from work.

Before long, the many new shopping malls began to compete strongly with established downtown stores because it was so much more convenient for people to shop near home. Some of the older stores countered by building branches in the new malls. Few malls of that period of fast growth were as architecturally distinctive as that of Old Orchard.

Overhauling the Education System

By the time World War II was over, the Illinois school system needed major attention on all levels. Elementary school districts were inefficient and short of funds, the high school curriculum was undergoing profound changes, and higher education was taking on greater importance as new technology demanded a more highly trained work force.

The Last of the Little Red Schoolhouses

Late in the 1920s laws were passed that extended the school year from six to eight months and required all children to complete elementary school before going to work. Thousands of one-room schools were built in small towns and villages to provide for the educational needs of rural children. By 1942 Illinois had 12,000 school districts, more than any other state. It also had more than 10,000 one-room schools.

At first many of these schools were able to offer students a good education, but as the population shift to the cities continued, the rural families that stayed behind could not continue to support their small schools. Then the war brought about an acute shortage of teachers. The one-room schools were the first to feel the pinch, losing their teachers to city schools that could pay more. More than one-fourth of the rural schools were left with teachers who had no training beyond high school. Books and materials were also scarce.

After the war, many school districts chose to solve their problems through consolidation. By pooling their resources, districts adjacent to each other could afford to build one modern school with several classrooms, buy more books and supplies and better equipment, and offer higher salaries to attract better teachers. They expanded the curriculum by hiring specialists in physical education, art, music, special education, foreign languages, shop, and other areas.

Not everyone was happy about consolidation, however. Some rural parents felt they would have less control over their children's education and were sorry to see the one-room schools, which had also served as community centers, disappear. But the newly consolidated districts were able to offer extracurricular activities, especially sports, which helped maintain a sense of community. Statewide tournaments became a highlight of the school year.

By 1948 the number of school districts in Illinois had been cut in half, and twenty years later there were only six hundred separate districts left in the state. The state shouldered a larger share of the financial burden for the new consolidated schools and made funds available for busing children to them.

A New Emphasis on High Schools

For many Illinoisans, graduating from high school had not been a high priority before World War II. During the Great Depression any chance to earn a little money seemed more important than getting an education. When war plants in the state were permitted to hire people of high school age, many teenagers left school for the factories. However, the war speeded up technological development, familiar occupations became more complicated, and new occupations evolved. Many workers found that they needed more education and a higher level of technological training than before. A high school diploma came to be seen as a passport to a better job.

Vocational education had become part of the secondary curriculum during World War I. Large numbers of riveters, welders, and machinists had to be trained quickly, and high schools were ready-made environments for such training. Another surge in vocational education occurred during World War II, and for the same reason. The idea that the high school curriculum should include practical courses that would prepare graduates for jobs in factories, stores, and offices carried over into peacetime.

The Junior College Movement

After the war more people could afford to send their children to college, and the GI Bill of Rights made it possible for veterans to receive a tuition-free college education. In Illinois, as in other states, campuses were swamped. Educators saw the community college as a way of relieving some of the pressure on the four-year colleges and universities.

Illinois had pioneered in the junior college movement. (Joliet Junior College began in 1901 as an extension of Joliet High School and is the oldest junior college in the nation still in operation.) But Illinoisans were slow to follow up on this early start. In 1940 there were only twelve public junior colleges in the state, most of which were in or near Chicago. After the war, differences of opinion on what the function of junior colleges should be and who should be in charge of them stymied the growth of the movement. In 1965 the General Assembly finally passed the Junior College Act, which established a state junior college board and set up guidelines for funding these institutions. After that the community college movement mushroomed.

Community colleges made higher education more accessible to people who had previously been unable to afford a college education. A student could live at home during the first two years of college, thereby saving the expense of boarding at a more distant institution. Men and women who had families to support and care for could continue their education in a community-based college. Schedules to accommodate those who worked and could not attend classes during the day became common. Today community college students can improve their literacy and occupational skills or prepare to transfer to a four-year institution. Many community colleges also serve as cultural centers, offering theatrical and musical events, art exhibitions, sports events, and public affairs forums.

The Universities Expand

So rapid was the postwar increase in student population that the University of Illinois soon ranked eighth in the nation in the number of full-time students enrolled. In 1965 the new Chicago Circle Campus opened, and within ten years had a student population 60 percent as large of that of the Champaign-Urbana campus.

Originally the state normal schools had been built as teacher-training institutions and could legally graduate only teachers. In 1947, after a long struggle, Southern Illinois State Normal School in Carbondale achieved full university status and became known as Southern Illinois University. The first state teachers' college at Normal became Illinois State University but continued to specialize in teacher training. The normal schools at DeKalb, Macomb, and Charleston became state colleges, then universities. During Governor Otto Kerner's administration, funds were appropriated for the building of Governors State and Sangamon State universities.

Private universities also thrived. The University of Chicago and Northwestern University continued to grow in prestige and attracted top-ranking professors and students. Chicago developed such a concentration of medical facilities that during the postwar decade one out of every five physicians in the United States received all or part of his or her training there. Today, Illinois continues to be a major center for biomedical research.

A New Generation of Illinois Writers

Chicago journalist Studs Terkel's gift for getting people to talk about themselves has formed the basis of some of his best books. In *Working* he recorded interviews with people who discussed their on-the-job experiences, good and bad. *Hard Times* is a collection of interviews with people who lived through the Great Depression. Terkel's lifelong interest in social issues and his empathy with the common people have won him a large audience.

In the late 1920s Ernest Hemingway, a young Illinoisan who had served as a war correspondent in World War I, published two novels about the devastating effects of war on the personal lives of people: *A Farewell to Arms* and *The Sun Also Rises*. A restless person who was always seeking adventure and challenge, Hemingway participated in the Spanish Civil War, about which he wrote *For Whom the Bell Tolls*. Some critics consider it his best novel. Hemingway hunted big game in Africa and in the American West and lived for a time in Cuba, the lush tropical setting for his short novel, *The Old Man and the Sea*. Several of Hemingway's novels were made into movies. In 1954 he won the Nobel Prize for Literature.

John Dos Passos's style was quite different from Hemingway's short, crisp sentences. Dos Passos used popular songs, news items, headlines, and fragments from the lives of many unrelated characters to give his panoramic trilogy, *U.S.A.*, a collagelike texture.

Several socially conscious writers of this period used Chicago's slums as the setting for their novels. The *Studs Lonigan* trilogy by James T. Farrell portrayed life in an Irish Catholic neighborhood on Chicago's south side in the 1930s. When Richard Wright's *Native Son* came out in 1940, it shocked readers who until then had been able to ignore the plight of young blacks growing up in the violence and hopelessness of the ghetto. Nelson Algren's 1949 novel, *Man with the Golden Arm*, gave many readers their first glimpse of the terrifying, dead-end life of a heroin addict. Frank Sinatra starred in the movie of the same name.

A Jewish writer who grew up in Chicago, Saul Bellow, won the Nobel Prize in 1976. Among his best-known novels are *The Adventures of Augie March*, *Henderson the Rain King*, and *Dr. Sammler's Planet*. Bellow's often bewildered main characters are drawn with wry touches of humor.

Gwendolyn Brooks, the first black woman poet to win the Pulitzer Prize. After Carl Sandburg's death, she became poet laureate of Illinois. Courtesy of the Illinois State Historical Library.

Gwendolyn Brooks came to the public's attention in 1945 when her collection of poems, *A Street in Bronzeville*, was published. It was followed by many more poems and several plays with Afro-American themes. Brooks became the first black woman poet to receive the Pulitzer Prize, an honor bestowed on her for her book, *Annie Allen*. For almost half a century Brooks has been writing, teaching, speaking, and reading her poetry to audiences throughout Illinois and other states. When Carl Sandburg, the poet laureate of Illinois, died in 1968, she was chosen to succeed him.

❧

Illinoisans were ready for peace when it came. They were in a hurry to put their disrupted lives back in order. For many, the dream of owning a home came true, and they were able to buy new cars and appliances that had been unavailable during the war.

More changes in architecture took place, and once again Chicago became a showcase of the new. Transportation improvements made it possible for people to live some distance from where they worked, which brought about another shift of population to the suburbs.

After the war more Illinoisans wanted a college education or advanced technical training. Demands on the educational system were so heavy that it had to be renovated. The state's normal schools became full-fledged universities, universities built new facilities and branches, and the community college movement opened up new possibilities for people who had only had limited access to higher education before. The high school curriculum was also revamped, and many small rural school districts consolidated.

The postwar years brought many positive changes, but they were punctuated with unrest and conflict. In the next chapter we will look at some of the problems that kept American society in a state of turmoil.

For Further Exploration

LeRoy Hayman. *American Ambassador to the World: Adlai Stevenson*. New York: Abelard-Schuman, 1966.

Adlai Stevenson's wisdom, character, and engaging sense of humor come through in this biography, which sums up his accomplishments as governor of Illinois and leader of the national Democratic party. That he was so well-informed about foreign affairs and was able to take a nonpartisan approach increased his stature from that of a politician to that of a statesman as he promoted peace and understanding during this era of conflict.

Richard J. Jensen. *Illinois: A Bicentennial History*. New York: W. W. Norton, 1978. In cooperation with the American Association for State and Local History.

Chapter 6, "The Suburban Era," deals with the postwar years of prosperity and the signs of trouble looming ahead, especially for the cities.

25

The Decades of Conflict

The Cold War

Although they had been allies during World War II, the Soviet Union and the United States spent the next four decades in confrontation. Americans were particularly alarmed by the fact that by 1949 the Soviets were capable of manufacturing atomic bombs. The two superpowers never directly attacked each other, but they carried on a cold war characterized by threats and accusations, the closing of borders, and attempts to influence or control smaller nations.

In Illinois, as in other states, municipal governments began educating people about what to do in case of atomic attack. Civic leaders in densely populated urban areas worked out evacuation routes so that people could, if necessary, leave the cities in as safe and efficient a manner as possible. A few worried homeowners even built underground bomb shelters.

The Korean Conflict

Americans' worst fears seemed about to be realized when war broke out in Korea. At the end of World War II, Korea had been partitioned into two zones, North Korea under Soviet control, and South Korea under the control of the United States. North and South Korea had been assured that within five years they would be reunited and given their independence. However, in 1950 North Korean troops, backed by the Soviets, invaded South Korea. The U.N. Security Council voted to send troops to prevent South Korea from being overrun. Sixteen member nations, including the United States, sent soldiers; another forty-one sent supplies.

Three years later, after more than two million people had been killed or injured, a truce ended the Korean conflict. Americans suffered substantial losses (54,000 killed and 103,000 wounded), and many Korean civilians were uprooted and their cities and farms devastated. Still, many Americans believed that the objective of keeping Communism from spreading had been achieved.

Vietnam

By 1954 Vietnam had also become a divided country. Backed by Communist China, the North Vietnamese were determined to take over non-Communist South Vietnam. At first many Americans supported a strong military presence in Vietnam and elected politicians who favored sending troops there. But as the war dragged on, people began to question how the war was being conducted and whether our troops should have been sent there in the first place.

A ceasefire agreement finally ended American involvement in Vietnam on January 25, 1973. American casualties had reached 57,000 killed and 300,000 wounded, but these figures did not represent the full impact of the war. The Vietnam conflict divided our country as it had not been divided since the Civil War.

Returning Vietnam veterans were not welcomed home with the enthusiasm that the veterans of other wars had received. Most had gone to Vietnam believing it was their patriotic duty to do so, but now they

Memorial in Springfield's Oak Ridge Cemetery honoring Illinoisans who died in Vietnam. Courtesy of the Illinois State Historical Library.

were told that Vietnam had been a pointless exercise. In some cases they were made to feel irresponsible and immoral for having participated in the war. Almost a decade passed before Americans began to start to sort things out and see how unfair it was to blame the war on those who had done the fighting. In a belated effort to honor the fallen, a monument to those who died in Vietnam was erected in Washington, D.C., in 1982. Illinois, too, chose to honor its 147 citizens who died in the Vietnam conflict. A monument in Springfield's Oak Ridge Cemetery, the same cemetery in which Lincoln is buried, was dedicated May 8, 1988.

Internal Conflicts

Our involvement in foreign conflicts came at the same time as an upsurge of political and social movements at home. The antiwar movement built to a climax in the late 1960s just as the civil rights movement was gaining momentum. Women's rights advocates also became more active at this time.

The Antiwar Movement

During the Vietnam War, the casualty figures given out by government officials suggested that the South Vietnamese and their American allies were winning. Consequently, many Americans believed that the sacrifice of so many lives would in the end be justified. However, many American journalists in Vietnam had another story to tell. They insisted that the North Vietnamese forces were having more success than the American government was willing to admit. Some began reporting the terrible consequences the war was having for Vietnamese civilians. When word began leaking out that some American soldiers had massacred civilians, the American public became confused and dismayed.

In Illinois, as well as in other states, college campuses became centers for antiwar protests. Taking their cue from the civil rights movement, some students organized vigils, teach-ins, and peaceful demonstrations. Others became more militant, occupying buildings, wrecking state property, and clashing with police and state militia.

Many young people turned against the establishment, by which they meant those in authority who had committed the nation to war. Some became hippies or flower children, "dropping out" of society and starting a subculture of their own. Men and women wore long hair, tie-dyed shirts, sandals, exotic jewelry, and even American flags. Their professed goals were to lead a simple life of peace and harmony. But to conventional Americans the hippies, especially those who lived in communes and used drugs, seemed different and dangerous.

Fear led many people to vote for law-and-order candidates who advocated stopping all protest movements. Nevertheless, opposition to the war continued to spread, and the use of force to stop demonstrations continued. Once again some citizens felt that their constitutional rights were being threatened just as they had been during previous wars. The whole nation seemed to be an intellectual and philosophical war zone with physical violence constantly hovering in the background.

The Civil Rights Movement

Americans who belonged to minority groups could not understand why soldiers should be sent abroad to fight for the freedom of others when not everyone in this country was free. In Illinois the General Assembly had repeatedly failed to pass civil rights legislation. Republican William Stratton, who served as governor from 1953 to 1961, proposed creating a Fair Employment Practices Commission, but the state senate killed the bill just as it had killed every similar bill since 1945. The next governor, Democrat Otto Kerner, tried to get an open-occupancy law passed to prohibit discrimination in the sale and rental of property. Again, the Senate refused to act. Governor Kerner finally issued an executive order to achieve his goal.

While the Illinois General Assembly was resisting civil rights legislation, an Illinoisan was leading the fight for new civil rights laws in the U.S. Senate. Born in Pekin, Illinois, Senator Everett Dirksen had been elected to the House of Representatives in 1932 and had successfully run for reelection six times. He then served for many years in the Senate. Known for his homespun humor and somewhat dramatic manner of speaking, Dirksen was also a thoughtful and astute politician. His talent for compromise helped clear the way for the passage of the Civil Rights Act in 1964 and the Voting Rights Act in 1965.

During these decades of conflict, many blacks and whites rallied behind Doctor Martin Luther King, Jr., a minister of great oratorical gifts who advocated nonviolent resistance based on the teachings of India's great leader, Mahatma Gandhi, and on those of the nineteenth-century American naturalist, Henry David Thoreau. In the summer of 1966 Dr. King came to Chicago, hoping to begin the process of breaking down patterns of housing segregation. He led marches into white neighborhoods on the southwest side and took over an apartment building to draw attention to the conditions in which white absentee owners expected their tenants to live. Resentment against his efforts ran high, and for several weeks sporadic violence broke out. He announced a plan to march through all-white Cicero, but then canceled this event to avoid violence.

When Dr. King was assassinated in April 1968, his death touched off a new round of violence. For three days desperate blacks on Chicago's south side went on a rampage, shooting, setting fires, and looting. They were convinced that nonviolence did not work and thought they had nothing to lose. Nine people died, some 500 were injured, and 3,000 were arrested. Property damage reached into the millions. Small-scale violence broke out in Evanston, Maywood, East St. Louis, Alton, Aurora, Joliet, Chicago Heights, and Carbondale. Other cities across the nation experienced similar upheavals.

The Democratic Convention of 1968

In August 1968 the Democrats convened in Chicago to choose candidates for the upcoming presidential election. As the delegates began to arrive, they were joined by thousands of demonstrators who wanted to use the convention to dramatize and publicize their views. Groups protesting the Vietnam War, racial and gender discrimination, the disparity between rich and poor, and the power of those controlling the economic and political structures of the nation converged on the city. Some had announced beforehand that they intended to disrupt the convention.

President Lyndon B. Johnson had already said he would not run for another term, so Vice-President Hubert H. Humphrey expected to be nominated. A peace candidate, Eugene McCarthy, was also on hand with his supporters, many of whom were college students who wanted an end to a war they considered illegal and immoral.

Mayor Richard J. Daley, the last of the powerful political bosses in Chicago, had served five consecutive terms since 1955. Chicagoans had consistently reelected him because he was able to get things done. While other cities were being overwhelmed with urban problems, Daley kept Chicago moving. He made alliances with ethnic leaders and kept his promises to them. When disagreements arose between various groups, he served as mediator. Businessmen appreciated the relative calm and order he maintained in the city.

Mayor Daley had no intention of allowing groups of obstreperous young people to challenge his authority or disrupt the life of the city. During the convention he ordered the Chicago police to stop any demonstrations and break up any large gatherings of protesters. When one group of demonstrators began a peace march for which they had not obtained a city permit, the police moved in with clubs and tear gas. They cleared the streets and the parks, beating, dragging, gassing, and arresting demonstrators. The crowds taunted the police, chanting, "The whole world is watching," and threw rocks, bottles, and other objects. When someone threw debris out of a Hilton Hotel window, the angry and nervous police rushed in and began beating McCarthy's supporters who were staying there, even though they had not been involved in the protests. It took McCarthy himself to get the police to stop.

After the convention, the leaders of the most militant protesters, the "Chicago Seven," were tried. Their activities in court made a farce of the trial, and they took advantage of the publicity it provided them. Eventually all of them were acquitted.

The end result of the Democratic convention of 1968 was that an already divided nation was further destabilized. Although people deplored the brutality the police had used, they were at the same time frightened by the rebellious young. Almost everyone felt uneasy about the increasing violence in American society in general.

The ERA in Illinois

In March 1972 Congress passed the Equal Rights Amendment (ERA). It stated that "equality of rights under the law shall not be denied or abridged by the United States or by any State on account of sex."

In order for the amendment to become part of the Constitution, it had to be ratified by thirty-eight states within seven years. ERA supporters in Illinois immediately set to work, with members of NOW (the National Organization for Women) leading the effort to round up local support across the state.

At that time, Illinois had only four women legislators: three in the house and one in the senate. Women lobbyists were rare and were not taken seriously at first. While some male legislators were supportive, others treated them in a demeaning manner. In April ratification bills were introduced into both houses of the Illinois legislature, but while the senate agreed to the reading of such a bill, the Executive Committee in the house tried to block it from being heard before the full house. Finally, with pressure from Governor Richard Ogilvie, the house did agree to consider the bill. In May seventy-five members of the house voted in favor of it, but eighty-nine votes were needed for passage. Backers of the bill felt betrayed because twenty-one legislators who had promised to vote for it either voted no or did not vote at all.

The ERA supporters then turned their efforts toward the fall election, in hopes of electing more women and more men who supported women's rights. Eleven women were elected, three in the senate and eight in the house, but that was still not enough. To complicate matters, one of the leading opponents of ERA on the national scene, Phyllis Schlafly, organized a "Stop ERA" movement based in Alton, Illinois.

She represented women who were satisfied with their traditional roles and saw the ERA movement as dangerous and ungodly. In 1973 efforts to ratify the ERA in Illinois failed again.

In spite of these setbacks, supporters tried again in 1976. Labor unions, church groups, civil rights groups, and business, professional, and campus organizations joined NOW members in a mass rally in Springfield which included 10,000 supporters from thirty states. But again the amendment failed in the Illinois senate.

Thirty-four states had ratified the ERA by 1977, and only four more states were needed in order for it to become part of the Constitution. Illinois was one of sixteen states that did not ratify the amendment. Although the amendment failed, it brought women's problems to the attention of a wide public and resulted in the passage of many specific laws to improve the situation for women.

꿔

The cold war made Illinoisans as uneasy as it made people in other states. The Korean and Vietnam wars were fought to contain Communism, but after the loss of many American lives people began to question the wisdom of such involvement. The antiwar movement coincided with other powerful social movements, especially the civil rights movement and the women's movement. The nation was torn by internal strife, which came to a climax at the 1968 Democratic convention in Chicago. When the commotion died down, Illinoisans turned to matters of pressing concern within their state.

For Further Exploration

Adade M. Wheeler with Marlene Stein Wortman. *The Roads They Made: Women in Illinois History*. Chicago: Charles H. Kerr Pub. Co., 1977.

Beginning with a chapter on Indian women, this book contains descriptions of the lives of women from pioneer days through the Civil War and the industrial revolution. It covers the woman suffrage movement in Illinois, including the unsuccessful struggle to have the ERA ratified by the Illinois General Assembly.

26

Contemporary Illinois

Creating a Modern Constitution

In 1965 Marjorie Pebworth, who had been president of the League of Women Voters and was at the time serving a term in the state house of representatives, launched the movement that eventually resulted in the writing of a new constitution for the state of Illinois. Several governors had unsuccessfully urged the General Assembly to take action, but lawmakers now began feeling pressure from citizens who felt that the one hundred-year-old constitution needed updating. The General Assembly put the question of calling a constitutional convention on the next ballot, and voters indicated that they did want a convention to be called and later chose delegates to attend it. The first meeting of the convention was held in Springfield on December 8, 1969.

The Constitutional Convention

No previous constitutional convention had had such a varied group of delegates. The unsuccessful constitutional convention of the 1920s had had only two black delegates and no women. The 1969 convention had thirteen blacks and fifteen women. The number of delegates from each party was nearly equal. Out of a total of 118 delegates, thirty-five were Catholic, fifty-six Protestant, and five Jewish. Lawyers outnumbered all other professions with a total of fifty-six, but there were also eleven teachers and educational administrators, five bankers, five farmers, and two labor union officials. Most of the delegates were well educated.

They began by chosing Chicago attorney Samuel W. Witwer as president of the convention. One of the first important decisions the delegates made was that the new constitution would not include anything but the most basic laws of the state. This may sound self-evident today, but the delegates had studied the 1870 constitution and realized that one reason it was so long and unwieldy was that it included so much extraneous material. For example, one section pertained to the preservation of military records, banners, and relics; another provided funding for the Columbian Exposition of 1893; and another specified the amount to be spent on the new capitol building. These matters had all been taken care of, and references to them only cluttered the document.

Fairly simple matters, such as how much tax a county could collect, became more complicated when written into the constitution because they could not be changed without the long and expensive process of writing an amendment and having voters approve it. It made more sense to have such matters covered by separate laws, which the General Assembly could easily change simply by voting on them in a regular session.

The next step was to set up standing committees to work on specific parts of the new constitution. Meanwhile, public hearings in Springfield and other cities gave citizens a chance to voice their concerns. When the standing committees had finished their assignments, they brought recommendations to the floor to be debated before the convention as a whole. Under Witwer's skillful leadership, the delegates were able to complete their task in just one year. Illinois voters ratified the new constitution on December 15, 1970.

Highlights of the New Constitution

By 1970 the responsibilities of the governor had increased so much that he or she needed to be able to act quickly and decisively. The delegates therefore gave the governor more power to do so. Governors can now veto just a part of a bill rather than the whole bill. They can reduce the amount of money appropriated for a specific program and create or reorganize agencies by executive order rather than by going through the General Assembly.

Previously the governor and lieutenant governor could be from different parties. But when people of opposite parties were elected to these top offices, it was difficult for them to work as a team. Partisan competition slowed down and even stymied the law-making process. The new constitution states that the governor and lieutenant governor must be of the same party and run for office together.

An innovative home rule article was included to reduce confusion and red tape between government agencies. At the time of the constitutional convention, Illinois had more governmental units than any other state—6,400. These included counties, cities, townships, school districts, and special districts. Because it was possible for one resident to come under the jurisdiction of three or four of these units, people needing government services or wanting to make complaints or suggestions often did not know which unit of government to consult. The wheels of government turned slowly because the only authority cities had to carry on their business was that delegated to them by the state. Even the simplest change or the passage of a new ordinance that only pertained to one community required action by the General Assembly. The home rule article allows cities with a population of at least 25,000 to levy taxes, issue certain licenses, borrow money, and pass ordinances without consulting the General Assembly. Not only does this provide more flexibility and efficiency for city governments, but it also relieves the General Assembly of a time-consuming burden.

Mindful of the social movements of the 1960s, the delegates wrote several civil rights provisions into the new constitution. Section 17 of Article 1 forbids "discrimination on the basis of race, color, creed, national ancestry and sex in the hiring and promotion practice of any employer or in the sale or rental of property." This is followed by a provision giving women equal protection under the law and another forbidding discrimination against the handicapped.

To keep the state government solvent, the income tax law that Governor Richard Ogilvie had urged the General Assembly to pass in 1969 was incorporated into the new constitution. In addition, the governor is now required to present an annual balanced budget for the approval of the General Assembly.

The General Assembly is required to put the question of whether or not to call a constitutional convention before the voters at least once every twenty years. If it fails to do so, the question is automatically put on the ballot. In 1990 Illinois voters decided against calling a convention.

The Four-Time Winner

The General Assembly had decided that beginning in 1978 governors would be elected in nonpresidential election years so that voters could concentrate on state candidates. Because 1976 was a presidential election year, whoever ran for governor would serve only a two-year term, filling in the gap before the new law went into effect. James Thompson decided to run in that election.

His opponent, Michael Howlett, said he would not raise taxes and that if taxes went up during his two years in office, he would not run

James Thompson, the first person to be elected to four consecutive terms as governor of Illinois. Courtesy of the Illinois State Historical Library.

for a four-year term. Thompson took a much different approach. He frankly admitted that he was inexperienced and would have to learn on the job and therefore was not prepared to make any promises.

Thompson has been called the best campaigner Illinois has ever had. A Republican who could take an independent point of view, he attracted many Democratic voters. He also had a way of speaking that made potential voters feel at ease with him. He appeared at parties and dinners, fairs and wiener roasts. As he put it, "People need to know that you're a regular guy, that they can trust you, feel comfortable with you—even if they don't always agree with you." Adding to his popularity was the fact that during his first campaign for governor he married Jayne Carr, an attorney who had been a student of his at Northwestern. Their daughter, Samantha, was the first child in seventy-two years to be born to an Illinois governor and his wife while they occupied the governor's mansion. Thompson was reelected in 1978, 1982, and 1986.

Historians will eventually assess Governor Thompson's years in office in detail, but meanwhile he is viewed as a doer and builder. In 1985 he pushed through the Build Illinois public works program, which funded major highway improvements. He more than doubled the capacity of state prisons. His support for state fairs not only provided

needed funds but also brought a wave of new interest in rebuilding a
sense of community in Illinois. Money for special projects in specific
communities brought him support and provided much needed community centers, health care facilities, and other social agencies.

Critics pointed out that Thompson reverted to spoils politics by
giving jobs to supporters and pork barrel projects to their communities.
Thompson responded by saying that this is the way politics works and
that as long as the people he appointed were competent and honest and
the projects he approved were valuable, he did not feel uncomfortable
with the patronage system. None of his top aides became the subject
of a public scandal or went to jail, and many have gone on to even more
responsible positions in government, business, and law. Critics acknowledge this, but point out that a less scrupulous successor could set the
state government back many years by misusing patronage.

The State of Illinois Center

Until recently, people in the state's largest and most prestigious city
had no central location to which they could go for services offered by
the state government. That changed in 1985 when the State of Illinois
Center in Chicago was completed and dedicated. Designed by architect
Helmut Jahn, the steel and glass structure has three floors of shops and
restaurants topped by thirteen floors of state offices that house various
agencies, boards, and commissions. Balconies face out into an atrium
flooded with natural light. The rotunda, a large multi-purpose space,
is available for public events, performances, receptions, and fund-rais-
ers.

The State of Illinois Center also serves as a cultural showcase. The
museum that the Illinois State Museum and the Illinois Arts Council
operate there has the largest collection of work by contemporary Illinois
artists anywhere. The arts are very much alive in Illinois, as a list of
just some of the top artists will show.

Painters and printmakers currently working in Illinois include Vera
Klement, Gladys Nillson, Ed Paschke, Carolyn Plochmann, Seymor
Rosofsky, Barbara Rossi, and Hollis Sigler. Sculptors include Don Baum,
Red Grooms, Richard Hunt, Jerry Peart, and Mark de Suvero. Art
Sinsebaugh, Aaron Siskind, and Charles Swedlund are among the many
fine professional photographers in the state.

In recent years Illinois has played a leading role in the revival of old
crafts and their innovative use in contemporary pieces. Sculptor Brent
Kington has been one of the leading figures in a nationwide revival of
interest in the art of blacksmithing. Illinoisans doing outstanding work

in metals include Mary Lee Hu, Richard Mawdsley, and Jim Wallace. Harris Deller and Ruth Duckworth have received awards for their innovative use of clay, and Bill Boysen and Bill Carlson have become well known both as practitioners and teachers of the art of glassblowing. Claire Ziegler has received wide recognition for her work in the fiber arts.

The State of Illinois Center in Chicago gives Illinois artists and craftspeople a chance to have their work viewed by Illinoisans and by people from all over the world. A large and attractive sales gallery provides visitors with a chance to purchase work they like.

Another President from Illinois

Ronald Reagan was born into a middle-class family in Tampico in 1911. He came of age just as the Great Depression was descending on the nation. For a while he worked as a sportscaster in Iowa. Then moving to Hollywood, he began a long and rewarding career as a movie actor. Next he became a highly visible political figure as governor of California.

Elected to his first term as president in 1980, he soon became known as the "great communicator." His manner of speaking and his sense of humor seemingly made him one of the most popular presidents in history. He was reelected in 1984.

Two Firsts for Chicago

During the 1980s Chicago elected its first woman mayor and its first black mayor. When Mayor Richard Daley died in 1976, Michael Bilandic completed Daley's term and fully expected to win reelection in 1979. But he was challenged by Jayne Byrne, a Daley appointee who had served as commissioner of Consumer Sales, Weights, and Measures until Bilandic fired her in 1977. He did not consider her much of a threat, but she proved to be a tireless campaigner who thoroughly covered the city.

One of the worst winter storms in several decades also helped Byrne's cause. During Daley's years in office, Chicagoans had gotten used to having such emergencies dealt with quickly and efficiently, but Bilandic seemed unable to get the city dug out and moving again. With transportation shut down, offices, factories, and stores suffered losses, and people became impatient. The discovery that political favoritism and graft had been involved in the letting of contracts for the city's snow-removal program clinched Bilandic's defeat. Byrne won the Democratic primary in February and received over 80 percent of the votes in the mayoral election. She was inaugurated in April 1979.

By the time of the next city election in 1983, Chicago was still not running as smoothly as when Mayor Daley had been in office. Its tax base continued to shrink as the shift of people to the suburbs continued, yet the demand for city services grew. Minorities were still unhappy with their limited role in the political arena and with their opportunities in housing and jobs.

Mayor Byrne was challenged by several opponents, one of whom was Harold Washington, a seasoned black politician with twenty years of legislative experience in the General Assembly and the U.S. Congress. He wanted to reform the Democratic party in Chicago and make it work for all segments of the population. Political observers did not believe he could win because he had broken with machine politics and was running as an independent. However, Washington and his more than 6,000 workers succeeded in forming a coalition of minorities that included blacks, Latin Americans, and Asians. Some whites also supported Washington, although he did not actively court the white vote.

Although Washington won the Democratic primary, the Democratic party did not fully support him. Nevertheless, when he faced off against his Republican opponent, Bernard Epton, he won and became Chicago's first black mayor.

Mayor Washington said that he wanted to be mayor for twenty years. He had many ideas for reorganizing the city government and was intent on giving blacks and other minorities a more equitable role in running it. Some of his appointees were well educated and able administrators; others had no background or experience to do the jobs they were given. Part of the problem lay in the fact that so few Chicago blacks had had a chance to develop political and leadership skills.

Had Washington been given more time, he might have realized some of his goals. Unfortunately, he died suddenly of a heart attack in 1987 without having completed his first term.

New Challenges for a New Century

Governor Thompson decided to return to the private practice of law rather than run for a fifth term as governor. In January 1991 Republican James Edgar became the thirty-eighth governor of Illinois. Edgar had been involved in politics since his college days, serving as an assistant in the state house and senate, then holding his first elective office in 1976 when he became a member of the General Assembly.

When Illinois Secretary of State Alan Dixon was elected to the Senate, Governor Thompson chose Edgar to fill the resulting vacancy. Edgar was subsequently elected secretary of state two more times, serving in that post until 1990. Now that he is governor, he must face

Cleaning up the environment is one of the great tasks of the immediate future. Here a team is removing toxic waste from a site under the direction of the Illinois Environmental Protection Agency. Illinois Environmental Protection Agency.

a number of stubborn problems that previous administrations have been chipping away at.

The financial situation is the most critical. Illinois has been steadily losing industries, jobs, and people to the Sunbelt states. Although the revenue base is shrinking, voters want the government to provide such services as medical care, aid to dependent children, unemployment compensation, day care for the children of working single parents, drug rehabilitation programs, improvement in public housing, aid to the elderly, better roads, better schools, more police protection, and many other benefits. The old question of who is going to pay for this is still with us. Some citizens feel that taxes are already too high and that a lot of tax money goes to waste; others insist that it will be impossible to balance the state budget and provide all the expensive services people want without increasing taxes. Attempts to stop waste and limit spending have not been very effective so far. One alternative to higher taxes is the combining of overlapping or related programs into more efficient and less wasteful agencies. Another approach is to recruit new industries that will broaden the state's tax base. Many Illinois counties can provide a genial small-town atmosphere, a work force, and good transportation. Unemployed coal miners and industrial workers would gladly participate in retraining and apprenticeship programs.

Illinoisans are also coming to realize that ecology is not just a buzzword. If Illinois is to continue to be a state of abundance and the good life, laws to protect the environment have to be passed and enforced. These include clean air and water laws, laws protecting agricultural land from erosion, waste, and contamination, and laws to solve the acid rain problem fairly. The list could be much longer.

Politicians, educators, and citizens alike are grappling with such questions as: How can we prepare students for a wide variety of highly technical jobs? How can we achieve excellence in education? Where will the funding come from? Can government and industry cooperate to meet educational needs? What is the best way to prepare students for active participation in politics and government? How can the poor be given improved educational and occupational opportunities? How can education be designed to make people happier and give them a better life?

In the continuing search for answers, mistakes are bound to be made. But Illinoisans have a history of problem solving that bodes well for the future, even though the problems to be faced seem more complex than ever before. It helps to know that previous generations have felt just as challenged and have consistently come up with gifted leaders and innovative solutions.

❧

While looking for solutions to some of the conflicts of the postwar decades, Illinoisans turned to the task of updating the state constitution. The new document streamlined the state government and made the amendment process easier.

Governor James Thompson became the first governor to be elected to four consecutive terms. Another Illinoisan, Ronald Reagan, served as president. Chicago elected its first woman mayor and followed that by electing its first black mayor.

As they prepare to enter the new century, Illinoisans are reevaluating their priorities and trying to come up with a fair and realistic program for the future.

For Further Exploration

Illinois Issues. Springfield: Sangamon State University. Published eleven times a year.

If you want to know what your elected and appointed officials are doing and what laws and policies are being acted upon, this magazine provides reliable and up-to-date information. Many libraries subscribe to it.

Frank Kopecky and Mary S. Harris. *Understanding the Illinois Constitution.* Springfield: Illinois Bar Association, 1970.

It is not easy to write about legal matters in a clear, lively, and concise manner, but these authors have succeeded in doing so. Their discussion of constitution-making in general and the Illinois Constitution of 1970 in particular informs us about areas that profoundly affect our lives.

APPENDIX 1

State Symbols

THE GREAT SEAL OF ILLINOIS

The state seal pictures an eagle on a rock, against which a shield of stars and stripes leans. The eagle holds a streamer in its mouth on which is printed the state motto.

STATE FLAG

The state flag consists of the state seal on a white background.

MOTTO	"State Sovereignty—National Union"
SONG	"By Thy Rivers Gently Flowing, Illinois"
NICKNAME	"The Prairie State"
SLOGAN	"Land of Lincoln"
TREE	White Oak
FLOWER	Meadow Violet
MINERAL	Fluorite
BIRD	Cardinal
INSECT	Monarch Butterfly
FISH	Bluegill

APPENDIX 2

Governors of Illinois

Shadrach Bond	Dem.	1818–22
Edward Coles	Dem.	1822–26
Ninian Edwards	Dem.	1826–30
John Reynolds	Dem.	1830–34 (resigned to run for Congress)
William Ewing	Dem.	Nov.–Dec. 1834 (completed Reynolds's term)
Joseph Duncan	Dem.	1834–38
Thomas Carlin	Dem.	1838–42
Thomas Ford	Dem.	1842–46
Augustus French	Dem.	1846–53 (1848 State constitution changed election dates to coincide with presidential elections. French served two years, then was reelected to a regular four-year term.)
Joel Matteson	Dem.	1853–57
William Bissell	Dem.	1857–60 (died in office)
John Wood	Rep.	1860–61 (completed Bissell's term).
Richard Yates	Rep.	1861–65
Richard Oglesby	Rep.	1865–69
John Palmer	Rep.	1869–73
Richard Oglesby	Rep.	Jan. 13–23, 1873 (resigned to become U.S. Senator)
John Beveridge	Rep.	1873–77 (completed Oglesby's term)
Shelby Cullom	Rep.	1877–83 (resigned to become U.S. Senator)
John Hamilton	Rep.	1883–85 (completed Cullom's term)

Richard Oglesby	Rep.	1885–89
Joseph Fifer	Rep.	1889–93
John Altgeld	Dem.	1893–97
John Tanner	Rep.	1897–1901
Richard Yates	Rep.	1901–5 (son of the Civil War governor)
Charles Deneen	Rep.	1905–13
Edward Dunne	Dem.	1913–17
Frank Lowden	Rep.	1917–21
Len Small	Rep.	1921–29
Louis Emmerson	Rep.	1929–33
Henry Horner	Dem.	1933–40 (died in office)
John Stelle	Dem.	Oct. 1940–Jan. 1941 (completed Horner's term)
Dwight Green	Rep.	1941–49
Adlai Stevenson	Dem.	1949–53
William Stratton	Rep.	1953–61
Otto Kerner	Dem.	1961–68 (resigned to become federal judge)
Samuel Shapiro	Dem.	May 1968–Jan. 1969 (completed Kerner's term)
Richard Ogilvie	Rep.	1969–73
Daniel Walker	Dem.	1973–77
James Thompson	Rep.	1977–91 (gubernatorial election dates were changed back to nonpresidential years. Governor Thompson was elected to one two-year term and reelected to three four-year terms.)
James Edgar	Rep.	1991–

APPENDIX 3

Important Dates in Illinois History

Boldface entries refer to national or international events that strongly influenced Illinois history.

c. 12,000 B.C.–1400 A.D.	Prehistoric tribes inhabit the Illinois country
c. 1500–1650	Illini tribes dominate Illinois country
1673–75	Explorations of Marquette and Jolliet
1679–90	Explorations of LaSalle and Tonti
1696–1700	Mission of the Guardian Angel built on present site of Chicago
1698	Church of the Holy Family built at Cahokia
1703	Founding of Kaskaskia
1720	French build Fort de Chartres
1756–63	**French and Indian War**
1763–65	**Pontiac's Uprising**
1776–83	**American Revolution**
1778–79	George Rogers Clark's campaign in the Illinois country
c. 1779	Jean Baptiste du Sable founds first permanent settlement at Chicago
1787	**Congress creates the Northwest Territory (which included the future states of Ohio, Indiana, Illinois, Michigan, and Wisconsin)**
1803	**The Louisiana Purchase (Illinois no longer**

	on the western border of the United States, but in the middle of the nation)
1809	Illinois becomes a separate territory
1810	First commercial coal mining, Jackson County
1811–12	New Madrid earthquake
1812–15	**War of 1812**
1812	Fort Dearborn massacre
1815	**Construction of the National Road begins**
1818	Illinois becomes the twenty-first state
1820	State capital moved from Kaskaskia to Vandalia
1825	**Erie Canal opens**
1832	Black Hawk's War. All Indian tribes expelled from Illinois
1836–48	Building of the Illinois and Michigan Canal
1837	John Deere invents the self-scouring plow
1837	Abolitionist Elijah Lovejoy killed at Alton
1837	The General Assembly passes Internal Improvements Act
1837	**Financial panic cripples the nation's economy**
1839–47	Mormons at Nauvoo
1840	Springfield becomes the state capital
1840	**National Road reaches Vandalia**
1846–48	**Mexican War**
1848	Second Illinois constitution ratified
1850–56	Building of the Illinois Central Railroad
1855	The General Assembly passes a law permitting the use of state taxes for the support of public education
1858	Lincoln-Douglas debates
1861	First national coal miners' union meets in West Belleville
1861	**Lincoln becomes president**
1861–65	**Civil War**
1865	General Assembly incorporates the Union Stock Yard

1865	Marshall Field and partners found department store
1868	Building of Illinois's first blast furnace for processing iron ore
1870	Third Illinois constitution ratified
1871	The Great Chicago Fire
1872	Montgomery Ward begins first mail-order business in Chicago
1873	**Financial panic**
1876	William Hulbert and Albert Spalding found the National Baseball League
1883	**Financial panic**
1885–1910	William LeBaron Jenney builds first skyscraper. Architects working in Illinois develop a truly American architecture
1886	Haymarket tragedy
1889	Jane Addams and Elizabeth Gates Starr open Hull House
1891	Chicago Symphony Orchestra founded
1893	Governor Altgeld pardons Haymarket prisoners
1893	The World's Columbian Exposition
1893	**Financial panic**
1894	Pullman Strike
1898	**Spanish-American War**
1900	Sanitary and Ship Canal opens
1901	United States Steel Corporation formed
1910	Illinois's worst coal mine disaster at Cherry Mine in Bureau County
1910	**Founding of the NAACP after race riot in Springfield**
1913	Illinois becomes first state east of the Mississippi to allow women to vote in municipal and presidential elections
1914–18	**World War I**
c. 1915	**The Great Migration of blacks from the South begins**

1917	Civil Administrative Code reorganizes state government
1918	Black musicians from New Orleans bring jazz to Chicago
1919	**18th Amendment prohibits manufacture, transportation, and sale of alcoholic beverages**
1919	The White Sox scandal
1920	**19th Amendment allows women in all states to vote**
1920	George Halas brings professional football to Illinois
1920s	Al Capone and other gangsters active in Chicago area
1929	**The Stock Market Crash**
1930–40	**The Great Depression**
1933	**Prohibition repealed**
1933–35	"A Century of Progress" Exhibition in Chicago
1939–45	**World War II**
1950–53	**Korean conflict**
1954–73	**Vietnam conflict**
1955	Richard J. Daley begins his twenty years as mayor of Chicago
1960s	**Civil Rights movement**
1968	**Assassination of Dr. Martin Luther King, Jr., sets off riots in Chicago and many other cities**
1968	Democratic National Convention in Chicago marred by violence
1970	Fourth Illinois constitution ratified
1977–91	James Thompson becomes first governor to serve four consecutive terms
1979	First woman mayor of Chicago, Jane Byrne, takes office
1983	Harold Washington becomes the first black mayor of Chicago
1985	State of Illinois building in Chicago is dedicated

Bibliography

Books

Adams, J. N. *Illinois Place Names*. Edited by W. E. Keller. Springfield: Illinois State Historical Society Occasional Publication #54, 1968.

Addams, Jane. *Twenty Years at Hull-House*. New York: Macmillan, 1910. Rpt. Urbana: University of Illinois Press, 1990.

Angle, Paul. *Bloody Williamson: A Chapter in American Lawlessness*. New York: Alfred A. Knopf, 1952. Rpt. Urbana: University of Illinois Press, 1992.

Atkinson, William. *The Next New Madrid Earthquake: A Survival Guide for the Midwest*. Carbondale: Southern Illinois University Press, 1989.

Baldwin, Leland D. *The Keelboat Age on Western Waters*. Pittsburgh: University of Pittsburgh Press, 1941.

Belting, Natalia. *Kaskaskia under the French Regime*. Urbana: Graduate College of the University of Illinois, Illinois Studies in the Social Sciences, Vol. XXIX, No.3, 1948. Polyanthos edition. New Orleans: Polyanthos, 1975.

Black Hawk. *Black Hawk: An Autobiography*. Edited by Donald Jackson. Urbana: University of Illinois Press, 1955.

Boewe, Charles. *Prairie Albion: An English Settlement in Pioneer Illinois*. Carbondale: Southern Illinois University Press, 1962.

Bogart, Ernest, and Charles Thompson. *The Industrial State: 1870–1893*. The Centennial History of Illinois, vol. 4. Springfield: The Illinois Centennial Commission, 1922.

Bogart, Ernest, and John Mathews. *The Modern Commonwealth: 1893–1918*. The Centennial History of Illinois, vol. 5. Springfield: The Illinois Centennial Commission, 1920.

Brose, David, James Brown, and David Penney. *Ancient Art of the American*

Woodland Indians. New York: Harry N. Abrams, in association with the Detroit Institute of Arts, 1985.

Brush, Daniel Harmon. *Growing up with Southern Illinois, 1820–1861*. Edited by Milo Milton Quaife. Chicago: Lakeside Press, R. R. Donnelley, 1944.

Buck, Solon J. *Illinois in 1818*. Springfield: The Illinois Centennial Commission, 1917.

Burg, David F. *Chicago's White City of 1893*. Lexington: University Press of Kentucky, 1976.

Cavanagh, H. M. *Funk of Funk's Grove*. Bloomington: Pantagraph Printing, 1952.

Chidsey, Donald Barr. *The French and Indian War*. New York: Crown Publishers, 1969.

Clark, George Rogers. *The First American Frontier: Col. George Rogers Clark's Sketch of His Campaign in the Illinois in 1778–9*. Cincinnati: Robert Clarke & Co., 1869. Reprint, Dale Van Every, advisory editor. New York: Arno Press and the New York Times, 1971.

Clayton, John. *The Illinois Fact Book and Historical Almanac, 1673–1968*. Carbondale: Southern Illinois University Press, 1970.

Corliss, Carlton J. *Main Line of Mid-America: The Story of the Illinois Central*. New York: Creative Age Press, 1950.

Cornelius, Janet. *A History of Constitution Making in Illinois*. Urbana: Institute of Government and Public Affairs, 1969.

Duis, Perry. *Chicago: Creating New Traditions*. Chicago: Chicago Historical Society, 1976.

Edmunds, R. David. *Tecumseh and the Quest for Indian Leadership*. Boston: Little, Brown and Company, 1984.

Eifert, Virginia S. *Louis Jolliet: Explorer of Rivers*. New York: Dodd, Mead & Co., 1962.

Farnham, Eliza W. *Life in Prairie Land*. New York: Harper, 1846. Prairie State Edition. Urbana: University of Illinois Press, 1988.

Flanders, Robert B. *Navoo: Kingdom on the Mississippi*. Urbana: University of Illinois Press, 1965.

Freedman, Russell. *Lincoln: A Photobiography*. New York: Ticknor & Fields. A Houghton Mifflin Co., 1987.

Ginger, Ray. *Altgeld's America*. New York: Franklin Watts, 1973.

Goodnough, David. *Pontiac's War, 1763–1766*. New York: Franklin Watts, 1970.

Grossman, James R. *Land of Hope: Chicago, Black Southerners, and the Great Migration*. Chicago: University of Chicago Press, 1989.

Hallwas, John E., ed. *Illinois Literature: The Nineteenth Century*. Macomb: Illinois Heritage Press, 1986.

Hastings, Robert. *A Nickel's Worth of Skim Milk: A Boy's View of the Great*

Depression. Carbondale: Southern Illinois University Press (University Graphics and Publications), 1972.

Hayman, LeRoy. *American Ambassador to the World: Adlai Stevenson*. New York: Abelard-Schuman, 1966.

Hicken, Victor. *Illinois in the Civil War*. Urbana: University of Illinois Press, 1966.

Horrell, C. William, Henry Dan Piper, and John Voigt. *Land between the Rivers: The Southern Illinois Country*. Carbondale: Southern Illinois University Press, 1973.

Howard, Robert P. *Illinois: A History of the Prairie State*. Grand Rapids, Mich.: Eerdmans, 1972.

———. *Mostly Good and Competent Men: Illinois Governors, 1818 to 1988*. Springfield: Illinois State Historical Society, 1988.

Hubbard, Gurdon Saltonstall. *The Autobiography of Gurdon Saltonstall Hubbard*. Chicago: Lakeside Press, R. R. Donnelley, 1911.

Hunt, Irene. *Across Five Aprils*. Chicago: Follett Publishing Co., 1964.

Hutchinson, William T. *Lowden of Illinois: The Life of Frank O. Lowden*. Vol. 1, *City and State*. Chicago: University of Chicago Press, 1957.

Isaksson, Olov, and Soren Hallgren. *Bishop Hill, Ill.: A Utopia on the Prairie*. Stockholm, Sweden: LT Publishing House, 1969.

Jagendorf, M. A. *Sand in the Bag and Other Folk Stories of Ohio, Indiana, and Illinois*. New York: Vanguard Press, 1952.

Jefferies, Richard W. *The Archaeology of Carrier Mills: 10,000 Years in the Saline Valley of Illinois*. Carbondale: Southern Illinois University Press, 1987.

Jensen, Richard J. *Illinois: A Bicentennial History*. New York: W. W. Norton, 1978. In cooperation with the American Association for State and Local History.

Johnson, Judi. *The Illiniwek*. Illinois State Museum. American Indian Pamphlet Series #2, n.d.

Keiser, John H. *Building for the Centuries: Illinois, 1865–1898*. Urbana: University of Illinois Press, 1977.

Kinzie, Juliette. *Wau-Bun: The "Early Day" in the North-West*. New York: Derby and Jackson, 1856. Reprint. Urbana: University of Illinois Press, 1992.

Koeper, Frederick. *Illinois Architecture from Territorial Times to the Present: A Selective Guide*. Chicago: University of Chicago Press, 1968.

Kogan, Herman, and Robert Cromie. *The Great Chicago Fire: Chicago 1871*. New York: G. P. Putnam's Sons, 1971.

Kopecky, Frank, and Mary S. Harris. *Understanding the Illinois Constitution*. Springfield: Illinois Bar Association, 1970.

Lantz, Herman R. *People of Coal Town*. With the assistance of J. S. McCrary. N.p., 1958. Reprint. Carbondale: Southern Illinois University Press, 1971.

McDermott, John Francis. *Frenchmen and French Ways in the Mississippi Valley.* Urbana: University of Illinois Press, 1969.

Madden, Betty I. *Art, Crafts, and Architecture in Early Illinois.* Urbana: University of Illinois Press (in cooperation with the Illinois State Museum), 1974.

Naden, Corinne J. *The Haymarket Affair: Chicago, 1886.* New York: Franklin Watts, Inc., 1968.

Neely, Mark E., Jr. *The Abraham Lincoln Encyclopedia.* New York: McGraw-Hill, 1982.

Onuf, Peter S. *Statehood and Union: A History of the Northwest Ordinance.* Bloomington: Indiana University Press, 1987.

Parkman, Francis. *La Salle and the Discovery of the Great West.* Modern Library Edition. New York: Random House, 1985.

Pooley, William V. *The Settlement of Illinois from 1830–1850.* Madison: Bulletin of University of Wisconsin, No. 220. History Series, Vol. 1, No. 4, 1908.

Pratt, Fletcher. *Civil War on Western Waters.* New York: Henry Holt & Co., 1956.

Redd, Jim. *The Illinois and Michigan Canal: A Contemporary Perspective in Essays and Photographs.* Carbondale: Southern Illinois University Press, 1992.

Rittenhouse, Isabella Maud. *Maud.* Edited by Richard Lee Strout. New York: Macmillan, 1939.

Ritzenthaler, Robert, and Pat Ritzenthaler. *The Woodland Indians of the Western Great Lakes.* New York: Natural History Press, 1970.

Rothert, Otto A. *The Outlaws of Cave-in-Rock.* Cleveland: Arthur H. Clark Company, 1924. Reprint. Evansville, Ind.: Whipporwill Publications, 1984.

Sandburg, Carl. *Abraham Lincoln: The Prairie Years.* Vols. 1 and 2. New York: Harcourt, Brace & Co., 1926.

Simon, Paul. *Lincoln's Preparation for Greatness: The Illinois Legislative Years.* Norman: University of Oklahoma Press, 1965. Illini Books Ed. Urbana: University of Illinois Press, 1971.

———. *Lovejoy: Martyr to Freedom.* St. Louis: Concordia Publishing House, 1964.

Struever, Stuart, and Felicia A. Holton. *Koster: Americans in Search of Their Prehistoric Past.* New York: Anchor Press/Doubleday, 1979.

Sutton, Robert P., ed. *The Prairie State: A Documentary History of Illinois, Civil War to Present.* Grand Rapids, Mich.: Eerdmans Publishing Co., 1976.

———. *The Prairie State: A Documentary History of Illinois, Colonial Years to 1860.* Grand Rapids, Mich.: Eerdmans Publishing Co., 1976.

Terkel, Studs. *Giants of Jazz.* New York: Thomas Crowell, 1957.

———. *Hard Times: An Oral History of the Great Depression.* New York: Random House, 1970.

Thomas, Benjamin P. *Lincoln's New Salem.* Springfield: The Abraham Lincoln

Association, 1934. New and rev. ed. Carbondale: Southern Illinois University Press, 1987.

Tillson, Christiana H. *A Woman's Story of Pioneer Illinois.* Chicago: Lakeside Press, R. R. Donnelley, 1919.

Tingley, Donald F. *The Structuring of a State: The History of Illinois, 1899 to 1928.* Urbana: University of Illinois Press, 1980.

Tunis, Edwin. *Frontier Living.* Cleveland: World Publishing Co., 1961.

Voigt, John W., and Robert H. Mohlenbrock. *Prairie Plants of Illinois.* Springfield: Department of Conservation, State of Illinois, n.d.

Wade, Louise C. *Graham Taylor: Pioneer for Social Justice, 1851–1938.* Chicago: University of Chicago Press, 1964.

Walton, Clyde C., editor. *An Illinois Reader.* Dekalb: Northern Illinois University Press, 1970.

Watters, Mary. *Illinois in the Second World War.* Vol. 1, *Operation Home Front.* Springfield: State of Illinois, Illinois State Historical Society, 1951.

———. *Illinois in the Second World War.* Vol. 2, *The Production Front.* Springfield: State of Illinois, Illinois State Historical Society, 1951.

Wendt, Lloyd, and Herman Kogan. *Give the Lady What She Wants! The Story of Marshall Field and Company.* Chicago: Rand McNally and Co., 1952.

Wheeler, Adade M., with Marlene Stein Wortman. *The Roads They Made: Women in Illinois History.* Chicago: Charles H. Kerr Pub. Co., 1977.

Wright, Frank Lloyd. *An American Architecture.* Edited by Edgar Kaufmann. New York: Horizon Press, 1955.

Wyman, Mark. *Immigrants in the Valley: Irish, Germans, and Americans in the Upper Mississippi Country.* Chicago: Nelson-Hall, 1984.

Young, Bob, and Jan Young. *Reluctant Warrior: Ulysses S. Grant.* New York: Julian Messner, 1971.

Periodicals

Illinois Historical Journal. Springfield: Old State Capitol. Illinois Historic Preservation Agency. Published four times a year.

Illinois History: A Magazine for Young People. Springfield: Illinois State Historical Society. Published monthly during the school year, October through May, by the Illinois Historic Preservation Agency in cooperation with the Illinois State Historical Society.

Illinois Issues. Springfield: Sangamon State University. Published 11 times a year.

Index

Abolition: Emancipation Proclamation, 110–11; first state constitution, 42–44; Lincoln-Douglas debates, 99; Lovejoy, 96; Republican convention (1860), 100; Thirteenth Amendment, 128

Addams, Jane, 169–73, 192

Addams, John, 169

Ade, George, 161

Adler, Dankmar, 159

Agricultural equipment, 70–71, 139–40

Agriculture: early pioneer, 50, 53, 57; grange movement, 130–31, 132–33; during Great Depresion, 208, 216; immigrant farmers, 65, 87, 88; Indian, 4, 7, 50–51; prairie farming, 69–76; in World War I, 189–90; in World War II, 223

Albion, 68

Algonquian Indians, 6, 14. *See also* Illini Indians

Algren, Nelson, 235

Altgeld, John Peter, 150–52, 172

Alton, 14, 80, 85, 96, 99, 140, 242

Amendments to U.S. Constitution: Thirteenth (outlawing slavery), 128; Fourteenth (conferring citizenship), 128; Fifteenth (voting rights), 128, 129; Eighteenth (prohibition), 201; Nineteenth (woman suffrage), 183, 195; Twenty-first (prohibition repealed), 215

American Baseball League, 200

American Railroad Union, 151–52

American Red Cross, 224

American Revolution. *See* Revolutionary War

Anarchists, 147, 148–50

Anderson, G. M., 196

Anna, 205

Antietam, battle of, 111

Anti-Saloon League, 201

Antiwar movement: Vietnam, 239–40, 242–43

Appalachian Mountains, 11, 19, 20, 22, 25, 28, 32, 49, 50, 130

Appomattox Court House, 119

Arbeiter-Zeitung (newspaper), 148

Architecture: at Century of Progress Exhibition, 214; Chicago school, 157–60; post–World War II, 230–32; State of Illinois Center, 249; at World's Columbian Exposition, 161, 163

Argonne National Laboratory, 222, 227

Armory Show (New York), 155

Armour, Philip, 139, 179
Armstrong, Louis, 199
Army of Northern Virginia, 106
Army of the Potomac, 118
Art Institute (Chicago), 154–55
Artists: Bacon, 120; Bauhaus, 230; contemporary, 249–50; Krans, 68; Picasso, 230. See also Architecture; Cartoonists
Astaire, Fred, 223
Atomic bomb, 221–22, 225, 238
Aurora, 105, 147, 242
Automobiles, 228, 231; manufactured in Illinois, 179. See also Hard-road system
Aviation: industry, in Illinois, 195–96, 227; O'Hare, 227–28; World War I, 189; World War II, 219, 220

Backwoodsmen. See Settlers, American
Bacon, Henry, 120
Bad Axe, battle of, 52
Baltimore (Md.), 100, 101
Banks, 81, 208, 211
Barbed wire, 140
Bardeen, John, 227
Barnstormers, 195–96
Baseball, 200–201
Baseball bats: Spalding Company, 141
Bathhouse John, 168
Bauhaus, 230
Baum, Don, 249
Bell, John, 100
Belleville, 140. See also West Belleville
Bellow, Saul, 235
Benny, Jack, 197
Berlin (Ger.), 224
Bessemer, Henry, 140
Bickerdyke, Mary Ann, 115–16
Bilandic, Michael, 250
Biloxi (Miss.), 18
Birger Gang, 206
Birkbeck, Morris, 68
Bishop Hill, 65, 68
Bismarck, Otto von, 87
Black Hawk, 52

Black Hawk's War, 50–53
Black Laws, 43, 95, 128
Black Thursday, 207
Black troops: in Civil War, 112; in World War II, 218
Bloomington, 62, 89
Blue Lake, 152
Boats and ships: civil war riverboats, 109, 113; Columbus's ships (replicas), 161; ferryboats, 60–61; flatboats and keelboats, 54–55, 59, 61; steamboats, 55, 56, 61, 64, 80. See also City of New York; Griffon; Lusitania; Seneca Chief
Bond, Shadrach, 42
Bonfield, John, 148
Boodlers. See Machine politics
Boone, Daniel, 54
Booth, John Wilkes, 119
Bootlegging, 201–2
Border (of Illinois): northern, 40, 86
Boss politics. See Machine politics
Boston Red Stockings, 200
Bowman, Joseph, 27
Boysen, Bill, 250
Bradwell, Myra, 130
Brattain, Walter, 227
Breckenridge, John C., 100
Brooks, Gwendolyn, 236
Brownson, Jacques, 230
Brush, Daniel Harmon, 91
Buchanan, James, 101
Buckner, Simon, 109
Buena Vista, battle of, 85
Buffalo (N.Y.), 56
Build Illinois program, 248
Bureau County, 182
Burnham, Daniel, 159, 161, 163
Byrne, Jane, 250–51

Cabot, John, 19
Cagney, James, 223
Cahokia, 18, 25
Cahokia Indians, 6, 18. See also Illini Indians
Cahokia Mounds, 4–5

Cairo, 80, 91, 128, 134; in Civil War, 101–2, 105, 107, 121

California, 107, 139, 162, 196, 250

California Gold Rush, 139

Cameron, Simon, 101

Camp Butler, 105

Camp Douglas, 105

Camp Ellis, 219

Camp Grant, 219

Camp Robert Smalls, 218

Camp Yates, 105

Camron, John, 60

Canada, 30, 35, 36, 162. *See also* New France

Canals: Erie Canal, 56, 90; Illinois and Michigan Canal, 77–80, 82, 88, 178; Panama Canal, 141; Sanitary and Ship Canal, 177–79; Suez Canal, 179

Capitals of Illinois. *See* Kaskaskia; Springfield; Vandalia

Capitol buildings, 85, 126–27

Capone, Al ("Scar Face"), 202

Carbondale, 89, 91, 125, 147, 234, 242

Carlson, Bill, 250

Carnegie, Andrew, 155, 181

Carrier Mills, 10

Carrier pigeons, 219

Carrollton, 105

Cars. *See* Automobiles

Carthage, 67

Cartoonists, 205–6

Cattle kings, 71–72

Cave-in-Rock, 38, 74

CCC (Civilian Conservation Corps), 211, 212

Cedarville, 169

Centralia, 229

Central Park (New York City), 161, 231

Century of Progress Exhibition, 213–14

Cermak, Anton, 213

Champaign County, 126

Chanute, Octave, 195

Chanute Air Field, 189, 195, 219

Chapin, John, 136

Charleston, 89, 99, 117, 234

Charleston (S.C.), 100

Chattanooga (Tenn.), 111, 119

Checker Taxi, 179

Cherry Mine No. 2, 182

Chester, 96, 205

Chicago, 70, 71, 77, 80, 87, 140, 141, 142–43, 151, 171, 192, 227–28; architecture, 157–60, 230–32; Century of Progress, 213–14; Cermak, 213; Civil War period, 96, 100, 101, 105; Democratic convention of 1968, 242–43; early history, 36–37, 40, 63–65; education, 88–89, 234; great fire of 1871, 135–37; and high culture, 154–65; Hull-House, 170–72; jazz, 199; labor troubles, 146–50; meat-packing industry, 138–39, 179; movie-making in, 196–97; during prohibition, 201–3; race relations, 185–86, 190, 218, 241–42; recent mayors, 250–51; Sanitary and Ship Canal, 177–79; State of Illinois Center, 249; World's Columbian Exposition, 161–65; in World War II, 218, 219, 220, 221, 222, 223; writers, 160–62, 235

Chicago Art Institute, 154–55

Chicago Bears, 200

Chicago Circle campus (University of Illinois), 234

Chicago Civic Center, 230

Chicago Civic Opera, 157

Chicago construction, 158–60

Chicago Cubs, 200

Chicago *Daily News*, 160

Chicago *Evening Post*, 160

Chicago Fire (1871), 135–37, 155, 158

Chicago harbor, 64

Chicago Heights, 242

Chicago Iron Company, 140

Chicago *Legal News*, 130

Chicago Opera Company, 157

Chicago *Post and Mail*, 140

Chicago Public Library, 155

Chicago River, 15, 177

"Chicago Seven," 243

Chicago Symphony Orchestra, 155–57, 223

Chicago Trades and Labor Association, 146
Chicago *Tribune*, 152, 167, 205
Children's Bureau, 172
Churchill, Winston, 217
Church of the Holy Family, 18
Cicero, 221, 241
Cincinnati Reds, 200
City of New York (ship), 214
Civil Administrative Code (1917), 184
Civil defense: during World War II, 222
Civil rights, of women: barred from professions, 130; battle for suffrage, 182–83; after Civil War, 128–29; constitutional convention of 1869–70, 132; constitution of 1970, 247; ERA, 243–44
Civil service system, 184, 229
Civil War, 95–121, 135, 139
Clark, George Rogers, 25–30, 31, 32
Cleveland, Grover, 152, 162, 229
Coal mine disasters: Centralia, 229; Cherry Mine No. 2, 182; New Orient Coal Mine No. 2, 229
Coal Mine Safety Act (1952), 229
Coal mining. *See* Mining
Cold war, 238
Coles, Edward, 43
Colleges and universities: private, 89, 234; public, 89, 126, 233–34. *See also* *individual names*
Collinsville, 4, 192
Colosimo, "Big Jim," 201
Columbian clubs, 162
Columbian Exposition. *See* World's Columbian Exposition
Columbus, Christopher, 161
Columbus (Ky.), 110
Columbus (Ohio), 56
Comic strips, 205
Commerce (town), 66
Communists, 193, 194, 239. *See also* IWW
Community colleges, 233–34
Compton, Arthur, 222
Coney Island (New York City), 164

Confederate States of America, 100, 101, 107
Consolidation: of schools, 232
Constitution. *See* Illinois Constitution; United States Constitution
Constitutional conventions (Illinois), 40–42, 43, 117–18, 245–46, 247
Cook, Daniel Pope, 39
Copperheads, 116–17
Corinth (Miss.), 110
Coughlin, John, 168
Court: first juvenile, 171
Cowboys, 71–72
Crab Orchard, 220
Cracker Jack, 163
Cullom, Shelby, 133, 147, 148
Cumberland (Md.), 56
Cumberland Gap, 54
Cumberland Pike, 55–56
"Cyclone in calico." *See* Bickerdyke, Mary Ann

Daley, Richard J., 242, 250–51
Danville, 80
Debs, Eugene V., 151–52
Debt: internal improvements, 84
Decatur, 125, 126, 200, 228
Deere, John, 70, 139
DeKalb, 89, 140, 234
Deller, Harris, 250
Democratic party, 150, 229, 248, 250, 251; convention of 1968, 242–43; election of 1860, 97–100; in Great Depression, 210–12; Peace Democrats, 117–18
Deneen, Charles S., 180, 184
Denkman, C. A., 141
Department stores, 142
Depression. *See* Financial panics; Great Depression
De Priest, Oscar, 186
Des Plaines River, 15
de Suvero, Mark, 249
Detroit (Mich.), 28, 36, 179
Dever, William, 202
"Dick Tracy," 205

Dirksen, Everett, 241

Discrimination against blacks: in Chicago, 185–86; Civil War soldiers, 112; in factories, during World War I, 190–91; post–Civil War, 127–28; Springfield riot, 184–86; World War II soldiers, 218. *See also* Slavery

Disney, Roy, 196

Disney, Walt, 196

Dixon, Alan, 251

Dodge Plant (Chicago), 220

Dooley, Martin, 160

Dos Passos, John, 235

Douglas, Stephen, 89, 97–101

Dreiser, Theodore, 204

Du Bois, W. E. B., 185

Duckworth, Ruth, 250

Duncan, Joseph, 79, 81

Dunleith (East Dubuque, Ill.), 91

Dunne, Edward F., 180, 184

Dunne, Peter Finley, 160

Du Sable, Jean Baptiste Point, 64

Earlville, 128

Earthquake. *See* New Madrid earthquake

Eastern Illinois University, 89, 234

East St. Louis, 140, 147, 190–91, 229, 242

Ebony Film Corporation, 196

Edgar, James, 251

Edison, Thomas A., 196, 213

Education: attitudes toward, 57–58; land grant universities, 126; post–World War II reform, 232–35; struggle for public education, 73, 88–89

Edwards, Ninian, 34, 36, 40

Edwardsville, 36, 140

Effingham, 147

"Egypt" (nickname), 104

Eiffel Tower (Paris, Fr.), 163

Eighteenth Amendment, 201; repeal of, 215

Eight-hour leagues, 146

Eisenhower, Dwight D., 229

Elgin Watch Company, 221

Eliot, T. S., 205

Elwood/Kankakee, 220

Emancipation Proclamation, 110–12

"Embalmed beef" scandal, 179

Emmerson, Louis Lincoln, 209–10, 212

England, 191, 217. *See also* English in the New World

English in the New World, 13, 19–20, 49; defeated by Clark, 25–30; in Illinois country, 22–25; War of 1812, 36–38

Epton, Bernard, 251

ERA (Equal Rights Amendment), 243–44

Erie Canal, 56, 90

Evanston, 130, 242

Fairlie, John, 184

Fallen Timbers, battle of, 33

Famine: in Ireland, 88

Farm machinery and equipment, 70–71, 139–40

Farnham, Eliza, 73, 75

Farrell, James T., 235

Federal Steel Company, 181

Fermi, Enrico, 222

Ferris, George Washington Gale, 163

Ferris wheel, 163

Field, Eugene, 160

Field, Marshall, 142, 165

Field, Marshall III, 223

Field Museum of Natural History, 165

Fifteenth Amendment, 128, 129

Financial panics, 181; of 1837, 81, 84, 88; of 1873, 146–47; of 1883, 148; of 1893, 151. *See also* Great Depression

Fink, Mike, 55

Florida, 30, 101

Flower, George, 68

Fluorspar (fluorite), 142

Football, 199–200

Foote, Andrew, 109

Ford, Henry, 179

Ford, Thomas, 67, 84

Ford's Theatre, 119

Fort Clark, 36

Fort Crevecoeur, 16

Fort Dearborn, 36, 37, 64
Fort de Chartres, 18, 22, 24
Fort Donelson (Ky.), 109
Fort Frontenac (Can.), 16
Fort Grant, 189
Fort Henry (Ky.), 109
Fort Massac, 26
Fort Miami (Ind.), 16
Fort Michilimackinac (Mich.), 36, 64
Fort Monroe (Va.), 52
Fort Russell, 36
Fort St. Louis (Starved Rock), 17
Fort Sheridan, 219
Fort Sumter (S.C.), 101
Fort Wayne (Ind.), 33
Four-Minute Men, 191
Fourteen Points, 193
Fourteenth Amendment, 128, 129
Fox, Carol, 157
Fox Indians, 9, 50–53
Fox River, 14, 87
Franklin, Benjamin, 22
Freeport, 99
Free Soilers, 97
Frémont, John C., 107
French, Augustus, 90
French and Indian War, 19–20
French in the New World: competition
    with English, 11–12, 19–20, 23, 24;
    exploration of Mississippi Valley, 13–
    17; relationship with Indians, 14–15,
    23; settlements in Mississippi Valley,
    18. See also Spanish in the New
    World
Frontenac, Louis, 13, 16
Frost, Robert, 205
Fuller, Henry, 161
Funk, Isaac, 71
Funk's Grove, 71
Fur trade, 9, 13, 16, 23, 37, 64, 76, 137

Gale, George Washington, 63
Galena, 61–62, 80, 87, 88, 91, 96, 105,
    107, 119, 141
Galesburg, 62, 99, 115, 204
Galveston (Tex.), 17

Gandhi, Mahatma, 241
Gangsters, 201–2, 213, 229
GAR (Grand Army of the Republic), 125
Garden, Mary, 157
Garland, Hamlin, 161
Garland, Judy, 223
Gary, Joseph, 149
Gateway Amendment, 229
General Trades Assembly, 146
Georgia, 49, 101
Gettysburg Address, 224
Gibault, Pierre, 27
Gilded Age, 147
Glidden, Joseph, 140
Goodman, Benny, 199
Gould, Chester, 206
Governors of Illinois, 257–58; Altgeld,
    150–52, 172; Bond, 42; Coles, 43;
    Cullom, 133, 147, 148; Deneen, 180,
    184; Dever, 202; Duncan, 79, 81;
    Dunne, 180, 184; Edgar, 251; Ed-
    wards (territorial governor), 34, 36,
    40; Emmerson, 209–10, 212; Ford,
    67, 84; French, 90; Green, 218, 229;
    Horner, 210, 212; Kerner, 234;
    Lowden, 180, 184, 185, 189, 191,
    192, 194; Ogilvie, 247; Oglesby, 119,
    126, 128, 150; Small, 180–81, 209,
    212; Stevenson, 229; Stratton, 241;
    Thompson, 247, 251; Yates, 101,
    104, 106, 112, 117, 119
Governors State University, 234
Grand Detour, 70, 71, 139
Grand Tower, 140
Granite City, 140
Grand Prairie, 69
Grange, Red, 200
Grange movement, 131
Grant, Ulysses S.: in Civil War, 96, 110,
    111, 115, 118; early years, 107, 109;
    response to Chicago fire, 137
Great Depression, 157, 207–13, 225, 250
Great Lakes, 13, 23, 40, 56, 64, 140, 178
Great Lakes Naval Training Station,
    189, 218, 219
Great Migration, 185, 187, 221

Great Northern Railway, 151
Great Western Mail Route, 80
Green, Dwight Herbert, 218, 229
Green Bay (Wis.), 14, 15
Gregory, John Milton, 126
Grierson, Benjamin, 111
Griffon (boat), 16
Grooms, Red, 249
Gulf of Mexico, 15, 17, 19, 74, 77, 178

Haines, Elijah, 132
Hall, Jennie, 64
Halleck, Henry, 107
Hamilton, Alice, 172
Hamilton, Henry, 28, 30
Hancock County, 66
Hanford (Wash.), 222
Hardin County, 142
Hard-road system, 180–81, 209
Harlem Airport, 218
Harper's Magazine, 136
Harrison, Carter, 148
Harrison, William Henry, 34, 35
Hastings, Robert, 216
Haymarket tragedy, 148–50
Heald, Nathan, 36
Hearst, William Randolph, 60
Hemingway, Ernest, 235
Henry, Patrick, 25–26
Henry County, 228
Herrin Massacre, 202–4
Hertz, John, 179
Hickok, James Butler ("Wild Bill"), 72
Hinky Dink, 168
Hiroshima (Jap.), 225
Hitler, Adolf, 217, 224, 230
Hodges, Jennie, 114
Hollywood (Calif.), 196, 250
Home Insurance Company, 158
Home rule, 246–47
Hook, Frances, 114
Hoover, Herbert, 209–10
Horner, Henry, 210, 212
Hovey, Charles, 89, 105
Howlett, Michael, 247
Hu, Mary Lee, 250

Hubbard, Gurdon Saltonstall, 76, 137
Hulbert, William, 200
Hulett, Alta, 130
Hull-House, 170–72
Humphrey, Hubert H., 242
Hunt, Richard, 249
Hutchinson, Charles, 154

Ice ages, 3, 69, 141
Illini Indians, 5–9, 13, 14, 15, 18, 36, 52
Illinois: border, 40, 86; Civil War regiments, 105, 106, 112, 119, 120–21; origin of name, 13
Illinois and Michigan Canal, 77–80, 82, 88, 178
Illinois Arts Council, 249
Illinois Central Railroad, 80–81, 88, 90–91, 98, 208
Illinois Constitution: of 1818, 40–45, 95–96; of 1848, 86; of 1870, 131–32; of 1970, 245–47. *See also* Gateway Amendment
Illinois *Herald*, 39
Illinois Industrial University, 126
Illinois Institute of Technology, 230
Illinois Law (woman suffrage), 183
Illinois National Guard, 147, 148, 185, 189, 190–91
Illinois River, 15, 16, 50, 77, 80, 81, 83, 87, 88, 220
Illinois State Federation of Labor, 146
Illinois State Museum, 218, 249
Illinois State Teachers' Association, 89
Illinois State University, 89, 105, 234
Illinois Steel Company, 181
Illinois Territory, 34–38, 42
Immigrants, 105, 147, 155, 157, 179, 213, 222; Bishop Hill, 65; black, 128, 185, 187, 197–99; German, 87, 92, 150, 191, 230; Irish, 79, 87–88, 92. *See also* Hull-House
Income tax, state, 247
Indenture, 42–43, 95
Indiana, 32, 35, 80, 137, 141, 214
Indianapolis (Ind.), 56
Indiana Territory, 34, 35

Indians, 3–5, 9, 14, 20, 23–24, 28, 33, 35, 36–38, 50–53, 61, 64, 119
Industrial revolution, 130, 145, 170, 177
Industries, 125, 135, 137–42, 227; agricultural equipment, 70–71, 139–40; automotive, 179–80; meat-packing, 137–39; steel industry mergers, 181; in World War II, 220–21
Insull, Samuel, 191
Internal improvement projects, 77–83, 84
Internal Improvements Act, 80, 81, 83
International Harvester, 220
Inventions: by women, 163
Inventors. See Scientists and inventors
Ireland, 79, 88
Iron and steel industry, 140, 181
Iroquois Indians, 9, 14
IWW (International Workers of the World), 192

Jackson County, 141
Jackson Park (Chicago), 164
Jacksonville, 85
Jahn, Helmut, 249
James I (king of England), 25
Jansson, Erik, 65
Japan: in World War II, 217–18, 224–25
Japanese-Americans: in Chicago, 222–23
Jenney, William LeBaron, 158
John Deere Company, 231
John Hancock Building, 230
Johnson, Bushrod, 109
Johnson, Lyndon B., 242
Joliet (city), 179, 233, 242
Joliet Iron and Steel Company, 140, 181
Joliet Junior College, 233
Jolliet, Louis, 13–15
Jonesboro, 99
Journalism, 39, 60, 100, 115, 136, 140, 148, 152, 203, 205–6, 235; Chicago journalists, 160–61; Chicago Legal News, 130; Haymarket reporting, 149; Lovejoy, 96; Prairie Farmer, 72–73; Stead, 167; telegraph used, 99; Vietnam, 240
Journals and diaries: Addams, 172–73;

Birkbeck and Flower, 68; Black Hawk, 52; Brush, 91; Clark, 31; Farnham, 75; Grant, 107; Hall, 64; Hastings, 216; Hubbard, 76; Kinzie, 76; Marquette, 15; Rittenhouse, 134; Tillson, 59
Jug towns, 141
Junior colleges, 233–34

Kane, Elias Kent, 40
Kankakee, 220
Kankakee River, 16
Kansas Territory, 72
Kaskaskia: American conquest of, 25, 26–27, 28, 33; under English, 24; first state capital, 44; under French, 11, 18; territorial capital, 34, 40
Kaskaskia Indians, 6, 15, 52. See also Illini Indians
Kaskaskia Island, 11, 27
Kaskaskia River, 44, 80
Kelley, Florence, 172
Kelley, O. H., 131
Kenna, Michael, 168
Kennedy, John F., 229
Kentucky, 25, 28, 34, 38, 50, 54, 109
Keokuk (Indian chief), 51, 52
Kerner, Otto, 234
Kewanee, 62
Kickapoo Indians, 9, 36
Kinetoscope, 196
King, Martin Luther, Jr., 241
King Oliver, 199
Kington, Brent, 249
Kinzie, John, 37, 64
Kinzie, Juliette, 76
Klement, Vera, 249
Knights of Labor, 146
Knox College, 63
Korean War, 238–39
Koster site, 10
Krans, Olof, 68
Ku Klux Klan, 202

Laffont, Jean, 27
Lake Erie, 56

Lake Michigan, 14, 40, 77, 137, 178
Landis, Kenesaw Mountain, 201
Land offices, 34
Land Ordinance Act (1785), 32
La Salle, Robert Cavelier (sieur de), 15–17, 18, 19
La Salle (city), 83
Lathrop, Julia, 171
Laval, François, 18
Lawrence, Charles, 132
League of Five Nations, 9
League of Nations, 193
League of Women Voters, 245
Lee, Robert E., 106
Leiter, Levi, 142
Leland Hotel, 127
Lester, William, 202
Liberty Bell of the West, 27
Libraries, 155
Lincoln, Abraham, 96, 101, 107, 126, 127, 169, 185, 204, 224, 240; death, 119–20; at New Salem, 60–61; reelection, 118–19; rise to presidency, 97–101
Lincoln-Douglas debates, 97–100
Lincoln Memorial (Washington, D.C.), 120
Lindsay, Vachel, 204
"Little Egypt" (dancer), 163
"Little Giant." See Douglas, Stephen
Little Wabash River, 80
Livermore, Mary, 100, 115
Lockport, 83
Logan, John A., 104, 118, 125
London (U.K.), 170
London Company, 25
"Long Nine," 97
Louis XIV (king of France), 16
Louisiana, 17, 18, 101
Louisville (Ky.), 25, 26
Lovejoy, Elijah, 96
Lovejoy, Owen, 96
Lowden, Frank O., 180, 184, 185, 189, 191, 192, 194
Lowell, Amy, 205
Lusitania, 188

McCarthy, Eugene, 242–43
McClean County, 228
McClellan, George B., 118
McClernand, John, 104
McCormick, Cyrus, 71, 139
McCormick Harvester Plant, 148
Machine politics, 167–69, 213, 242, 251
Macomb, 89, 234
Madison, James, 34, 40
Mail order companies, 143
Maine, 53
Manchuria, 228
Marietta (Ohio), 32
Marine Corps' Women's Reserve, 219
Marquette, Jacques, 13–15
Marx, Harpo, 223
Mason, Roswell B., 90
Massachusetts, 72
Masters, Edgar Lee, 204
Mattoon, "Big Bill," 90
Mattoon (city), 90
Mature, Victor, 223
Mawdsley, Richard, 250
Mayors (of Chicago): Bilandic, 250; Byrne, 250–51; Cermak 213; Daley, 242, 250–51; Harrison, 148; Thompson, 202, 213; Washington, 251
Maywood, 242
Meat-packing industry, 137–39
Medical education, 234–35
Memorial Day: first celebrated, 125
Memorial Stadium (University of Illinois), 200
Memphis (Tenn.), 116
Menard County, 61
Meredosia, 81
Mergers, business, 181–82
Mesabi Range, 140
Metamora, 62
Mexican War, 84, 97, 105, 107, 139, 218
Miami (Fla.), 213
Miami Indians, 9, 33
Michigamea Indians, 6. See also Illini Indians
Michigan, 13, 28, 32, 36, 214
Mickey Mouse, 197

Midway, the, 163, 214
Mies van der Rohe, Ludwig, 230
Miller, Frank, 114
Mine safety laws, 182, 229
Mining: coal, 141, 146, 148, 182, 202–4, 208, 229; fluorspar, 142; lead, 18, 61–62, 141
Minnesota, 140, 141, 181
Mission of the Guardian Angel, 63
Mission of the Immaculate Conception, 15
Mississippi (state), 101, 110, 111
Mississippi River, 32, 49, 51, 52, 61, 66, 77, 87, 97, 139, 183; Civil War, 101, 107, 111, 121; exploration of, 14–18; floods, 11, 24, 27; New Madrid earthquake, 35; World War II, 220
Mississippi Valley: first teachers' college in, 89; French in, 13–20; in Revolutionary War, 25–30
Missouri, 66, 106, 107, 110, 139
Missouri River, 17
Mix, Tom, 196
Modoc Rock Shelter, 3
Moline, 71, 139, 179, 220, 231
Monks' Mound, 4
Monroe, Harriet, 204
Monroe, James, 42
Montgomery (Ala.), 101
Montgomery Ward Company, 143
Montréal (Can.), 15
"Moon Mullins," 205
Moran, "Bugs," 202
Mormons, 65–67
Morning News (Chicago), 161
Morrill Act, 126
Morris, Nelson, 139, 179
Moskowitz, Henry, 185
Mother Bickerdyke. See Bickerdyke, Mary Ann
Mounds, 113
Mount Carmel, 80
Mount Hope, 62
Movie actors: and war bond drive, 223. See also Benny, Jack; Reagan, Ronald; Sinatra, Frank

Movie producers, 196
Mulligan, James, 105
Munn, Ira, 133
Murphysboro, 141
Museum of Science and Industry, 165
Music, 155–57, 197–99

NAACP (National Association for the Advancement of Colored People), 185
Nagasaki (Jap.), 225
Nashville (Tenn.), 109
National Association of Baseball Players, 200
National Baseball League, 200
National Football League, 200
National Guard. See Illinois National Guard
National Road, 55–56
National Stockyards, 139
Natural resources, 69, 137, 141–42
Nauvoo, 65–67
Negro Business League, 186
New Deal, 211
New England, 49, 53, 56, 73. See also Settlers, American
New France, 13, 18, 19, 20
New Hampshire, 53
New Madrid earthquake, 35, 38, 56
New Mexico, 222
New Orient Coal Mine No. 2, 229
New Orleans (La.), 18, 56, 121, 197, 199
New Salem, 60–61, 97
Newspapers (in Chicago): Daily News, 161; Evening Post, 160; Legal News, 130; Morning News, 161; Post and Mail, 140; Tribune, 152, 167, 205
New York (N.Y.), 56, 161, 164, 185, 196, 199, 231
New York (state), 56, 63, 64, 65, 96
New York Stock Exchange, 207
Nillson, Gladys, 249
Nineteenth Amendment, 183, 195
Nobel Prize, 192, 222, 227, 235
Normal, 234
North Carolina, 49, 54, 101, 119